THE WELSH LAW OF WOMEN

THE WELSH LAW OF WOMEN

Studies presented to Professor Daniel A. Binchy
on his eightieth birthday
3 June 1980

◆

Edited by

DAFYDD JENKINS and MORFYDD E. OWEN

PUBLISHED ON BEHALF OF THE BOARD OF CELTIC STUDIES

CARDIFF
UNIVERSITY OF WALES PRESS
1980

© THE CONTRIBUTORS 1980

British Library Cataloguing in Publication Data

The Welsh law of women
  1. Women—Legal status, laws, etc.—Wales
  I. Jenkins, Dafydd
  II. Owen, Morfydd E
  III. Binchy, Daniel Anthony
  342'.429'085   KD4058.W6

ISBN 0-7083-0771-X

Printed in Wales
by D. Brown & Sons Ltd.
Cowbridge

PREFACE DEDICATORY

to Professor Daniel Anthony Binchy

Annwyl Gyfaill,

This Welsh form of address seems to be the appropriate one, not only because it avoids all problems of the right degree of formality or familiarity, but because you have been so good a friend to the study of Celtic Law, and through that to all of us who are interested in that study, whether or not we have enjoyed your friendship at the personal level.

I have claimed the privilege of writing this Preface, but this volume owes its existence to the enthusiasm of my co-editor, who nearly ten years ago at the Third Colloquium on Welsh Medieval Law persuaded us to join in a series of seminars and suggested that the Law of Women would be an ideal subject for a seminar group. The Head of her Department at Cardiff (Professor A. O. H. Jarman) agreed to invite the seminars to the University College there, and the Board of Celtic Studies subsidised them; at a later stage some meetings were held at Corpus Christi College, Oxford, at the invitation of Dr. Charles-Edwards, and we had the invaluable help of Professor Foster.

When we began our study we knew very well that a shining example had been set us by the Thurneysen seminar whose fruit is preserved in the *Studies in Early Irish Law* which you edited. We hoped then that in time we might have something comparable—*si parva licet componere magnis*—to show for our labours, and we hope now that our labours will not suggest to you those of the mountains. We, at least, have learnt a great deal, and even in the process of preparing the collection for the press have learnt so much that we are particularly conscious of how much remains to be done.

The papers first offered to the Cardiff Seminar in private were revised for presentation to the Fourth Colloquium at Aberystwyth in 1974, and have been further revised since then, while the last of the studies is based on part of a paper given to the Fifth Colloquium (at Bangor in 1979) by a specialist in Comparative Law whom we count ourselves fortunate to have attracted to our company.

In now offering you this collection, we perhaps honour ourselves more than we honour you, but we believe that you will welcome the studies here published, not only for their intrinsic interest but perhaps even more as the sign of a growing devotion to the study of our field, and we ask you to accept them as a mark of the appreciation of us all for your inspiring example as our Father in Celtic Law.

On behalf of the contributors, and of all those whose
names appear in the list which follows,

DAFYDD   JENKINS

TABULA GRATULATORIA

Anders Ahlqvist, University College, Galway
Leslie Alcock, Glasgow
Rhian M. Andrews, Prifysgol y Frenhines, Belfast
Y Barnwr Hywel ap Robert, Penarth
G. M. Ashton, Y Barri
J. H. Baker, St Catharine's College, Cambridge
John Bannerman, Edinburgh University
Gareth Bevan, Aberystwyth
Margaret Bird, Cardiff
Padraig A. Breatnach, University College, Dublin
R. A. Breatnach, University College, Cork
Rachel Bromwich, Bangor
Constance Bullock-Davies, University College of North Wales, Bangor
Francis John Byrne, University College, Dublin
Enrico Campanile, University of Pisa
S. Caulfield, University College, Dublin
Johan Corthals, Hamburg
Wendy Davies, University College, London
Per Denez, Université de Haute-Bretagne, Rennes, Brittany
Tania M. Dickinson, University of York
D. N. Dumville, Girton College, Cambridge
The Rt. Hon. Lord Elwyn-Jones of Llanelli and Newham, lately
    Lord Chancellor
D. Ellis Evans, Jesus College, Oxford
D. Simon Evans, St David's College, Lampeter
John Hefin Evans, Trewallter
Léon Fleuriot, Paris
Patrick K. Ford, University of California, Los Angeles
Sir Idris Foster, Jesus College, Oxford
Edward Fox, Regional Technical College, Galway
J. D. Foy, Bath
Carys Gibson, Llangefni
William Gillies, University of Edinburgh
Margaret Nona Ginn, Welsh St Donats
J. W. Gleasure, University of Glasgow

Count Lysander de Grandy, Southampton
David Greene, Dublin Institute for Advanced Studies
R. Geraint Gruffydd, Llyfrgell Genedlaethol Cymru
Margot and Eric Hamp, Chicago
Geoffrey J. Hand, The European University Institute
Alan Harding, University of Edinburgh
Marged Haycock, Aberystwyth
Máire Herbert, University College, Cork
Donald Howells, University of Glasgow
Daniel Huws, National Library of Wales
Dafydd Ifans, Llyfrgell Genedlaethol Cymru
Richard W. Ireland, University College of Wales, Aberystwyth
B. S. Jackson, Liverpool Polytechnic
Kenneth Jackson, University of Edinburgh
Christine James, Bridgend
A. O. H. Jarman, Cardiff
David Jenkins, lately National Librarian of Wales
Nansi Jenkins, Harrow Weald
Bedwyr Lewis Jones, University College of North Wales, Bangor
E. D. Jones, Aberystwyth
Islwyn Jones, Politechnig Cymru
Joyce Jones, Haverfordwest
R. Brinley Jones, Llandovery College
R. M. Jones, Coleg Prifysgol Cymru
Fergus Kelly, Dublin Institute for Advanced Studies
A. Kiralfy, King's College, London
Peter Kitson, Birmingham University
Alfred, Zia, and Anne-Marie Kramer, Cilgerran, near Cardigan
Pierre-Yves Lambert, Ecole Pratique des Hautes Etudes, Paris
Aneirin Lewis, University College, Cardiff
Ceri W. Lewis, University College, Cardiff
D. Myrddin Lloyd, Aberystwyth
Nesta Lloyd, University College of Swansea
H. R. Loyn, Westfield College, University of London
A. T. Lucas, Dublin
Proinsias Mac Cana, University College, Dublin
Margery McDermott, Tondrugwaer
Liam Mac Mathúna, Coláiste Phádraig, Baile Átha Cliath
Yr Anrhydeddus Mr Ustus Mars-Jones, Rhosneigr, Ynys Môn, Gwynedd
Wolfgang Meid, Innsbruck

Daniel F. Melia, University of California, Berkeley
Ceridwen Lloyd Morgan, University of Exeter
Gerald Morgan, Abermagwr
Mererid Morris, Miskin
Filippo Motta, University of Pisa
Kay Muhr
Muireann Ní Bhrolcháin, Dublin Institute for Advanced Studies
Próinséas Ní Chatháin, University College, Dublin
Tomás Ó Cathasaigh, University College, Dublin
Donncha Ó Corráin, University College, Cork
Brian Ó Cuív, Dublin Institute for Advanced Studies
Proinsias Ó Fhaoileáin, St. Hilary
Cecile O'Rahilly, Dublin Institute of Advanced Studies
William and Anne O'Sullivan, Dublin
D. Hugh Owen, University College, Cardiff
Goronwy Wyn Owen, Bethesda
Trefor M. Owen, Welsh Folk Museum
Sir Thomas Parry, Bangor
Susan Pearce, City Museum, Exeter
John Percival, University College, Cardiff
John Phillips, Pontypridd
Jean-Michel Picard, University College, Dublin
Y Barnwr Watkin Powell, Radyr, Caerdydd
Nia Watkin Powell, Nantmor, Caernarfon
Gwyneth Pye, Bedford College, University of London
Elena Wyn Rea, Groesfaen
D. Harding Rees, Felinfoel, Llanelli
R. L. Rees, Nantgaredig
G. L. Rees, University College of Wales, Aberystwyth
Ann Rhŷs, Ystrad Meurig, Dyfed
W. J. St.E.-G. Rhŷs, Ystrad Meurig, Dyfed
B. F. Roberts, University College of Swansea
Enid Roberts, Bangor
Jenny Rowland
Eurys I. Rowlands, Cardiff
Wynne I. Samuel, Parc y Rhath, Caerdydd
R. M. Scowcroft, Cornell University
David Sellar, University of Edinburgh
Richard Sharpe, Trinity College, Cambridge
J. G. T. Sheringham, Machynlleth

Katharine Simms, Dublin Institute of Advanced Studies
Patrick Sims-Williams, St John's College, Cambridge
Elan Closs Stephens, Coleg Aberystwyth
Cl. Sterckx, Institut des Hautes Etudes de Belgique, Brussels
C. B. Sweeting, Université de Paris IV
Hans Thieme, Freiburg i.Br.
Ceinwen H. Thomas, University College, Cardiff
Charles Thomas, Truro
J. Gwyn Thomas, Denbigh
Peter Wynn Thomas, University College, Cardiff
R. George Thomas, University College, Cardiff
R. L. Thomson, Leeds University
Hildegard L. C. Tristram, Freiburg i.Br.
Máirín bean Uí Dhálaigh, Taithile, Co. Chiarraí
Charlotte Ward, University of Connecticut
Calvert Watkins, Harvard University
T. M. Ll. Walters, Loughborough
Aled Rhys Wiliam, Salford University
J. E. Caerwyn Williams, Aberystwyth
Noel K. Williams, Llanelli
Stephen J. Williams, Abertawe (Swansea)

ABERYSTWYTH:	National Library of Wales
	University College of Wales Law Library
	University College of Wales Library
BAILE ATHA CLIATH:	Colaiste na hOllscoile,
	Roinn Bhealoideas Eireann
CAMBRIDGE:	University of Cambridge, Library of the Department of Anglo-Saxon, Norse and Celtic
CARDIFF:	British Broadcasting Corporation Reference Library
	University College, Salisbury Library
LEEDS:	University of Leeds, Brotherton Library
LONDON:	Public Record Office
	University College London Library
PARIS:	Amis des *Etudes Celtiques*
PISA:	Universita di Pisa, Istituto di Glottologia
ST FAGANS:	Welsh Folk Museum Library

ACKNOWLEDGEMENTS

THE Editors acknowledge very gratefully the permission to use material, freely given by Sir George Meyrick, Bart., for the Bodorgan manuscript, The British Library for the Cotton manuscripts, and the National Library of Wales for the Peniarth manuscripts; by Mrs. H. D. Emanuel for the text of Latin Redaction A; and by the President and Fellows of Corpus Christi College, Oxford, for the frontispiece.

They also wish to record their great gratitude to those who have helped in the preparation and production of the book, and in particular to Howard E. F. Davies, Marged Haycock, D. Myrddin Lloyd, and J. E. Caerwyn Williams for illuminating discussion of various points; to Gareth Bevan and his colleagues of *Geiriadur Prifysgol Cymru* for access to the slips of the Dictionary and much useful information; to Nia Bonsall, Sabina Thompson, Alice Tudor, Anne Watkin-Jones, and Ann Watkins for patient work on the typescript, often under trying conditions; to Keith Williams and his colleagues (and especially Susan Jarvis) of the Computer Unit at University College, Cardiff, for invaluable help with the Index; to Gifford Charles-Edwards for an inspired handling of illustrations from the manuscript of Latin A (Peniarth 28) in her design for the dust jacket; to the Board of Celtic Studies of the University of Wales for undertaking the publication, and the staff of the University Registry and Press Board for help in carrying the process through; and to Keith Brown and his staff, whose enthusiastic collaboration has worked miracles in producing the final result.

NOTE ON REFERENCES

In references to periodicals the volume number appears in arabic numerals before the title (full or abbreviated) of the periodical; where a date appears in *square* brackets in that position, it is an essential part of the reference. For the mode of reference to the law texts see pp. 132, 147, 161. References to *Ancient Laws and Institutes of Wales* have wherever possible been to book, chapter, and section rather than to page.

CONTENTS

INTRODUCTION

WRITING in 1895, F. W. Maitland reminded us that "at any given moment the law of a nation contains things new and old", and warned of the difficulty of separating the new from the old in the law of the past: "We know the *caput mortuum* when we come upon it in modern times . . . But do we know the *caput mortuum* when we come upon it in ancient times?" Because of this difficulty, the medieval Welsh material would be dangerous to use "until the day comes (whether it ever will or ever can come I do not know) when those who are skilled in Celtic philology will have sorted that miscellaneous mass which we know as the Ancient Laws of Wales". If the sorting of the mass had to depend on philology alone, we might well admit that Maitland's day could never come; but Maitland himself had shown that a specialist in quite a different field could make some contribution to the sorting, and by now our hopes have been raised by the recognition that many other disciplines —History, Comparative Law, and Anthropology, to name only the most obvious—have a great deal to give to the process.[1] This probably means that no one student can ever again hope to have a complete mastery of the subject, but it means also that any student is much less likely to find himself entirely alone, though few of his colleagues will approach the study from quite the same angle as himself.

This collection of studies is the fruit of that kind of collaboration between specialists from different disciplines, though none of us would want to claim that as yet we have done much more than open the gate and cut a swath round the edge of a very extensive field. This disclaimer may suggest that we have been too eager to publish, and it is of course true that any conclusions we may seem to have reached must not be regarded as in any way definitive. Nevertheless, we believe that such a collection as this is of value now, because it makes available to a wider circle knowledge hitherto largely confined within a small group of specialists. If our studies do nothing else they may at least reinforce the

---

[1] Maitland himself would be delighted by a recent monograph of William Linnard, a specialist in the History of Forestry, showing how the natural distribution of beech in Wales is reflected in the different recensions of the lawbooks: W. Linnard, *Trees in the Law of Hywel* (1979).

lesson which Maitland was trying to teach, so many years ago, but we may also claim that our presentation and examination of some of the Welsh material will make the use of that material a little less dangerous for the non-specialists.

The main source of our knowledge of the Welsh law of women is the tractate which in some manuscripts is clearly marked off as containing *Cyfraith* (or *Cyfreithiau*) y *Gwragedd*; it is found in some form in all the most important books of *Cyfraith Hywel*. In Ior,[2] the tractate is introduced by the rubric "Eman e dechreun ny o kyureythyeu e guraged" (Here we begin the laws of women), and ends with the words: "Ac uelly e teruena keureyth e guraged" (and thus ends the law of women). In Cyfnerth the only rubric is the misleading "Gobreu guraged" of MS. *U*. In Lat A the first section begins *De lege puellarum* and each individual following section has its own heading. It is not easy to express simply what the concept of a "book" means to us, but we may start by saying that each of the five "Redactions" in Latin is usually treated as a distinct book, though the five are closely related—so closely, indeed, that they correspond to one of the three principal Welsh books, now usually referred to as the Books of Cyfnerth, Blegywryd, and Iorwerth, rather than by the names used by Aneurin Owen in his great edition of 1841, *The Ancient Laws and Institutes of Wales*, respectively "Gwentian Code", "Dimetian Code", and "Venedotian Code". Each of these books is represented by several manuscripts which differ, often very substantially, from one another, and there has been no serious attempt to reconstruct the ultimate common archetype of any of the three. That is why we have tended in this volume to speak for instance of the Iorwerth text or tradition, rather than of the Book of Iorwerth.[3] We must also make it clear that the use of these names does not imply any particular theory of the relation of the books to their eponyms.

The word *tractate* was introduced by the late Sir Goronwy Edwards as a convenient name for a collection of material dealing with one particular field, which may be very wide or very narrow. Until Sir Goronwy introduced this word, students tended to think of the Welsh lawbooks as amorphous masses, whereas it has long been the tradition to distinguish

---

[2] This rubric is not found in the G text and the reading is taken from MS B, see A. R. William, Llyfr Iorwerth (Cardiff 1960), §44/1.

[3] *Llyfr Iorwerth* and *Llyfr Blegywryd* are the names of printed editions. Ior and Bleg are used as abbreviations for these in the references. If "Bleg" seems to have been used in reference to "the Bleg tradition" it should be understood as meaning "the Bleg tradition as evidenced in the printed edition *Llyfr Blegywryd*".

tracts dealing with specific subjects as characteristic of the early Irish law material. The smallest Welsh tractates may have been compiled in their present form, but most tractates seem from their present appearance to have had a fairly long history of development. For it often happens that material which in one book or manuscript forms part of an ordered tractate appears in scattered fragments in various (often irrelevant) contexts in others.

The tractate *Cyfraith y Gwragedd* occurs in some form in all the books, but in every manuscript much material which is relevant to the Law of Women is to be found outside the compact tractate, and the most cursory comparison of the different versions will give an idea of the way in which the tractate has been built up, by the conglomeration of propositions of law derived from different sources and especially by the attraction to it of material which is also found in collections of triads or opinions on difficult cases (*Damweiniau*) or the like.

The process of development in the tractate is outlined in the study by T. M. Charles-Edwards which follows the three versions of the tractate here published. Those of the Cyfnerth and Iorwerth traditions are printed from manuscripts never before printed in full, while the Blegywryd tradition is represented by the Latin text of Peniarth MS. 28, which can be regarded as the oldest extant form of the tradition. None of these tractates contains all the relevant material, and we have shirked the formidable task of trying to gather the unassimilated fragments and to present them in an effective way. We hope, however, that all the relevant non-tractate material has been sufficiently presented in the studies in which it is cited.

The tractate is particularly valuable in its form, as an example of its *genre*; it is also particularly valuable in substance, because the juxtaposition of archaic and sophisticated in the Law of Women so often throws a revealing light on the development of society. The *caput mortuum* in the Law of Women did not lie quietly in its grave.

In the present volume an attempt has been made to begin identifying the old and new in our source material, and to apply historical and comparative techniques to its interpretation. The relevance to that attempt of some of the studies needs little comment: thus the archaic appears in its purest form in the *Naw Cynyweddi Deithïog* examined by Charles-Edwards. This legal fossil preserved in two of the Latin manuscripts and in three Welsh manuscripts, two of them late, lists nine types of marital union which invite comparison with similar classifications found, at opposite ends of the Indo-European periphery, in Ireland and India. A similar classification may also have provided the underlying framework for the tractate in its "Iorwerth" form, so that that particular form perhaps took shape for the first time very much earlier than the Iorwerth manuscript tradition would suggest.[4]

A more general comparison with Irish material is made by Christopher McAll, who traces the seven ages of the Celtic woman as reflected in Irish and Welsh law. The two editors have concentrated on what are really two facets of the same subject, the payments in cattle and money for which the tractate makes such detailed provision. Dafydd Jenkins's approach is that of a professionally-trained lawyer. His main interest is in the sophisticated development which justifies us in speaking of a classical period of Welsh law, and he is perhaps too ready to put the material into ready-made juristic categories. Morfydd Owen takes as her starting-point the two payments which are always treated as defining status in Welsh law, *galanas* and *sarhaed*. She relates them to the often unexpress-ed assumptions about social relationships which gave them their impor-tance, and shows (inter alia) that *galanas* had originally a much wider meaning than homicide, whereas *sarhaed* was only one of several technical terms relevant to the complementary concepts of insult and shame.

In the studies by R. R. Davies and D. B. Walters we take advantage of the expertise of two specialists from other disciplines. Davies has an en-viable mastery of the archival material from the marcher lordships; having skilfully used the lawbooks to help in interpreting the court records, he repays the debt by showing how those records testify to the survival and adaptation of Welsh law principles in the centuries between the Statute of Wales and the Act of Union. Walters, writing as a com-parative lawyer, gives us for the first time a detailed examination of a particular field of Welsh law in the light not merely of English and classical Roman law but also of the legal material of medieval western Europe. In some of the comparisons which he makes, we can see hints of a common origin for Welsh and other material, so that we are brought back very near to our Indo-European starting-point.

---

[4] The oldest law manuscripts in Welsh are of the Iorwerth text, but it is generally agreed that they are not very far removed in time from their archetype, which was probably compiled in the first half of the thirteenth century. As the pattern of our tractate sug-gests, however, any particular part of the compilation may have had a long history before it was incorporated into anything which can be recognised as a Iorwerth text.

There is inevitably overlapping between the studies and some inconsistency in the interpretations offered for the obscurities of the lawbooks. This is most evident in the treatment of the terms *priod* and *priodas*. There has been no editorial pressure to remove inconsistency, but we have made some comments in the Glossary.

The translators, too, have been allowed a freedom which means that though each has tried to be consistent with himself in his renderings of the technical terms, the same English word is not always used by different translators for a particular Welsh word. Welsh words occurring in the Latin Redaction A have been left untranslated in the English, but they have been transliterated into modern spelling (since there is no standard spelling of medieval Welsh). Welsh technical words and phrases occurring in the studies have likewise been modernised, save where they occur in quotations from a single manuscript or a printed edition. The translators of the two Welsh texts have agreed to differ about the best way of handling such a word as *wynebwerth*: one has left it in its Welsh guise, the other has used the literal rendering *face-value*.

The translators' greatest difficulty has been that of rendering in English the various Welsh words used for the human female. There is first of all the word *gwraig*, which may mean a female of any age.[5] More often it means a sexually-experienced female, and it is often used in contrast with *morwyn* which has the range of meanings still found in the word *maid* in some English dialects. In twentieth century literary English, one is forced to the choice between *girl* and *virgin*, according to the context, which is unfortunate because *virgin* is also needed as a translation for its cognate *gwyry*, used in Welsh only in the sense of the sexually-inexperienced girl. There is fortunately little doubt about the meaning to be given to *morwyn* in any particular passage, but the difficulties are prettily illustrated by McAll's discussion of the special term *morwynwraig*. Here, as often in the lawbooks and very often indeed in modern Welsh, *gwraig* has the meaning *wife*, that is, a woman having a husband, without any necessary implication that she has had sexual intercourse with him—or with anyone else. *Morwyn* has the meaning *virgin;* perhaps we should say *reputed virgin*, for the rule in question would apply to the *morwynwraig* even if it were afterwards shown that she was a *twyllforwyn*. The unregenerate lawyer is tempted to regret that we have no record among the *Damweiniau* of a solution to the problem

---

[5] As in the discussion of the compensation for a foetus destroyed, Ior §97/3.

which would arise if a defendant paid *sarhaed* to a *morwynwraig* for a non-sexual assault, and afterwards alleged that he had paid at the wrong rate because her husband has rejected her as not being a virgin, so that she never became in the full sense his wife.[6]

The last paragraph, peppered as it is with italics, reminds us to offer our defence for not treating such words as *amobr* as naturalised in English for the purpose of this volume. We have decided to italicise them for a simple practical reason, namely that in our experience it is often much easier to track down some statement in print when it contains an italicised technical term.

As we have already emphasised, we do not claim to have done more in these studies than open up the field, and we are conscious that there are corners of the field at which we have hardly cast a glance. If some readers feel that too many aspects of the Law of Women have been neglected, we hope that others will find answers to some of their queries in the Glossary or in some Excursus, where we have tucked away information for which no point in any of the studies seemed appropriate.

---

[6] It would be useful to have a study of the ambit of the various words, comparable with those for the German words in the same field, presented in diagram and comment in Werner König, *dtv-Atlas der deutschen Sprache* (Munich, 1978), 22-3, 112-13.

THE NORMAL PARADIGMS OF A WOMAN'S LIFE IN THE IRISH AND WELSH LAW TEXTS[1]

WOMEN IN the Irish and Welsh legal texts occupy, not unexpectedly, a position of considerable inferiority. In the earliest Irish material, however, this inferiority is to some extent alleviated by the fact that at at least one stage in her life, a woman enjoys equal status with her male coeval. Admittedly, the equality is somewhat short-lived, but until the age of seven a child's honour-price (the index of an individual's status) is fixed at a comparatively high level irrespective of the child's sex or social background. At that point a child is brought into line with the hierarchical structure of society, its honour-price being calculated as half that of its father, but still until the age of twelve a girl is of equal status with her brother.[2]

In this respect, Welsh law is considerably less generous to women, only allowing them such an equality of status while they remain indistinguishable from men, i.e. until birth, or more accurately in the eyes of the law, until baptism. At this point they suffer the characteristic indignity of having their *sarhaed* (compensation for insult) and their *galanas* (compensation owed to an individual's kindred in the event of his or her having been killed) calculated as half that due to or on behalf of a brother.[3]

Welsh law does not, therefore, recognise in quite the same way as the Irish the special sanctity attaching to children in their first seven years, defined in Irish law as *grád maice*, "the status of childhood", but it does recognise the age of seven as significant in the development of a child's legal responsibility. At that age a Welsh girl can "go on oath", while a boy can not only swear on his own behalf, but goes "under the hand" of a priest, and takes upon himself the "yoke of God".[4]

---

[1] In this paper I attempt to define and compare the normal paradigms of a woman's life in early Irish and Welsh society respectively in so far as they are ascertainable from the law texts. Since such a comparison is dependent upon there being rather a community of subject-matter than an established relative chronology, I beg the question of the precise periods to which the texts refer, except in so far as it is necessary—particularly in the Irish material—to distinguish between different chronological strata within the texts themselves. I should like to thank Dr. T. M. Charles-Edwards for having read through the original draft and for making many helpful comments.

[2] *Ir. Recht* 22; CG 125.

[3] Ior § 97, § 38/4, 5, § 110/9.

[4] (1934) 12 *Ériu* 8, Ior § 97/6, § 99/1.

It is at this point that the prospects facing a girl under the two legal systems take on a markedly different character. In Welsh law she is destined to remain at her father's knee (lit. beside his plate) until she has been successfully married between the ages of twelve and fourteen, and her brother does the same, only leaving the family circle at fourteen to be commended to and join the retinue of his feudal lord.[5] It is difficult to establish precisely the degree of metaphor with which *wrth noe y t(h)ad* ("beside his (or her) father's plate") should be translated. It could, for instance, simply imply in the case of a girl that her father retains ultimate responsibility for her up until the age of betrothal, but that she does not necessarily remain within her own family throughout this period. In the absence of evidence to the contrary, however, one has to presume that unlike their Irish counterparts, at the period of the law texts neither a Welsh girl nor her brother were normally subject to fosterage, and that therefore *wrth noe y t(h)ad* can be taken to suggest that they remain in the proximity of their immediate family.

The Irish evidence on the subject of fosterage is not exactly profuse, but the fragmentary information preserved in the tract *Cáin Íarraith* does establish that both a girl and her brother could be sent out on fosterage in that an *ócaire* (lowest grade of freeman) is described as having to pay three *séoit*[6] as fosterage fee for his son, and four for his daughter.[7] The text does not elaborate further on the reasons for this differential, although the later commentators are at no loss to provide a variety of explanations, and one can only assume, perhaps unfairly, that a foster-daughter was more of a liability than a foster-son. The *áes díailtri* ("age of unfosterage", i.e. age at which fosterage came to an end) is defined in *Críth Gablach* as fourteen years for a boy, although elsewhere in *Bretha Crólige* for example, and in the commentary on *Cáin Íarraith* generally, it is suggested that a boy could remain in fosterage until his seventeenth year. For a girl, fosterage ended at marriageable age, (*áes tóga*, "age of choice"), nowhere precisely defined in the texts, but the commentators are presumably right in giving it as fourteen years.[8] What proportion of children were actually sent out on fosterage for the full period is impossible to say on the evidence of the law texts, but fosterage was doubtless the peculiar prerogative of the grades of freemen, the *Féni*, and the

---

[5] Ior §§ 98, 99.
[6] *sét* (pl. *séoit*) is generally used in the texts of any chattel up to the value of one milch-cow.
[7] ALI ii. 150.
[8] CG 30-34; 12 *Ériu* 8; *Ir. Recht* 8.

ócaire would therefore have been the man of lowest rank for whom it was customary to have his son or daughter fostered.

There is not, therefore, a great deal of similarity between the prospects that faced an Irish and a Welsh girl respectively as they emerged from childhood. The one enjoyed equal status with her brother until the age of twelve and was subject to fosterage until she reached marriageable age at fourteen, while the other was entitled to only half her brother's status, and remained within her own family until the marriage negotiations had been satisfactorily concluded.

The importance, for Welsh law, of a girl being brought up in the proximity of her immediate family, becomes apparent when she reaches the *oed iddi ei rhoddi i ŵr* ("age for her to be given to a man"). Marriage in both legal systems involves a complicated exchange of wealth in which the prime commodity to change hands is the girl herself, but in Welsh law this commodity becomes of little or no value if the husband or prospective husband finds her not to be a virgin. If such is the man's claim on going to bed with the girl for the first time, the evidence of the girl's *cyfneseifiaid* ("next of kin"), defined as her parents and brothers and sisters, can be of paramount importance for the substantiating of her claim to virginity up until the point at which she went to her husband's bed. If she does not appeal to them in such a case, or if they are not prepared to be appealed to, or on appeal concur with the groom, the unfortunate *twyllforwyn* ("false virgin") as she is now called, is dealt with with remarkably little ceremony. Instead of her proper share of the marriage wealth in the form of *agweddi* due to her on her legitimate separation from her husband after nine nights of marriage, she is given a one-year-old steer with a greased tail. In the unlikely event of her being able to keep hold of the animal by its tail, she is allowed to keep it.[9] Obviously if the *cyfneseifiaid* are to be considered reliable witnesses in such a case, it is essential that they should have had the opportunity of observing the behaviour of the girl from close quarters over a considerable period of time, or at least, from the age of twelve onwards. To have sent her out on fosterage between the ages of seven and fourteen would inevitably give rise to serious doubts as to her marketability and would be unthinkable.

What then is the situation in the Irish context? One can only conclude from the allusive references to the establishment of marital relations in the Irish legal texts that virginity did not affect a girl's market-value in Irish society in the same way as it did in the Welsh, and that if it did, the

---

[9] Bleg. 61. 27-31; Ior § 47/5. Cf. pp. 80-81 and the article there cited.

fact that she parted company with her own family from early childhood onwards meant that they would not have been the most reliable witnesses to testify to her virginity. It is unfortunately the case, however, that there is no Irish legal text extant that concerns itself specifically with the establishment as opposed to the dissolution of marital relations, and if one concludes from such negative evidence that virginity was not as crucial a factor in the marriage contract in Irish as in Welsh society, it has to be recognised as being a conclusion arrived at *e silentio*.

Irrespective of whether a girl was or was not a virgin, a husband would have been even more interested as to whether she would or would not prove fertile, but before considering the implications of fertility and infertility it is necessary to describe the payments involved in the marriage contract and the various sorts of wife that an Irish or Welsh girl could expect to become.

Welsh law is the more informative as to the pecuniary exchange that took place at marriage. When a father is in the position of saying to his daughter *"Mi a'th roddais i ŵr"*, ("I have given you to a man"), a payment known as *amobr* becomes payable to the feudal lord. When she goes to her husband's bed for the first time, he (i.e. the husband) becomes liable to a payment known as *cowyll*, effectively a payment for her virginity, but just in case the marriage is not consummated to his satisfaction, he does not actually hand over the *cowyll* until the following morning, although the bride has to stipulate what she wants the payment to consist of before rising from the bed. If she forgets to make the stipulation, she forfeits exclusive rights to the *cowyll*. During the first night of marriage, the *neithiorwyr*, "wedding guests", remain in the vicinity as witnesses to the happy or unhappy conclusion to this particular part of the ceremony, and for the next nine days the wife remains secluded in the environs of the marriage-bed. At this point she emerges and returns to the world, and thenceforth until the end of the seventh year of marriage she is entitled to the payment of a sum known as *agweddi* from him in the event of her legitimately leaving him or his illegitimately leaving her.[10]

The Irish texts do not allow of such a clear-cut analysis of the payments made either to or on behalf of a prospective bride. That the girl in question was at one point considered to be a commodity to be exchanged for the appropriate sum is suggested by a passage in the *Gúbretha Caratniad*, " 'False' judgements of Caratnia", where Caratnia

---

[10] e.g. Bleg. 119. 8-18; but cf. Lat A § 52/65, 66.

mystifies the king by informing him of his judgement that a *ráth*-surety should stand for the payment of a debt owed by the son of a living father. "That was false", says the king; "It was correct", says Caratnia, "*ar ba creic cétmuintere*", ("for it was [lit.] the purchase of a *cétmuinter*").[11] It would be wrong to read too much into the expression "purchase" here in what is essentially a highly respectable form of gift exchange, but one cannot altogether ignore the commercial implications. The payment due from the bridegroom is generally known as *coibche*, (ultimately from *com* + *fíach*, "equivalent liability to payment", "mutual debt"),[12] and would appear to have been shared between father and daughter, (or, if the father is no longer alive, between the latter and the head of her kindred), in so far as concealment of the payment on the part of the girl would seem to lead to her forfeiting her share.[13] Originally there may have been some distinction between *coibche* and another payment that is mentioned, *tinnscra*, (from *to-ind-ess-cren-), which again, as a compound of *crenaid*, "buys", conveys the idea of purchasing something from somebody, but by the period of the texts they seem to have come to mean one and the same thing.[14]

Concerning the various categories of wife that a girl was liable to become, both legal systems present a relatively complicated aspect. For Irish law, I shall draw on the evidence of two texts. The first was itself considered by Thurneysen to consist of two tracts but for the sake of the argument will be considered as one,[15] and was published by him under the title *Díre*.[16] The second is *Cáin Lánamna*, which could be translated the "law of couples", and has particular reference to divorce and its implementation with respect to nine different categories of marital union.[17]

The most that an Irish girl could hope for at the period of the *Díre* tract was to become a *cétmuinter*, and it is therefore necessary to decide quite what a *cétmuinter* was. The *Díre* tract itself does not elaborate in

---

[11] (1925) 15 ZCP 311; for the meaning of *cétmuinter*, (a category of spouse), see further below.

[12] By way of *cobach* which not only has the sense of a payment owed as part of a contract, but can also refer to one of the parties to the contract; cf. *Bürgschaft*, p. 13.

[13] ALI iv. 60-62.

[14] Cf. also *tochre*, verbal noun of *do-cren*, apparently identical in meaning with *tinnscra* and *coibche*, but it does not seem to occur in the law texts.

[15] It remains a distinct possibility that the text in question was originally a unity; compare particularly the order of quotations from the text preserved in TCD H.3.17 cols. 425-429 which seem to follow a more logical (i.e. chronological) order than those in the other two MSS.

[16] *Ir. Recht* 1-60.

[17] Ed. R. Thurneysen, SEIL 1-80.

any detail on the status or peculiar qualities of the *cétmuinter*. It does, however, recognise three categories of wife: *cétmuinter*; *ben aititen*, "acknowledged wife"; and *ben bís for foxul*, "abducted wife". These three categories are further enlarged to five by the addition of the *cétmuinter* who does not produce sons, and the subdivision of the *ben aititen* into two categories: the "acknowledged wife" who is betrothed by her kindred, and she who is neither betrothed nor compelled to marry, but who marries on her own account with the approval of her kindred.[18] The "abducted wife", *ben bís for foxul*, specifically refers to a woman who marries against the express wishes of her father or her kindred. As the category of wife changes from the *cétmuinter* through the two types of *ben aititen* to the *ben bís for foxul*, so the involvement of the woman's kindred in the payment of any compensation owed by her, and, in the event of her death, the receipt of a share in her *díbad*, "estate", (and if she has been killed, her *éraic*, "wergeld"), increases, with the exception that in the case of an "abducted wife", her kindred have no obligation to share in the payment of any compensation owed by her, but are entitled to the whole of her *éraic* and her *díbad*. In the case of the second category of *ben aititen*, therefore, the woman's kindred shares the obligations and entitlements with her own offspring in the proportions of two-thirds to one-third. If she is a *cétmuinter*, however, the proportions are reversed. The fact that a *cétmuinter* was considered to be at a greater remove from her own kindred than any other type of wife is further emphasised by another passage in the *Díre* tract where she is described as being the only woman not entitled to decide whether the responsibility for the levying of any debts due to her should lie with her son, her kindred, or the "man of her thigh", (her husband). For a *cétmuinter*, the responsibility can only lie with her *cétmuinter*, her spouse.[19] The only other piece of information concerning these five categories of wife enumerated in this part of the *Díre* tract that will be mentioned here is that both times that it occurs, *ben aititen* is glossed *adaltrach urnadma*, "betrothed adulteress".

Cáin Lánamna presents a rather different picture. Its main departure from the *Díre* tract is that it describes a type of wife known as a *bé cuitchernsa*, ("woman of joint sovereignty"), in the first of its nine categories of marital union. The *bé cuitchernsa* contributes an equal amount to the marriage-wealth as does her husband, and, in addition, represents a phenomenon unheard of at the period of the *Díre* tract, in

---

[18] *Ir. Recht* 27-28.
[19] ibid. 34.

that she can enter into contracts independently of her husband provided that they do not serve to the overall detriment of the union; (the *Díre* tract states specifically that no woman is capable of entering into contracts independently of the man responsible for her).[20] It is apparent, therefore, that *Cáin Lánamna* dates from a later period in that it suggests at least the possibility of a woman attaining some degree of contractual independence.[21]

It is not until we arrive at the second category of marital union that we begin to see the relics of the system outlined in the *Díre* tract. The second category relates to a type of marriage in which the man makes the greater contribution of wealth, and it is apparent that such, at an early period, had been the normal form, in that the *bé cuitchernsa*'s accession to greater independence cannot be divorced from the fact that she herself brings considerable wealth into the marriage. In the context of the second type of marriage, three categories of wife are mentioned: *cétmuinter*; *ben urnadma*, "betrothed wife"; and *adaltrach*. In order to be a *cétmuinter*, a woman is described as having to be *comaith comcheniuil*, "of equal rank and of equal birth", and if she satisfies these requirements she is entitled to "disturb" those of her husband's contracts that she considers "foolish". Alternatively she might be simply a "betrothed wife" but not a *cétmuinter*, in which case she has no power to disturb her husband's foolish contracts, and he only has to consult his wife when selling clothes, food, cows, or sheep.[22]

There is, therefore, in the second type of marriage described in *Cáin Lánamna*, a distinction made between the *cétmuinter* and the *ben urnadma*, "betrothed wife", that reflects exactly that made in the *Díre* tract between the *cétmuinter* and the first of the two categories of "acknowledged wife", the one who was betrothed. The question needs to be considered as to whether the distinction between the two simply reflects the status of the two partners in marriage, or whether it has hitherto (in this paper) unconsidered implications for the nature of the marriage connection itself. Instructive in this context is the allusion (with reference to the same type of marriage) to the *adaltrach*.[23] A man in early Irish society was quite liable to have more than one wife, and *Cáin Lánamna* states that should a man take on an *adaltrach* in spite of his *cétmuinter*, not only is the *adaltrach*'s share of her *coibche* forfeit to the

[20] SEIL 18-19; *Ir. Recht* 35.
[21] Cf. Dr. Binchy's remarks in "The Legal Capacity of Women in Regard to Contracts" at SEIL 210.
[22] SEIL 45-46.
[23] ibid. 49.

cétmuinter but she is also obliged to pay to the latter her honour-price. The distinction here is quite apparently that between a wife to whom a man is already married and his additional or secondary wife. It is also probable, in view of the fact that the man has paid *coibche*, that the *adaltrach* was betrothed by her kindred and that she could therefore be described as a *ben urnadma*, "betrothed wife". In fact a passage of text at ALI v. 480 specifically refers to *adaltracha íarna n-urnaidm nó aidite dia finib fria firu*, "*adaltracha* after their betrothal or acknowledgement by their kindred with respect to their husbands". This passage not only suggests that an *adaltrach* was generally a *ben urnadma*, (i.e. betrothed), but also a *ben aititen*, (acknowledged). We have already seen that in the *Díre* tract *ben aititen* is glossed *adaltrach urnadma*, "betrothed adulteress", and the conclusion that is forced upon one by these passages is that *ben urnadma, ben aititen*, and *adaltrach* all refer, at different stages, to one and the same category of wife. It is significant that from the moment that she appears in the texts, the *ben aititen* is described by the glossators as an adulteress. The explanation can only be that generally speaking such indeed was the case, that the *ben aititen*, (or, as she is later known, the *adaltrach*), was taken on by a man "in spite of" his *cétmuinter*.

One could, therefore, conclude on the basis of the discussion so far, that at the period of the *Díre* tract (and to a lesser extent at that of *Cáin Lánamna*), a man had his *cétmuinter* who was characterised by the fact that (i) she came from a family of equal status to his own, and (ii) the man to whom she was married did not already have a *cétmuinter* or any other wife, and conversely that he might also have a *ben aititen* (or *adaltrach*) who was taken on by him with the approval of her kindred in addition to a *cétmuinter* or other wife whom he already possessed. Such an additional wife was, therefore, by definition, (at least in the eyes of the Church), an adulteress.

If one accepts that, at least at the period of the *Díre* tract, the terminology concerning married women reflects the essentially polygynous nature of marriage in early Irish society, one has yet to establish the precise meaning of *cétmuinter* itself. *Cétmuinter* refers not only to the category of wife defined above, but also to her husband. *Muinter* itself can mean both "household" and "member of a household", and the prefix could either be taken to be the ordinal numeral *cét-*, "first", or the less well attested preposition *cét-*, "with". Since *cétmuinter* is invariably used in a personalised sense, it is therefore either to be translated "first (i.e. 'principal') member of a household" or "joint member of a household". Although the second translation might be considered to underline the shared responsibility of the two spouses within the household, the first would seem to be the more acceptable since (i) the translation "principal member of a household" accurately reflects the position of the *cétmuinter*; (ii) the preposition *cét-* "with" used as a prefix is of only limited attestation, whereas the ordinal numeral *cét-* (as a compositional prefix) is of frequent occurrence; and (iii) the translation "joint member of a household" is not sufficiently exclusive of other members of the household, all of whom can be referred to by the term *muinter*.[24]

Having to some extent managed to disentangle ourselves from the undergrowth of Irish law with respect to the sorts of wife that a woman was liable to become, we must now return to the thicket of the Welsh. The situation relating to married women in the latter is, however, mercifully simplified by the fact that by the period of the texts a man was only allowed to have one wife at a time. The generic word for "wife" in Welsh law is *gwraig*, but the word can have other implications depending on context, and it is important initially to establish its various areas of meaning.

Gwraig refers primarily to a "woman" as opposed to a "man", and can therefore be used of a woman of any age. It can also be used to describe a "woman" as opposed to a "girl", (*morwyn*), the latter being considered a *gwraig* in this sense only when she reaches maturity, when the *teithi oedran gwraig*, ("characteristics of womanhood"), have come to her. But the most crucial distinction in a legal context is the third opposition between *gwraig*, "non-virgin", and *morwyn*, "virgin". If a man takes a wife on the understanding that she is a virgin, (*ar fraint morwyn*, "with the status of a virgin") and finds her not to be so, (*a hithau yn wraig*, "and she a woman"), he can not only divest himself of her through the procedure outlined above involving the steer and its greased tail, but he can give her a *gwg*, "injury", for which no compensation is payable.[25] Having come through the various categories of *gwraig* to the point of being *gwraig* X, "X's wife", she now enters upon

[24] Although Meyer understood *cét-* in *cétmuinter* to be the prep. "with" (used as a prefix) (*Contribb.* 355), both Thurneysen and Binchy take it to be the ordinal numeral. Thurneysen comments: "es bedeutet den Ersten oder die Erste der *familia*, den Vorstand des Haushalts; ich übersetze es mit Hausvorstand (Hausvorsteherin)" (SEIL 46); Binchy translates " 'head of the household' (chief spouse)": CG.

[25] WML 137. 16-18; the various meanings of *gwraig* can give rise to some apparently oxymoronic terminology. For instance, a girl who has been betrothed but whose marriage has not yet been consummated is described as a *morwynwreic*, which could be translated "virgin-non-virgin", but in fact presumably means "virgin-wife".

a preliminary seven-year period of marriage during which time *agweddi* is payable to her by her husband should she legitimately separate from him or wrongly be abandoned by him. After seven years of cohabitation she is entitled to a half share in the marriage-wealth, and *agweddi* is no longer payable to her on separation. Similar rights to a share in the marriage-wealth extend to a woman in any marital union that has survived seven years, however disreputable its origins. After seven years, the law recognises the partners in any such union as man and wife.[26]

There are, therefore, at least three categories of women in a legally recognised relationship with a man: a woman who is properly betrothed and married but who is still *a dan ei hagweddi*, lit. "under her *agweddi*", (i.e. who has not yet been married for seven years); a woman cohabiting with a man who was not originally betrothed or married and who is not yet officially recognised as his wife since the seven-year period has not yet elapsed; and a woman in any marital union after seven years. One would expect the important legal distinction between these three to be reflected in the vocabulary by which they are described, but although there are several terms descriptive of marital unions and the partners involved in Welsh law, their precise areas of meaning are not entirely clear. On one level, the first three of the nine categories of union enumerated in Latin Redaction B could be taken to reflect such a basic three-fold distinction.[27] The third, *caradas*, "illicit affair", could well refer to an irregular union that has not yet been made legitimate under the seven year rule; the second, *agweddi*, could be an accurate description of any properly entered-into marriage before the end of the first seven years, when the woman is still entitled to receive *agweddi* on separation; and the first *priodas*, any marriage after the first seven years have elapsed.[28]

Whether or not it had originally been the case that the lapse of seven years was considered sufficient for any union to be considered fully established and legitimate, it is clear that the Church took a different view of what constituted legitimacy. *Llyfr Iorwerth* states quite clearly:

> *Keureyth eglues a dyweyt na dele un mab tref tat namen e mab hynaf e'r tat o'r wreyc pryaut* "Church law states that no son is entitled to his father's holding except the father's eldest son from the *gwraig briod*".[29]

---

[26] e.g. Ior § 52/5.
[27] Lat B 244. 37-9.
[28] One quite literal translation of *priodas*, "property", would indeed make it an apt description of the process that took place after the seven year period when the woman became entitled to a half share in the marriage-wealth.
[29] Ior § 87/5.

Gwraig briod here can only refer to the wife who is legitimate in the eyes of the Church, that is, who was married according to Church law and who became a *gwraig briod* at the moment she married and not seven years afterwards. The same interpretation need not necessarily be put upon the term in another passage from *Llyfr Iorwerth*:

> *Ny dele gureyc na prynu na gwerthu ony byd pryaut; o byd pryaut hy hagen, hy a dele prynu a guerthu* "a woman is not entitled to buy or sell unless she is *priod*; if she is *priod*, however, she is entitled to buy and sell".[30]

On analogy with the Irish *bé cuitchernsa* one could lay it down as axiomatic that the rights of a *gwraig briod* to enter into contract are directly related to the fact that she is a woman of property in her own right. Either, therefore, she is a woman who has acceded to her due share of the marriage-wealth after seven years, or she is a woman who was properly endowed with the *gwaddol*, "dowry", due to her when she first entered the marriage.

Again on analogy with the Irish evidence, one could set up the following hypothesis as to the developing significance of *priodas* in marriage. Originally the man would have brought the larger proportion of wealth into the marriage, the bride being simply a commodity to be exchanged by her kindred for the requisite marriage-payments. The bride herself had no property of any quantity until after the seven year period had elapsed, when she became entitled to half the marriage-wealth. At that stage in the marriage she became known as a *gwraig briod* and her rights increased accordingly.[31] This would have been the system obtaining at the period of the nine unions, and one could perhaps translate *gwraig briod* quite literally as "woman of property". As in Irish society, the position of women under Welsh law gradually improved to the extent that they became entitled to *gwaddol*, a share in their father's wealth consisting of moveable property and worth half that due to a son, (more particularly in the form of land). A woman had ceased, therefore, to be simply a commodity, and was in effect a "woman of property", *gwraig briod*, as soon as she entered marriage. Both partners were, therefore, suitably endowed at the commencement of marriage, and it may well have been at this stage that a husband became known as a *gŵr priod* by analogy with his wife. The seven year period would, presumably, have

---

[30] Ior § 53/4 (B).
[31] The husband at this period would, presumably, not necessarily have been known as a *gŵr priod*, since he would by definition have had to have been a man of property since the beginning of the marriage.

become somewhat academic, since the wife's moveables (livestock etc.) would have become inextricably involved with the husband's land from the earliest days of the marriage. The husband's liability to the payment of *agweddi* on separation would also have been somewhat irrelevant since the woman was well enough endowed without it, (at the early period she would have had nothing but her *agweddi*), but the law texts still mention it, although in the case of *Llyfr Blegywryd* it is described as a payment made by the bride's father to the bridegroom.[32] *Gwraig briod* had by this stage, therefore, simply come to mean a married woman who had been properly endowed, and, in the eyes of the Church, properly married according to Church law, effectively its modern meaning.

Such is one possible explanation that could be put upon the evidence of the Welsh texts, and it has the advantage that it corresponds closely to the development of marriage under Irish law, but the task of definitive differentiation between the chronological strata within the two systems remains a tenuous exercise, and any conclusions based on such differentiation, particularly with respect to the Welsh evidence, can only be of a tentative nature.

Having contrived, if circuitously, to reach that point in a woman's life where she has become successfully married, it may be instructive to compare her rights under Irish and Welsh law with reference to entering into contracts, giving gifts, acting as witness, and inheriting.

The general rule in both systems is that her rights in such situations are either severely limited or non-existent. In contract, for instance, at the period of the *Díre* tract, a woman is described as:

> *ní túalaing reicce na creice na cuir na cundruda sech óen a cenn* "she is not capable of selling or buying or contract or transaction without one of her heads" (i.e. one of the men responsible for her)[33]

while the Welsh Latin Redaction E has the statement:

> *mulier non potest mercari nec vendere sine licencia viri sui.*[34]

In both laws, therefore, any purchasing or selling that a woman might wish to do on her own account is strictly controlled by the man under

---

[32] Bleg 119. 14, cf. Col § 1 n (pp. 43-5); Professor Dafydd Jenkins suggests to me that the reference in *Bleg* to the payment of *agweddi* by the bride's father may have arisen from a practice of requiring with a wife a dowry which would pay the *agweddi* if it ever became due.

[33] *Ir. Recht* 35.

[34] Lat E 475.

whose aegis she stands, whether it be her father, her husband, her son, or the head of her kindred, with the exception in Irish law of the *bé cuitchernsa*, and in Welsh of the *gwraig briod*, both of whom are women of property in their own right, and both of whom can therefore be considered to represent innovations over an otherwise obtaining incapacity.

One area in which a married woman in both legal systems is able to act without reference to her husband and her lord is in the giving of gifts. The parallel between the two laws is a fairly close one. A married woman in Irish law, according to a passage of text in TCD H.3.17,[35] is prohibited from buying and selling but is allowed to make a *tabairt cach mná fo míad*, "gift of every woman according to rank". The Irish law texts do not elaborate further on such gifts, but an exactly similar rule applies in Welsh law and could almost be an expansion of the brief Irish statement. The wife of a Welsh king can give away without permission one-third of the *dofod* (casual acquisitions) that comes to her from the king; that of an *uchelwr* various articles of clothing in addition to food and drink, as well as being able to lend as much of the household equipment as she chooses; while the wife of a villein can only give her headgear and lend her sieve, and then only under severe restrictions.[36]

As witnesses women are also virtually legal non-entities in both systems. They are specifically banned in the Welsh context from acting as witnesses in relation to men, (*na eyll gureyc bot en vybedyat ar vr*), and in Irish law a woman is considered to be one of seven persons completely incapable of giving evidence as an eye-witness, (although Caratnia produces the exception of a case involving men in Holy Orders).[37]

There is also a close similarity between a Welsh and Irish woman's rights in inheritance, or rather, the absence thereof. Only in the event of there being no surviving heir to the family property does a woman become liable to inherit it, and in the Irish context anyway, she only inherits a life-interest. There was only one way in which an Irish heiress was able to pass the family property on to her children, which was by taking the precaution of marrying the nearest surviving agnatic relative to whom the property would otherwise have gone on her death.[38]

---

[35] Quoted by Professor Binchy at SEIL 214.
[36] Ior § 51/6-8.
[37] Ior § 77/16; ALI v. 284; 15 ZCP 345.
[38] Bleg 75. 24-5; Myles Dillon, "Relationship and the Law of Inheritance", SEIL 150-151; the figure of the *banchomarbe*, "heiress", in Irish law, does in fact throw the generalised subservient position of women (at least at the early period) out of kilter, in that there is no question of her being considered in any way dependent upon her husband, but since she must have been a comparative rarity in early Irish society I shall not confuse the issue further by elaborating upon her peculiar position.

Should a woman discover that she is dissatisfied with the legal persona that has been imposed upon her by marriage, or simply wishes to be separated from her husband, she can do so legitimately under Welsh law by proving that he has been discovered with another woman not less than three times, has leprosy or bad breath, or is impotent. In Irish law, she can legitimately divorce her husband if he turns out to be in Holy Orders, or is too fat or impotent, or if he persists in revealing secrets about their intimate life to third parties.[39] It had been, at the early period, in the interests of married women under both laws to bear with it for a certain period of time; in Welsh law, seven years, and in Irish law an undisclosed quantity of time referred to allusively by Caratnia as the *ré téchte*, "proper period".[40] Originally in Welsh law, or at least at the earliest period for which evidence is forthcoming in the law texts, the marriage-wealth was shared between the two parties after seven years. Divorce after that point entailed the complete division of the moveable property as outlined in the law texts, while in the first seven years if the woman left on legitimate grounds she only took with her her *agweddi*, her own personal possessions, (*argyfrau*), and her *cowyll*, (the payment for her virginity that she had received from her husband). If she left her husband for another man, she lost everything except her *cowyll*, her *wynebwerth*, (honour-price), and her *gowyn*, (such compensation as she might have received for having found her husband with another woman).[41]

In Irish law, in the *Gúbretha Caratniad*, a wife is described as losing her *tinnscra*, (perhaps to be translated "dowry"), if she leaves her husband before the *ré téchte*, "proper period". Thurneysen follows d'Arbois de Jubainville and suggests that such a period of time may well have been of one year's duration, and have been designed to establish beyond doubt the fecundity or infecundity of the partners. There is a distinct possibility, however, that it too was a seven year period; and that such a length of time need not be considered excessive for establishing whether or not the partners were fertile, or acting in good faith, or both, is suggested by a parallel passage in the Laws of Manu, where a man is prohibited from divorcing his wife before the end of seven years even though she may be barren.[42]

---

[39] Ior § 45/4; ALI v. 132.
[40] 15 ZCP 345.
[41] At a later stage, when a woman took a considerable dowry into marriage with her, it is not certain that the seven year period still operated in quite the same way, as has been mentioned above; in any case, in such a situation, whenever she legitimately separated from her husband, she would have taken her own dowry with her.
[42] *The Laws of Manu*, trans. G. Bühler, *Sacred Books of the East* xxv, Oxford 1886, Book ix, section 81; (I am grateful to Dr. T. M. Charles-Edwards for this reference).

I shall not attempt to describe in detail the division of the marriage-property on divorce in Irish and Welsh law, but there are still two instances not entirely unrelated to the subject of separation that provide grounds for comparison between the two laws before we are able to complete the paradigms in hand and see our subjects safely interred. In Irish law, should a man's *cétmuinter* draw the blood of a woman whom her husband has taken on "in spite of" her, the injury is free from compensation. In Welsh law the same rule applies, in that a man's wife can injure or even kill her husband's *cywyres*, ("mistress"), with her two hands, and remain free from having to make any compensatory payments.[43] In addition, should a Welsh wife leave her husband on the grounds of his taking another wife, she may legitimately do so and take everything that she is entitled to and he is powerless to stop her, *kany byd karrdychwel*, "since there is not car- (or "sled-") -return". One of the legitimate seizures in Irish law of a person emigrating, and involving the unyoking of that person's cart (or carts), is that of a woman who absconds from the law of marriage.[44] The implication of the Welsh passage is that should a woman abscond from marriage illegally, she, too, is subject to "car-return". It must remain at least possible that the institution of "car-return" is a common inheritance in both laws from a period at which it was a regular form of distraint made to prevent illegal emigration.

The women are now approaching the end of their productive life, their husbands may have died, or they may have long since been divorced. In any event, they cease to be of much interest to the Irish and Welsh lawyers. Welsh law does show some interest in mentioning that a woman who has separated from or outlived her husband still has her *sarhaed* (honour-price) calculated according to the status of the man with whom she was last known to have publicly cohabited, while Irish law only chooses to mention her equivalent, the *fedb*, ("widow", or perhaps "single woman"), in the doubtful company of an *aindir* ("non-virgin") and a *bé carna* ("woman of flesh"), in that they are all three described as being payable in "chattels of innocence" (in their honour-price) if they have done adequate penance for the innumerable cohabitations that they have been guilty of.[45]

---

[43] ALI v. 142; Bleg 116. 27-9.
[44] Ior § 52/5; ALI v. 260.
[45] Ior § 110/9; ALI v. 448.

The Welsh lawyers do not concern themselves with the presumably straightforward question of who inherits what after a woman's death, but one contributor to the Irish *Díre* tract does see fit to modify the legitimate claims of a woman's kindred to her estate, and in so doing not only adds a certain poignant reminder of the gradually improving social position of women, but also provides eloquent testimony as to precisely which group of learned men were most responsible for the written preservation of the Irish laws:

> *Cach ben nad-faccaib cin na ciniud na soethar i túaith, is meise torad a da llám do chor fri eclais* "Every woman who does not leave liability to fines nor offspring to be supported nor any other trouble among her people is entitled to leave the fruit of her two hands to the Church".[46]

CHRISTOPHER MCALL

[46] *Ir. Recht* 32-33.

NAU KYNYWEDI TEITHIAUC

IN TWO of the Latin versions of the Welsh Laws, Redactions B and E, and in three other legal manuscripts there is a collection of "nines", mnemonic lists of nine items and other standardised uses of the numeral nine. The collections include a wide variety of topics from the "novem occisionis pertinentie, id est, *nau affeith galanas*" to the *nau nos guesti*. One of the lists of nine items is that of the *naw kynywedi teithiawc*. In this case all nine, or at least most of them, are set out in full. In this accidental fashion we have preserved for us a remarkable legal fossil which can be interpreted best by comparison with a similar list in an Irish law tract of about A.D. 700, *Cáin Lánamna*. More than forty years ago Professor Binchy noted the resemblance between this Irish list and similar lists in Hindu legal texts;[1] and it is, therefore, a particular pleasure to offer an analysis of the Welsh list as a small return for the many hours he spent guiding a faltering novice past, or at least out of, the many snares of Old Irish Law, and into its richer pastures.

I. TEXT

Versions of the list have been printed already. That of Wynnstay MS. 36 (now deposited in the National Library of Wales), was published by Aneurin Owen in the second volume of his *Ancient Laws and Institutes of Wales*; and he also gave there the more important variants of a second MS., B.L. Add. MS. 22,356.[2] In the same volume he published the list as given by one of the Latin versions of the laws, Redaction B, from B.L. Cotton Vespasian MS. E.XI.[3] This was re-edited by Emanuel, who also printed another version, that of Redaction E.[4] In the latter case the archetype is not extant so that Emanuel's text is edited from a number of manuscripts. One early version has not been published, that of Peniarth MS. 35.[5] The customary sigla and approximate dates of the manuscripts in Welsh are as follows:

---

[1] SEIL vi.
[2] X.viii.6
[3] AL Lat B II.xlvii.6, vol.ii, p. 874.
[4] LTWL 244, 495.
[5] f.16v.

Peniarth MS. 35 (G) : s.XIV[1]
Wynnstay MS. 36 (Q) : s.XV[1]
B.L. Add. MS. 22,356 (S) : s.XV

The manuscript containing Redaction B is dated by Emanuel to the mid-thirteenth century. The earliest manuscript of Redaction E is fifteenth century.[6]

These manuscripts, including the reconstructed text of Redaction E treated as a single witness, fall into two groups distinguished by several textual variants : G and Q are extremely close even in detail, but probably independent; the Latin Redactions B and E and the Welsh manuscript S form a second group, less closely related than the first but still sharing a number of features in common. In this second group S derives from a Latin version, but has further peculiar errors. It does not share any peculiar and significant errors with Redaction B against Redaction E or vice versa. It seems likely that all these versions derive from a single archetype: that they all derive from one written version is suggested by their occurrences as part of a collection of "nines", and by the probability, as I shall argue later, that they share at least one common error. The proposed stemma is, therefore, as follows:

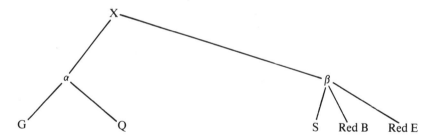

Emanuel regarded Redaction E as largely copied from a manuscript of Redaction B, very probably Cotton Vespasian E.XI.[7] It is very difficult to be sure whether a scribe is copying but trying to improve a particular exemplar, or is copying another manuscript closely related to the first, but with some superior readings. My own judgement, in this case, is in favour of the second alternative.

Since the interpretation of part of the *Naw Cynyweddi Deithïog* is uncertain I have thought it best to set out the reconstructed texts of (α)

[6] LTWL 172-4, 408-10.
[7] LTWL 74-5.

and (β) separately. G and Q differ so little that I have given all the variants of Q other than 6 for w and v for u, while using G for the text. The greater variation in the β group means that only variants which are not trivial matters of orthography are given. Punctuation and numbering are editorial.

(α) Na6 kynegwedi[1] teithia6c:

1. priodas,
2. agwedi,
3. caradas,
4. deu lysuab llathlut,
5. llathlut goleu,
6. llathlut t6yll,
7. beichogi t6yll yr6g[2] ll6yn a pherth,
8. kynniwedi[3] ar li6 ac ar oleu[4],
9. t6yll uor6yn.

[1]kynyg6edi
[2]r6ng
[3]kyne6edi
[4]olei

(β) Nau kynywedi teithiauc, *scilicet*,

1. priodas
2. aguedi
3. karadas
4-7. *duo privigni* ladrut twill beichogi twyll *mulieris* llwyn *et* perth,[1]
8. nau affeith[2] kennewedi ar lu ac[3] aruoll,
9. twyll morwyn[4].

[1]*duo privigni* et ladrut twill beichodi twyll *mulieris* lluyn *et* perth, Red. B;
duo privigni lladlut twyll ueichiogi tuyll *mulieris* llwyn a perth, Red. E;
deu privei a lladryd gida hynny a gwreic ll6yn a pherth, S.
[2]g6eith, S.
[3]*omitted in* S.
[4]tuyl uoroyn, Red. B; t6ylluor6yn, S.

The confusion in (β) 4-7 I take to be caused by a scribe jumping from the *llathlut* (or *llathrut*) which corresponded in his exemplar to the *llathlut* of (α) 4 to the *llathlut* corresponding to that of (α) 6. He thus omitted 5 entirely and produced confusion in the rest. The Latin versions have changed the resulting text very little but the version of S represents an attempt to make some sense out of chaos. Redaction E does not reproduce Redaction B's error, *beichodi*, but introduces a mutation unlikely to have been in (β); this may show initiative rather than independence. S has shown so much independence that were it not for *privei*, it could hardly be shown to be closely related to the Latin versions. But a comparison with the (α) text shows that *deu privei* must be a bungled version of *duo privigni*, for the latter agrees with *deu lysuab*. Hence (β) must have been a mixed Latin/Welsh manuscript.

In (β) 7 and 8 there is further trouble. I suggest that *nau affeith* in the Latin Redactions is a scribal error caused by (1) *llwy[n a fferth]* in an earlier exemplar and (2) the occurrence of other items such as *naw affaith galanas* in the collection of *nawoedd*, "nines". If the first part of this explanation is correct, it becomes probable that the archetype, X in my stemma, was in Welsh. The text of (β)7 probably read *lluyn* et *perth* as in Redaction B, since Redaction E does not show the expected mutation in his *llwyn a perth*. The *na6 g6eith* of S is not easy to explain. It can hardly be separated from the *nau affeith* of the Latin versions, but it is as strange interpreted as conscious emendation as it is if taken as mere error.

On the whole, the text of (β) seems greatly inferior to that of (α), but on one point (β) may well preserve the better version. In 7 G has *yr6g ll6yn a pherth* and Q *r6ng ll6yn a fferth*. Instead of *yr6g/r6ng* (β) had *mulieris*. The standard description of one category of woman is *gwreic llwyn a pherth*, "woman of bush and brake", whereas the phrase *yr6g ll6yn a pherth*, "between bush and brake" is without parallel. It is perhaps just possible that a scribe wrote *rug* for *gur(eic)*.

The other differences between (α) and (β) can only be understood after a detailed investigation of the nature of the list. They will, therefore, be left until the commentary.

There is one indication of the date of the archetype (X), provided by the spellings *kynegwedi* (G) and *kynyg6edi* (Q). These seem to derive from an Old Welsh *ciniguedi* or *cinniguedi* with *gu* for /w/, but this hardly pushes the date of X back much beyond the date of Cotton MS. Vespasian E.XI, since it is clear that such remnants of OW orthography appear in manuscripts written in the mid-thirteenth century such as Peniarth 28.[8]

---

[8] D. Huws, "Leges Howelda at Canterbury", (1976) 19 NLWJ 342-3.

II. COMMENTARY

One or two of the items in the list are extremely obscure. The best approach must be to discuss, first, the general character of the list, relying on those items that are easier to interpret, and, secondly, each difficult item at greater length.

The term *kynywedi* is generally understood as *cyn + dy-weddi*.[9] This must be correct in spite of such spellings as *kynniwedi* in (*a*) 8. The Q variant *kyne6edi* suggests that an OW *cin(n)iguedi* has been imperfectly modernised in G. The spelling in Q, -*e*- for /ə/, suggests an exemplar of the second half of the thirteenth century which used an orthography similar to that of Cotton Titus D.II. (B). The same spelling appears in G's *kynegwedi*. *Kynywedi* may, therefore, be taken to contain *dyweddi* and not an unattested **diweddi*. From AL V.ii.100, it appears that *dyweddi* did not mean "betrothal", but rather the whole process by which a woman was united with a man. The force of *cyn-* is unclear, but if we take it as **kom-* (**kon-* before a dental) it would only confirm the sense of *dyweddi*. The list would appear to be one of nine lawful unions in the sense of nine processes by which a man and a woman were sexually united in the eyes of the law; in this sense the unions were *teithïawc*.

The textual problems of the list itself only begin with item 4. If the analysis of (*β*) 4-7 given above is correct, we can rely at this stage of the discussion on the text of (*a*); and it suggests that 4-7 are all different forms of *llathlud*. Similarly, the textual analysis implied that in 7 we should read *beichogi twyll gwreic llwyn a pherth*. This is enough to suggest strongly that the list is organised as a sequence of unions of declining legal status. It may be compared with the tractate on the law of women in the Iorwerth text. There §§ 44-46 are devoted to the *gwraig o rodd cenedl*, §§ 47-48/7 to the *gwraig lathlud*, § 48/8 to the woman with whom a man sleeps for three nights, § 49 to the *gwraig o lwyn a pherth* and § 50/1-4 to *trais*. Here again the tractate is organised as a sequence of unions of declining status. From § 50/5 to the end of the tractate there is no discernible order : in effect we have a series of *damweiniau gwragedd* interspersed (as in *Llyfr y Damweiniau*) with triads and other scraps of legal tradition. The tractate falls into two parts: an organised part, §§ 44-50/4, and a disorganised part §§ 50/5-55/15. The first part will help us to interpret the *Naw Cynyweddi Deithïog*.

Priodas is the first of the nine. Although in Modern Welsh this is the standard word for "marriage" there is no corresponding general term in

---

[9] GPC s.v.

the laws. Lawyers use the phrases *gŵr priod* and *gwraig briod* but they are only beginning to use *priodas* in the modern sense.[10] *Llyfr Blegywryd* uses *priodas* as a translation for Latin *coniugium* in Redaction D, but this is the later sense of the word.[11] In Ior § 87/5 the *gwraig briod* seems to be the woman legitimately married in the eyes of the canon lawyers. In Ior § 53/4 we are told that "no woman is entitled to buy or to sell unless she is *priod*; if, however, she is *priod*, she is entitled to buy and to sell". A greater legal capacity, then, is the consequence of a woman being a *gwraig briod*; moreover, it is a greater capacity in relation to property. This, however, does not tell us what it is to be *priod*; it merely states one consequence, for a woman, of being *priod*. In the medieval laws, as later, a man may be *priod*; but the evidence will not tell us whether, if a woman was *priod*, so too was her husband, and their union was then *priodas*. At all events the power to buy and to sell will not be the characteristic which makes a husband *priod*.

It has been suggested that a *gwraig briod* was a woman given in marriage by her kindred, *g6reic a rodyeit arnei*, Ior (G) § 48/8.[12] This will not explain the *priod* of the *Naw Cynyweddi Deithïog*.

The second union, *agweddi*, must also be of a woman given in marriage. Admittedly the tractates on the law of women speak of an *agweddi* to which even a woman in a *llathlud* union is entitled, but the *agweddi* union in the *Naw Cynyweddi Deithïog* is of higher status than the *llathlud* unions, (nos. 4-6), and of higher status than the *caradas* union (no. 3). The *agweddi* union must therefore be of a woman by gift.

It has also been suggested that the *gwraig briod* may have been the woman who contributed more goods than the man.[13] It would then be unsurprising that she should have greater powers in relation to property. At this point it is essential to distinguish between land and movable goods. The Welsh law of the thirteenth century assumes that a woman given in marriage will bring with her movable goods. For seven years the husband has no right to alienate or consume the wife's contribution, the *argyfrau* or *cynhysgaeth* or *gwaddol*; but after seven years it passes into the common pool. Subsequently, in the event of *ysgar*, termination of the union, the wife no longer has an exclusive right to the *argyfrau*, but takes half of the common pool of movable goods. A daughter receives a

---

[10] e.g. Col § 48, *gureic priaut* = *gwreic vria6c* of Ior § 54/6. But cf. LlA 159.11, *at wyry bria6t* = ad virginem desponsatam of the Vulgate, Luke i.27.
[11] Bleg 79.11 = Lat D 385.9.
[12] Col § 34n, citing Gwilym Prys Dafis, "Rhwymedigaethau Cytundebol . . .", LL.M. Thesis, University of Wales, 1952.
[13] Col § 34n.

share of movables, but only half the value of that received by a son (Ior § 53/8). Hence in a union between spouses whose families are of approximately equal wealth and equal numbers of sons and daughters, the *argyfrau* will be roughly half the portion of movables to which the husband is entitled, though he may not yet have acquired this portion if he marries in his father's lifetime. No daughter inherits land except in special circumstances. In the normal union, therefore, the wife's material contribution is doubly unequal: she contributes no land and less movable wealth. A union, in which either or both of these circumstances did not exist, might well have the consequence that the wife would be entitled to buy and to sell. In a normal union, after the initial seven year period, the husband appears to have unrestricted powers to administer the common pool of movable wealth. If the wife's *argyfrau* were of equal or greater value than the husband's movables, that might be enough to give her special powers in relation to the sale and purchase of movables. It is not necessary to assume that she contributed land: buying and selling would normally be of movables, and if her contribution of movable wealth was greater that would be a natural reason why she should have greater powers in this aspect of the marriage. The difficulty is that such a situation seems to imply that the husband's family is appreciably poorer than the wife's family, or that the husband has more brothers and sisters with whom he must share. This is hardly the basis for the highest of the nine unions. It is more likely that *priodas* is a union in which the *argyfrau* is at least half the husband's portion of movables, but not much more.

Another possible explanation is suggested by *Llyfr Iorwerth*'s use of *gwraig briod* in § 87/5-6: "The law of the church says that only the eldest son born to the father of the *gwraig briod* is entitled to a patrimony. The law of Hywel adjudges it (patrimony) to the youngest son as to the eldest, and declares that neither the father's sin nor his illegal act should prejudice his son in relation to patrimony". If we may suppose that early Welsh custom allowed polygyny then the *gwraig briod* might be the first wife united to the man by gift of her kin or other process which the Church recognised as establishing a regular union. This suggestion may take support from the translation *domina principalis* in Latin Redactions D and E (LTWL 369, 475) and the phrase *rhoddi X yn briod i Y* "to give X *yn briod* to Y".[14] Yet there are difficulties in the way of this proposal. The supposition of polygyny is not so great a difficulty, as we shall see, but it is nevertheless difficult to see how a canonically acceptable union

[14] e.g. WM 174. 13-14.

might be one of the nine *cynyweddi*. A *llathlud* union might be acceptable to the Church just as a union by gift of kin might be acceptable;
both, if the man were already married, would be unacceptable. The
criteria of the Church were not easily harmonised with the fundamental
distinctions implied by the list of nine *cynyweddi*.

The second union, *agweddi*, and the third, *caradas*, pose fewer
difficulties. In the union by gift of kin, the value of the *agweddi* was fixed
in accordance with the status of the bride's father: if she was the
daughter of an *uchelwr* (*breyr*) the *agweddi* was equivalent to twelve
milch cows; if she was the daughter of a *taeog*, it was equivalent to six
milch cows.[15] The tractates on the law of women prescribe, as we have
seen, a payment often called *agweddi* even for a *llathlud* union, but this
is of less value. We may assume that the *agweddi* in a *llathlud* union was
disregarded by those who termed the second of the nine unions in our list
agweddi; or we may suppose that, at the period from which the list
stems, *agweddi* was confined to unions by gift of kin.

Caradas appears to be neither a union by gift nor a union by *llathlud*,
elopement or abduction.[16] MS. Q contains a triad which helps to define
caradas[17] : *Teir g6raged ny dyly eu g6yr ia6n gantunt am y godineb*,
"three women whose husbands are not entitled to compensation from
them for their adultery". The first is the woman taken in *llathlud*; the
second is the woman "who is slept with *ygkaradas*," in *caradas*, "and
that publicly". The third is the *gwraig lwyn a pherth*, "woman of bush
and brake". The position of *caradas* in this triad and in the list of nine
unions suggests (1) that it is a public and regular union (there is no mention of *twyll* and it is *yn gyhoedd*), (2) that it is not a union by gift of kin
(by contrast with *agweddi*), and (3) that it is a union in which the woman
stays at home (by contrast with *llathlud* as well as *agweddi*).

The fourth union, *deu lysuab llathlut* or *duo privigni* (*ladrut*), is one of
the most difficult to identify. This is partly for textual reasons. At this
point we come to the part of the list which had become corrupt in (β)
through the omission of a number of words. The only full witness is (α)
and it is precisely in the fourth union that (α) first seems questionable.
The *llathlut* of *deu lysuab llathlut* precedes *llathlut goleu*, and the latter is
clearly opposed to *llathlut twyll*. It is not obvious how *deu lysuab llathlut*
might be superior to *llathlut goleu*. This raises the suspicion that a scribe

---

[15] Cyfn § 73/5, 7a; DwCol § 285.
[16] I have preferred *caradas* to *caraddas* (cf. GPC s.v., CA 281), though XIV.iii.28 has *o garaddas*. Elsewhere it is spelt *caradas* which is ambiguous. The comparison with Irish *carthach* (SEIL 64, 95-6) argues for *caradas* with *d*.
[17] DC II.xviii.54; cf. XIV.iii.28.

has repeated *llathlut*, and that the fourth union is simply *deu lysuab*. The explanation of the (β) text suggested earlier—that words were omitted by jumping from one *llathlut* to another—is not affected. If the earlier text had only *deu lysuab* then the jump was from *llathlut* (*goleu*) to (*llathlut*) *twyll*, thus simply omitting the bracketed words. Indeed the explanation is now rather simpler: otherwise the scribe would have had to jump from the *llathlut* of (*α*)4 *deu lysuab llathlut* to *twyll* of (*α*)6 passing over *llathlut goleu llathlut*. The syntax is possible on either interpretation: *deu lysuab llathlut* would be the same construction as *gwreic lathlut*. There are no strong textual or linguistic arguments for rejecting the *llathlut* of (*α*)4, but the argument that it makes no sense in that position in the list remains very powerful. I shall, therefore, proceed on the assumption that the archetype (X) read *deu lysuab*.

This is still not readily intelligible. If, however, *deu lysuab* may, in the context, be translated "two step-children" rather than "two step-sons" then the situation may be that depicted at the beginning of *Culhwch ac Olwen*. Cilydd's first wife, Goleuddydd, bears him a son, Culhwch, and then dies. After seven years have gone by Cilydd marries the wife of King Doged, having defeated her husband in a battle and having killed him. Doged and his wife had had a daughter, and her mother proposed that Culhwch should marry her daughter.

The situation was therefore as follows:

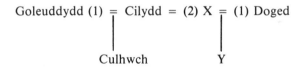

Goleuddydd (1) = Cilydd = (2) X = (1) Doged

Culhwch   Y

Culhwch is step-son of X, the former wife of Doged; the daughter of Doged is step-daughter of Cilydd. Such a union might well have been subject to canonical objection, but it is not so clear why, in the law of Hywel, it should rank below *caradas*. It is, however, true that such a union would tend to frustrate the prime object of many marriages, in that it would not create a new alliance between two kindreds. If Doged had died peacefully in his bed, and his wife had been given by his kin to Cilydd, an alliance would have been established. To this extent a marriage between Culhwch and Doged's daughter would have been redundant. This explanation, is, however, only a speculation, and the fourth union remains something of an enigma.

The next two unions, *llathlud golau* and *llathlud twyll* are straightforward. Although the Latin versions render *llathlud* as *rapina* there is usually no suggestion of violence: it is not so much the consent of the woman as the attitude of her kindred which is at issue. A late text (AL XIV.x.32) uses *llathlud* in an unusually broad sense to cover a range of unions: *llathlud* is either with or without the consent of the woman; if it is without her consent it is rape, *trais*. If *llathlud* is with her consent, intercourse may take place either within a house or in the open, in "bush and brake". The distinctions made in this passage are old, but the wide uses of *llathlud* to cover all such unions is not the normal usage of the older texts. There it is customarily used for the union in which a woman is taken from her home, without having been given by her kin, and is then taken to a house where they sleep together. (Ior § 99/5: *O deruyd duen gureyc en llathlut o ty e that hyt en ty arall ac eno kescu genthy . . .*) *Llathlud* is a higher form of union than that in "bush and brake", and higher still than *trais*.

The distinction between *golau* and *twyll* seems to be that between open and public *llathlud* on the one hand and a secret *llathlud* on the other. If it is open and public the kindred of the woman may passively consent to the union even though it is not by gift of kin. For example, it is stated in the tractates (Ior § 50/5; Cyfn § 73/13a, 13b), that if a virgin goes in *llathlud* without the consent of her kin, they and her lord (Ior), or her father (Cyfn) can bring her back against her will; but if she is not a virgin she cannot be compelled to return. This implies that a kindred may consent to a *llathlud* union by not exercising their right to bring back a virgin. Furthermore, the version of this rule in Cyfn (*W*) defines the *llathlud* to which the rule applies as *llathrut heb canhat kenedyl, llathrud* without consent of kindred. Presumably if they were aware of the planned elopement and did nothing to prevent it, they would forfeit any right subsequently to bring back their kinswoman against her will. In such a case knowledge would imply consent. This, then, is probably the distinction between *llathlud golau* and *llathlud twyll*.

The seventh union is probably, as we have seen, to be read as *beichogi twyll gwreic llwyn a pherth,* "secret pregnancy of a woman of bush and brake." The emphasis on her pregnancy arises from the lawyer's concern with the legal consequences of a relationship: if a relationship that is of its nature secretive is undiscovered no legal consequence will follow; but if the woman becomes pregnant then *amobr* is due (Ior § 51/10), and it is the father's duty to rear the child (Ior § 49/1; AL IV.iv.3). This form of union is necessarily *twyll*. According to some texts (Bleg 112. 3-8; WML 127.25-128.4), the son of *gwreic o lwyn a pherth, mab llwyn a pherth*, is not to share land with a son born of a subsequent marriage in which his mother was given to a man by her kindred. The legitimate son gets all. Whether this was the general rule is doubtful, for only if the subsequent marriage was with an *alltud* ("foreigner" or "alien") would the legitimate son inherit through the mother,[18] and only if the paternity of the *mab llwyn a pherth* was undeclared or disputed would he inherit through his mother. If either of these conditions did not hold, there would be no question of the two sons sharing with each other. Whereas if the paternity of the *mab llwyn a pherth* were accepted he would inherit from his father (cf. Ior § 102/16: *gnotaf yu guadu mab er tref y tat*). This union is, therefore, one in which (a) the partners do not sleep together in a house, (b) it is, therefore, a secretive and furtive union, and (c) legal consequences normally flow from it only because the woman's pregnancy has made further concealment impossible, (though the union might be discovered directly: cf. the triad *tri chadarn enllip gwreic*, WML 127. 7-11; Bleg 111. 24-28).

The eighth union is perhaps the most mysterious of all. The two versions differ radically: (α) has *kynniwedi ar li6 ac ar oleu*, (β) *nau affeith kennewedi ar lu ac aruoll*. The phrase *nau affeith* in (β) has been rejected on purely textual grounds; but that still leaves the further difference between *ar li6 ac ar oleu* and *ar lu ac aruoll*. The only clue is that this is a union of very low status. *Llw ac aruoll* is a phrase which occurs elsewhere: in the Red Book version of *Brut y Brenhinedd*, Geoffrey's *Historia Regum Britanniae*, Gwrtheyrn suggests to Constans a plan whereby Constans may become king; Constans is delighted at the plan, *ac adaw trwy lw ac aruoll rodi idaw bop peth o'r a vynnei*, "and promised by oath and vow to give him everything that he wanted".[19] The phrase *trwy lw ac aruoll* corresponds to *jurejurando* in the Latin. But this will not give good sense in the present context: such an inferior union could hardly be identified as a union "upon oath and vow". It is perhaps conceivable that we have here a different meaning of *arfoll*, namely "acceptance, reception". In this case one might hazard the guess that this union arises—or rather becomes legally operative—by the oath of the woman that so-and-so is the father of her child and his acceptance of paternity. But this is a desperate speculation: *arfoll* is not used for acceptance of a fact or assertion.

The other reading has perhaps rather more to be said for it. *Lliwo* is to accuse, to impute blame, (*lliwaw idaw hynny*, PKM 37; *lliwa6 arna6 y*

---

[18] Ior § 86/3-6.
[19] RBB 127.18; the corresponding passage in *Brut Dingestow* (ed. H. Lewis, Cardiff, 1942) 87, has only *aruoll*.

welet, WML 100. 15-16). It corresponds exactly to the Old Irish *liid for X Y*, "he accuses X of Y"; this phrase is used when the offence is sexual (*S.Cano*, 1. 210; *Liad & Cuir*, p. 18, 6-20; *B. Crólige* 29). In Bleg 122. 20-25, (= Lat D 356. 33-36) *ar y liw* means "openly": a "hand-having" thief, one caught with the stolen object openly in his possession, is said to be caught with the object *ar y liw gantaw*. The theft is indisputable and cannot be concealed (cf.PKM 37: *lliwaw idaw hynny a heb y gelu*). In this sense *ar liw* seems to mean much the same as *ar olau*; for example, Ior § 110/24 fixes the *sarhaed* of a woman according to that of the last man she has *ar oleu*. A *cynyweddi ar liw ac ar olau* must be an open and undeniable union. But here again we meet the same difficulty: why is this a separate union with so low a status? If the woman has not left home it should be *caradas*; if she has, it is *llathlud golau*. And if *llathlud twyll* ranks below *llathlud golau*, why should *cynyweddi ar liw ac ar olau* rank below *beichiogi twyll gwraig lwyn a pherth*? The only way to explain the low position of this union is to attribute to it a characteristic which its title does not imply; most obviously, this might be an open and public abduction of a woman against her will, whereas all superior unions were with her consent.

The last union is in (*a*) *t6yll uor6yn*, in (*β*) *twyll morwyn*. In (*β*) only Redaction E has the unmutated form, *tuyl morwyn*, whereas Redactions B and S have mutated forms, *tuyl uoroyn* and *t6ylluor6yn*. By the ordinary rules of textual criticism a mutated form should have been attributed to (*β*); but since the tendency at this period is all the other way, namely to show more mutations in the orthography, I have preferred the unmutated form. In the first place this has been done for purely textual reasons; but there are other grounds for suspecting that *twyll forwyn* would not have been the correct reading. The compound *twyllforwyn* refers to a woman given in marriage, purporting to be a virgin, but being nothing of the kind (Lat A § 52/25; Lat B 224.3-13; Ior § 47/2-5; WML 132. 10-19 = Bleg 116.29-117.6 = Lat D. 374.26-32; Bleg 61.27-31 = Lat D. 342.13-16). In the triad *tri hwrd ni diwygir*, there is even mention of a *mach ar y mor6ynda6t*, "a surety as to her virginity". In a *llathlud* union there can be no *twyllforwyn* for in such a union there are no *neithiorwyr*, "wedding guests", before whom the man can testify that he has found the woman not to be a virgin. In a *llathlud* union "her word is a word" upon her virginity and upon the value and nature of her *cowyll* her morning-gift (Ior § 56/7; cf. WML 41. 8-13); in other words, her testimony is, by itself, conclusive. A *twyllforwyn*, then, could only occur in a *priodas* or *agweddi* union. It is not so much a separate union as the invalidation of a union by gift because of a defect in the conditions of the union, conditions guaranteed by a surety. As such it is analogous to the *twyll* which may occur in a sale: in Ior § 124/13 the vendor of "a horse with a *twyll* in it" may, in certain circumstances, escape liability by an oath that he was ignorant of the *twyll*. If, however, we read *twyll morwyn* we may take *morwyn* as an objective genitive: "deception of a virgin" rather than "deception by a virgin". We have now reached the last union, and we should expect something like *trais*, "rape", to appear in this position. At least, it should be a union to which the woman does not consent. The only way to obtain something answering these requirements seems to be to read *twyll morwyn*. It is not, however, a particularly satisfactory solution, for there is no reason why it should be *twyll morwyn* rather than *twyll gwraig*: if the issue is whether or not the woman consents to the union, it should be irrelevant whether or not she is a virgin. Only a *putain*, a whore, has no right to compensation for rape (Ior § 55/11). The explanation may be that if a *morwyn* is raped, she is entitled to her *cowyll*, her *agweddi*, her *wynebwerth* and her *dilysrwydd*, whereas the *gwraig* is not entitled to her *cowyll* or her *agweddi* (Ior § 50/4). Rape of a *morwyn* is thus treated as a union which entails the usual payments; rape of a *gwraig* is treated as an offence, but not as a union.

We may also ask why this last union is *twyll morwyn* and not *trais morwyn*, "rape of a virgin". The answer may be that *twyll*, in the context, could be a broader term covering, for example, a case in which a man gets a girl drunk; this would involve deception rather than violence.

Several of the unions have received no explanation approaching certainty, but the preferred form of the text and the most likely explanations may be listed as follows:

A. Unions by gift of kin:

1. *priodas*: perhaps this is the union in which the *argyfrau* is at least half the value of the husband's share of movables.

2. *agwedi*: still a union by gift, but perhaps the *argyfrau* is less than half the value of the husband's share of movables.

B. Unions not by gift of kin, but with the consent of the kin and of the woman herself:

3. *caradas*: the woman does not leave her house but is openly visited there by the man.

4. *deu lysuab*: perhaps the union exemplified by Cullhwch's step-mother's proposal that he marry her daughter (his own father's step-daughter).

5. *llathlut goleu*: an open elopement by the couple to any house other than that of her own family. The lack of concealment may well imply passive consent by her kin.

C. Unions to which the woman's kin do not consent, but to which the woman herself does:

6. *llathlut twyll*: the same as *llathlut goleu*, except that the elopement is secret, presumably because the woman's kin actively oppose the union, or could be assumed to oppose it.

7. *beichogi twyll gwreic lwyn a pherth*: a secret union, again presumably because the woman's kin would oppose it if they knew of it. It involves no domestic habitation but is merely a secretive union which occurs out of doors. The woman continues to live at home.

D. Unions to which neither the woman nor her kin consent:

8. *kynnywedi ar liw ac ar oleu*: perhaps a union through the abduction of a woman by force.

9. *twyll morwyn*: a union by deception of a virgin, for example by getting her drunk so that she cannot resist intercourse.

If we compare this list with the classification implied by the tractate on the law of women in *Llyfr Iorwerth*, we have the following results:

1. *gwreic a rodyeit arnei/gwreic o rod*: this description covers *priodas* and *agwedi* (1 and 2).

2. *gwreic o lathlut/lathrut*: this covers *llathlut goleu* and *llathlut twyll* (5 and 6).

3. Woman slept with for three nights in a house: this might cover *caradas* (3) or be intended for a particularly transitory form of *llathlud*.

4. *gwreic o lwyn a pherth*: equivalent to no. 7.

5. *treis*: may cover both nos. 8 and 9.

Caradas is either omitted or demoted to a position below *llathlud. Dau lysfab* is, not surprisingly, omitted. Otherwise the assumptions are the same, but the distinctions are drawn more minutely in the list of nine unions than in the Iorwerth text.

One final caveat is in order before we move on to consider the relationship of the Welsh list of unions to its counterparts in Irish and Hindu law. Some of the unions in the Welsh list may plainly co-exist with other unions in which either or both parties are involved. If monogamy is the rule, then it is necessary to draw a firm line between proper marriages on the one side and illegitimate unions on the other. If, *de facto*, someone has entered into more than one union, only one, at most, of these unions can be a marriage in the eyes of the law. This is the doctrine towards which Welsh law is developing in the thirteenth century with the evolution of a concept of *priodas* as lawful marriage as opposed to the rest: in AL XIV.x.32, all the unlawful unions seem to be covered by the term *llathlud*. Ior § 52/4 specifically rules against bigamy, but it seems likely that polygyny had been recognised at a not very remote period. The underlying theme of a list such as the *Naw Cynyweddi* is that unions may be graded along a continuous line ranging from the most honourable at one end to the least honourable at the other. There is no sharp division between lawful and unlawful, but rather a gradual shading off. Even the tractates do not imply that a *llathlud* union is, of itself, unlawfully created or that elopement is an unlawful act. They only imply that the woman loses *braint*, "status", which she would have had as a *gwraig a rhoddiaid arni* (Ior § 48/3). This strategy for classifying sexual unions is natural in a society which permits polygamy. In the triads there are references which suggest that polygyny had been recognised (WML 132. 5-9 (MS.*V*.) = 133. 11-15 (MS.*W*.) = Bleg 116. 27-29 = Lat. D. 374. 25-26 = Lat. B 243.2; WML 126. 24-25 = Bleg 111. 21-22 = Lat D 371. 29).

Both the early Irish and Hindu societies recognised polygyny (the Irish *locus classicus* is *B. Crólige*, §§ 56-57). Both legal systems had lists corresponding to the Welsh.

The Irish list is as follows:[20]

1. *Lánamnas comthinchuir*: "union of joint input": a union by gift of kindred in which both parties contribute movable goods; *Cáin Lánamna (CL)* §§ 5-20.

2. *Lánamnas mná for ferthinchur*: "union of a woman upon man-input": a union by gift in which the woman contributes little or no movables; *CL* 21-28.

3. *Lánamnas fir for bantinchur*: "union of a man upon woman-input": a union by gift in which the man contributes little or no movables; *CL* 29-31.

---

[20] There are two versions in *Cáin Lánamna* (SEIL 1-75), one in § 4, the other in the rest of the tract. I have preferred the second. References are to paragraphs.

4. *Lánamnas fir thathigthe*: "union of a man of visiting"; a union by consent of the kindred in which the man visits the woman in her family's home; *CL* 32.

5. *Lánamnas airite for uráil*: "union accepted at the instigation (of the man)": a union in which the woman departs openly with the man to cohabit elsewhere, but is not given by her kin; *CL* 33.

6/7. *Lánamnas foxail* 7 *lánamnas táide*: "union by abduction and union by stealth": the woman's kin do not give their consent, but the woman is abducted (*foxal*) or secretly visited (*táide*); *CL* 34.

8. *Lánamnas éicne no sléithe*: "union by force or stealing up on (the woman)": rape or intercourse with a woman found asleep or drunk"; *CL* 35.

9. *Lánamnas genaige*: "union of mockery": a union of the insane; *CL* 36.

Of these (1) corresponds to *priodas*, (2) to *agweddi*, (4) to *caradas*, (5) to *llathlud golau*, (6) to *llathlud twyll*, (7) to *beichiogi gwraig llwyn a pherth*, (8) to *twyll morwyn*, and perhaps also to *cynyweddi ar liw ac ar olau*. There is no Irish counterpart to *dau lysfab*, and no Welsh counterpart to *lánamnas genaige*. The Irish list is, however, based on the same principles as the Welsh one: at the honourable end of the scale come unions by gift of kin; then unions to which the kin consents but which it does not initiate; thirdly, unions to which the woman consents but her kin does not; and finally, unions to which she does not consent. In effect, unions are mainly graded according to the degree to which the woman's side—herself and her kin—are responsible for the union.

The corresponding Hindu list is one of the standard features of both the *Dharmasūtras* and the generally later *Dharmaśāstras*. It occurs already in what may be the earliest of the *Dharmasūtras*, that of Gautama.[21] Gautama's version may be given in the form of a list as follows:

1. *Brāhma union*: union by gift to "a person possessing learning".

2. *Prājāpatya union*: union by gift; the bridegroom does not give cattle.

3. *Ārsha union*: union by gift; the bridegroom gives a cow and a bull to those who have authority over the bride.

4. *Daiva union*: union by gift to a priest.

---

[21] Tr. G. Bühler, Sacred Books of the East, ii. 194-5; IV, 1-15. For the date of this text see R. Lingat, *The Classical Law of India*, tr. J. D. M. Derrett (Berkeley/Los Angeles/ London, 1973), 19-20. Lingat discusses the list of unions on pp. 59-60. I have used the older transliteration, *sh*, for cerebral (lingual) *s*.

5. *Gāndharva union*: not by gift, but the woman is willing.

6. *Asura union*: those who have authority over the woman "are propitiated by money"—there consent is bought.

7. *Rākshasa union*: abduction by force.

8. *Paiśaca union*: if a woman is "deprived of consciousness".

This list bears the imprint of Hindu beliefs, notably in the implied hostility to bride-purchase or bride-wealth. The commentators had considerable difficulty in explaining away apparent references in the Veda to bride-purchase. The *Daiva* union may be compared to the Roman *confarreatio*, the form of union appropriate for priests. In general, however, this list is of the same character as its Irish and Welsh counterparts: unions by gift have higher status than unions by consent of the wife and her kin; the latter have higher status than those in which such consent is lacking. There is no sharp distinction between legitimate and illegitimate though fewer are legitimate for Brahmins than for other castes.

The existence of the Welsh list suggests that in many respects the Welsh law of women resembled the Irish until the gradual progress of Christian ideas on marriage caused a fundamental transformation. But even in the thirteenth century this transformation was still very incomplete, as the law on *ysgar* demonstrates. *Cyfraith Hywel* remained very different from *cyfraith eglwys* and had not yet conceded that the law of marriage was the proper sphere of the canonists.

T. M. CHARLES-EDWARDS

SHAME AND REPARATION;
WOMAN'S PLACE IN THE KIN[1]

IN A society dominated by kin groups of male agnates, as was that of medieval Wales, the position of woman was inevitably one of juridical inferiority and dual ties. The juridical inferiority sprang from the fact that, in most legal institutions, she, like the dumb and the mad,[2] was regarded as a non-person recognised by society only as an appendage to some male with whom she was connected by ties of blood or by bonds of marriage. Her links were dual. They lay both with the kin into which she was born and with the kin with which she was associated through her husband after marriage. Despite, or because of, this her rôle in society was an important and delicately balanced one, governed by subtle conventions of behaviour, for she was the genetrice in whose person lay the future of her husband's kin, and her own kin was well aware of this rôle and conscious of the need to preserve her honour. She served also as a unifying force between kins.

These aspects of the position of woman are high-lighted by the rules of *galanas* and *sarhaed*.[3] *Galanas* (life price) and *sarhaed* (insult price) are terms frequently coupled by commentators on Welsh law because they are used together for the two payments made when a homicide was committed in medieval Wales. Both terms have in fact a wide range of meanings and legal implications. I propose, in this paper, to deal with some of the rules concerning *galanas* and *sarhaed* as they affect women. First, I shall consider the status of woman as revealed by her *sarhaed* and *galanas* price; secondly, the place of compensation in the Law of Women and its implications for social attitudes in Welsh society towards what was considered shameful and honourable to woman in marriage; and finally, the light thrown on the place of woman in the kin by the rules for homicide.

---

[1] This paper is a developed version of material presented at the fourth Conference on Welsh Mediaeval Law in 1974.

[2] cf. *Tres sunt homines quorum quisque a rege debet habere prelocutorem, id est, tauodyauc, versus alios in curia, quem rex sibimet eligat; quia rex est solus homo cuius est eligere sibi prelocutorem de suis pre omnibus. Primus est raucus, id est cryc. Secundus est femina. Tercius, exul qui nesciat recte loqui Walensice.* Lat D 354.16 and also Lat E 504.7.

[3] Dafydd Jenkins, *Cyfraith Hywel* (1976), Pennod VI, 60-80.

The law of *galanas* is an immensely complicated mixture of elements, some of which derive from a common Celtic source and are paralleled by features in the laws of Ireland, while others are later innovations.[4] In the law texts of the thirteenth century, *galanas* is the usual word for homicide, normally compensated by the payment of composition also known as *galanas* or alternatively as *gwerth*; this payment varied according to the status of the victim. The original meaning of *galanas* was, however, feud or enmity, and this meaning is well attested in the literature and to a lesser extent in the law books. A state of enmity between kins could originally be created by various actions other than killing, as is suggested by the evidence of *Naw Affaith Galanas herwydd Gwŷr Powys*[5] preserved in Redaction B of the Latin texts. According to this list, land dispute, woman dispute, treachery, and insult were among the actions that could provoke feud between the kins of the offender and the victim. This enmity was perpetuated by *dial* (vengeance) until terminated by payment of composition (*diwyn*).[6] The composition was probably originally an amount settled by bargaining. By the thirteenth century and for some considerable period before, it was a standard sum whose amount was governed by the *braint* (status) of the victim and bore a fixed relation to the *sarhaed* (or insult price) which also varied according to the status of the victim.[7] The laws of *galanas* are therefore concerned with the status of individuals and the structure of the kin involved in the payment of composition.

Sarhaed, however, has as a payment wider implications than *galanas*, for it is usually payable as an addition to the compensation due for physical damage. Since any physical assault is damaging to the honour of the victim, *sarhaed* has come by the thirteenth century to function as a payment for intentional harm.[8] In homicide, where unintended killing is compensated by *galanas* alone, intent attracts *sarhaed* as well. The underlying idea behind *sarhaed* is very ancient, concerned with honour and shame, and corresponds to similar notions among other Celtic peoples, and in many primitive societies, an aspect to which we shall return later.

---

[4] T. M. Charles-Edwards, "Kinship, Status and the Origins of the Hide", (1973) 56, *Past and Present*, 26-33.

[5] Excursus I.

[6] Excursus II; T. M. Charles-Edwards, "The Seven Bishop Houses of Dyfed", (1970) 24 BBCS 247-262.

[7] On the principle "Amod a dyrr ddeddf", a contract breaks the law, the compensation might be negotiable (even at the time of the law books).

[8] DwCol §§169, 170. Distinctions between intent and non-intent are late in all legal systems.

A. *Status*

There are two chief sources in the law texts for knowledge of comparative status as reflected in *galanas* and *sarhaed* prices. The one is the Laws of Court which is basically a tract on status and may be compared with the Irish *Críth Gablach* and *Uraicecht Becc*.[9] Unlike the Irish tracts, however, it is concerned only with the members of the king's family and household and may derive as a specific section of the law books from the time of Hywel Dda.[10] The second Welsh source is a tract on *sarhaed*[11] which, in the Blegywryd text, follows significantly a list of values for compensation for damage to parts of the human body, a tractate primarily concerned with physical assault. In the Iorwerth text, it is annexed to the treatise on *galanas*. This tractate again enumerates the *galanas* and *sarhaed* of the king and queen and of the officials of the country including this time, the *maer* and *cynghellor* and the other members of medieval Welsh society, the *pencenedl* (chief of kin), the *breyr* (a free Welshman who has succeeded to his patrimony), the *bonheddig canhwynol* (the ordinary native freeman), the *bilain* (villein), the *alltud* (alien) and the *caeth* (slave). With the exception of the *galanas* and *sarhaed* of the king and his family, the value of the *galanas* is expressed in cattle and of the *sarhaed* in cattle and silver, in both these lists.

The following table shows the comparative values of *sarhaed* and *galanas* from the tractate on *sarhaed*. (Bleg 57-60).[12]

	GALANAS				SARHAED		
pencenedl	3 × 9 + 3	× 9	× 20 kine	3 × 9	kine + 9	× 20 silver	
breyr	6	+ 6	× 20 kine	6	kine + 6	× 20 silver	
bonheddig	3	+ 3	× 20 kine	3	kine + 3	× 20 silver	
king's bilain	3	+ 3	× 20 kine	3	kine + 3	× 20 silver	
breyr's bilain	1½ + 1½		× 20 kine	1½	kine + 1½	× 20 silver	
king's alltud	3	+ 3	× 20 kine	3	kine + 3	× 20 silver	
breyr's alltud	1½ + 1½		× 20 kine	1½	kine + 1½	× 20 silver	
bilain's alltud	¾ +	¾	× 20 kine	¾	kine + 1½	× 20 silver	
caeth overseas	(Price £1½)			12d			
native caeth	(Price £1)			12d			

---

[9] D. A. Binchy, *Críth Gablach*, (Dublin, 1970); Eóin Mac Neill, "The Law of Status or Franchise", (1923) 36 PRIA 281-306.

[10] J. G. Edwards, "The Royal Household and the Welsh Lawbooks", 13 TRHS/V 163-76; D. A. Binchy, *Anglo-Saxon and Celtic Kingship*, (Oxford, 1970).

[11] Bleg 57-60: Ior §110.

[12] The values given in Ior §110 are similar to these, but Ior uses the term *uchelwr* where Bleg uses *breyr*. The values given in the list are the basic values of sarhaed and galanas which could be increased by augmentation *(dyrchafael)*.

The king's *sarhaed* is a symbolic one, a golden plate as broad as his face, the symbol of his face value or honour, the silver rod of kingship and a cup of plenty.[13] The members of the lists can be divided into those who are free and have a place in society in their own right and the unfree whose dependence on another is essential to their status in society, like the *bilain* (villein) or the *alltud* (alien) who has no kin, the slave whose life has a price on it like an animal but who has no *galanas* and whose death does not cause feud; compensation for it is paid to his owner rather than to any blood relatives.

In both lists, no woman, not even the females who are officials of the king's court, is afforded both a *galanas* and *sarhaed* in her own right. With one exception a woman's *sarhaed* is half that of her brother before marriage when she is a *morwyn* and a third that of her husband when she is a *gwraig*.[14] The exception to this rule is a female slave, whose *sarhaed* depends on the nature of her occupation. If she is a sewing woman, her *sarhaed* is twenty four pence, otherwise her *sarhaed* is twelve pence. The *galanas* of all women except that of a queen is equal to half that of their brothers both before and after marriage. A female slave, like her male counterpart, has only a price. Thus, the galanas of a *bonheddig* is given as 63 kine, his sister's would then be 31½ kine; his *sarhaed* was 3 kine and 60d., his sister's 1½ kine and 30d.; his wife's *sarhaed* would be 1 cow and 20d.; her *galanas*, if she were the sister of a *bonheddig*, would be the same as his sister's. Should the *bonheddig* attain the status of *breyr*, the *galanas* of his sister would immediately rise in value, as would the *sarhaed* of his wife. These material manifestations of status, therefore, link a woman closely with the men with whom she is connected by ties of either blood or marriage. The reflected status of a married woman is shown in other ways, particularly in her right to make gifts, since whereas the king's wife may give away her share of the king's casual acquisitions, *dofod*, a villein's wife may only give her head-dress

---

[13] J. Loth "Un Genre Particulier de Compensation pour Crimes et Offences chez les Celtes Insulaires," (1931) 48 *Revue Celtique* 332-351, deals with the significance of the golden plate citing many parallels in Welsh and Irish literature. G. Dumezil, *Mythe et Epopée I,* (1973) 189, calls attention to the importance of the rod as a symbol of kingship originally possessing superhuman powers and compares Math and his rod in PKM with the rod bearer or *dandavara* of Indian tradition whose power was also closely connected with virgins. Possibly it is some such myth which underlies the nature of the *sarhaed* due to the king when a virgin is raped. In some texts, the king's *sarhaed* for this offence consists solely of a silver rod. For goblets as symbols of sovereignty, see Glenys Goetinck, *Peredur, A Study of Welsh Tradition in the Grail Legends,* (Cardiff, 1957) 182; T. F. Ó'Rahilly, "On the Origin of the Names, Érainn and Ériu", (1946) 14 *Ériu* 14.

[14] Ior §46/1; Bleg 61.7; Lat A §51/5. For the slave woman's *sarhaed*, see Bleg 59.25.

and lend a sieve.[15] In the case of a married woman, her dependence, as expressed in terms of *galanas* and *sarhaed*, is ambivalent since her *sarhaed* value reflects that of her husband and her *galanas* that of her natal kin: there is one exception to this rule, namely a queen whose *sarhaed* and *galanas* are always reckoned as a third of those of her husband.[16] The queen's position possibly reflects some privilege accorded to royal blood or it may be a survival from an archaic state in which the woman, who undergoes the most honourable degree of marriage, becomes more completely integrated into her husband's kin than the wives of a more inferior type of union. Rules concerning the king and his family are often notoriously archaic in all legal systems. Other references in Welsh law suggest that the Welsh, like the Irish, did at one stage recognise the different rights of a wife who had undergone the highest grade of marriage. For instance a *gwraig briod*, whatever that means, is the only wife allowed to buy and sell.[17] In Irish law the *cétmuinter*[18] was more firmly integrated into her husband's grade of kin than any other grade of wife.

For most women, however, it is the change in *sarhaed* which is the most obvious sign of the change in status which comes to a woman from union with a man, and in this context it matters not how the union was created, for the adjective used to define the woman is *gwriog* not *priod*.[19] So we turn to examine the concept of *sarhaed*.

B. *Insult and Shame*

The basic meaning of the verb *sarhau* is to insult. *Sarhaed* was originally the act of insult which brings shame and infringes honour, notionally represented among the insular Celtic peoples by the face, Welsh *wyneb*, Breton *eneb* and Irish *enech*.[20] Honour and shame are important social

---

[15] Ior §51/6-8; Bleg 62.9; WML 91.16, 90.17; Lat B 221.24; Lat D 342.23; Lat E 470.23.
[16] Col §305.
[17] Ior §53/4; Lat E 475.23.
[18] SEIL 182-3.
[19] Ior §46/1 cf. Bleg 61.7. There is some doubt regarding the exact juncture at which this comes about, since the lawyers seem to disagree as to whether a girl who has been given in marriage, but the union unconsummated should be compensated according to the status of her husband or of her brother: Ior §55/14, cf. also Lat B 223.6 *Si cum viro alio coierit, et hoc notum fuerit, a suo poterit libere repudiari, nec de iure quiquam habebit preter tria que sibi auferri non possunt. Adulter quidem viro prefato suum* sarhaet *reddat.*
[20] J. Loth supra.

concepts for the understanding of the ethos of any society.[21] They are the publicly declared valuation put on people by those who know them. The conduct which establishes the repute of any person depends on the rôle and status of that person in society. In all societies, the rôles of men and women imply different modes of conduct for each sex. A woman, in most traditionalist societies, is dishonoured by the tainting of her sexual purity, whereas a man is not. A man, in turn, is dishonoured if doubt is cast on his virility. Certain patterns of conduct are considered the exclusive virtues of one sex or another. A woman is obliged to preserve her purity, which has a physical basis, whereas a man is obliged to defend his kin, which includes the protection and restraint of the woman dependent upon him. Honour is the aspiration to status and the validation of status, shame is opposed to honour and is the restraint of such an aspiration and the recognition of the loss of status. Thus, just as honour is honour felt, claimed, and accorded, so shame is dishonour imposed, accepted, and felt. Shame, however, has another nuance of meaning. The attributes of this shame are blushing, timidity, shyness and modesty. These attributes are proper to a woman and can be evoked by events which necessarily expose her to sexual contact like the physical consummation of a marriage. This shame has no ethical connotations and does not imply loss of honour. Its sense is well conveyed by the Latin word *pudor*. Yet failure to preserve the bonds of propriety implied by this shame can lead to the shame which is dishonour.

Celtic society shows in its tradition of praise poetry a strong awareness of the importance of the public acclamation of repute which is honour, it also shows its awareness of honour and shame in that the laws of both Ireland and Wales equate these concepts with a material price which reflects the value of individuals according to their status in the hierarchy of society, and which is paid in compensation when insult is inflicted on them. In this, Celtic law shows a different emphasis from Anglo-Saxon law.[22] In Ireland the terms frequently used for this value contain the

---

[21] The studies of social anthropologists dealing with the importance of these concepts in Mediterranean societies throw considerable light on the workings of early Welsh society. See especially J. G. Peristiany, *Honour and shame: the Values of Mediterranean Society*, (London, 1965); Julian Pitt-Rivers, *The Fate of Shechem or the Politics of Sex*, (Cambridge, 1977); J. K. Campbell, *Honour, Family and Patronage*, (Oxford, 1976). T. M. Charles-Edwards has recently applied Pitt-Rivers principles to a study of forms of address used in Welsh and Irish stories as a reflection of relative status, T. M. Charles-Edwards, "Honour and Status in some Irish and Welsh Prose Tales", (1978) 29 *Ériu* 123-141.

[22] J. Pitt-Rivers, "Honour and Social Status" in J. G. Peristiany, *Honour and Shame: the Values of Mediterranean Society* (London 1965), 39.

element *enech*, literally face or honour; in Wales, *sarhaed*, a word with a converse meaning, is used, although there is evidence that it has displaced the older word *wynebwerth*, which means face or honour price. Thurneysen many years ago drew attention to the contrast between the Welsh and Irish terminology.[23] The semantic origins of the terms used in the Welsh law books suggest that the rules for the payment of *sarhaed* reflect the concepts of honour and shame held in early medieval Welsh society.

A series of triads define some of the different ways in which the insult which demanded reparation could be brought about:

> *Val hyn e traethun ny o'r sarhaedeu; en gyntaf o sarhaet brenhyn Aberfrau. Sef er edrechus e keureyth pa beth esyd sarhaet, ac ydau ef ac y paub; ac esef reweles e keureyth, nat sarhaet e nep namen un o try peth en enwedyc: guneythur guaratwyd ydau am e wreyc, neu lad e gennat neu torry e naud.*

This is how we treat the *sarhaedau*; first of the *sarhaed* of the King of Aberffraw. Namely the law looked what is *sarhaed* both for him and for everyone; and the law saw, that only three things constituted *sarhaed*, namely to do shame to him concerning his wife or to kill his messenger, or to break his protection.

> *O teyr ford e serheyr e urenhynes; o torry e naud, neu o'y tharau, neu o grybdeyllau peth o'y llau.*

In three ways the queen is insulted, namely by breaking her protection, or by striking her or by snatching something from her hand.

> *O teyr ford e serheyr pob den en e byt; o tarau a gossot, a duen treys e arnau, ac os gur uyd, o bedyr gan e wreyc, sarhaet yu ydau; keuoet gureyc uo, o cheyff hytheu wreyc gan e gur, sarhaet yu ydy hytheu: ac euelly ny dyeync nep hep ford y'u sarhau.*

In three ways is everyone in the world insulted; by blow and onslaught and bringing force against him, and if he be a man, if anyone lies with his wife, it is *sarhaed* for him; though she be a wife, if she finds a woman with her husband, it is *sarhaed* for her; and thus no one escapes without some way of being insulted.[24]

The thirteenth century compiler of the Iorwerth text still regards *sarhaed* as a recompense not merely for physical assault, though that was an obvious cause of its exaction, but also for infringement of the conventions of behaviour; such infringements were considered an insult to

---

[23] R. Thurneysen, *Celtic Law*, in CLP 67, originally published as *Das keltische Recht*, (1935) 55 ZRG 81-104.

[24] Ior §110/1-10. The *sarhaed* for misuse of a king's wife is augmented by a half: cf. Ior §3/1.

honour and prestige. This insult was felt not only by the individual but also by his kin and originally could cause kin feud. In the case of a woman it immediately affected any male on whom she was dependent. In the case of the king the greatest disgrace that could come to him was the misuse of his wife. One of the redactors of the Iorwerth text in an attempt to rationalise the implications of *sarhaed* when explaining the procedure followed in a case of *sarhaed* interprets the interaction of insult, shame, and reparation in terms which would be familiar to many social anthropologists:

> *Puybynnac a dywatto sarhaet, try pung esyd yaun ydau y wadu: na wnaeth na meuyl na sarhaet ydau nac y'u genedel nac y'u argluyd. Sef paham e guedyr rac er argluyd, rac dyrue er argluyd a rac talu ydau enteu e sarhaet a rac dyal e kenedel. Paham e guedyr ef rac e genedel ac na cheyff e genedel dym o'r sarhaet a talher ydau? Llyna er achaus: pan sarhaer eu kar guaratwyd yu udunt huy a kyureyth yu udunt huenteu dyal eu guaratwyd; ac urth henne e mae yaun guadu racdunt na sarhauyt eu kar; o thelyr ydau enteu y sarhaet, dywaratwyd yu e'r kenedel, a'r lle ny bo guaratwyd nyt oes haul.*

Whosoever may wish to deny *sarhaed*, it is right that he denies on three points: that he did no blemish or insult to him or his kin or his lord. It is denied before the lord, because of the lord's *dirwy* and lest *sarhaed* be paid to him and lest the kin take vengeance. Why is it denied before the kin and the kin receives none of the *sarhaed* which may be paid to him? This is the reason: when their kinsman is insulted, it is shame for them and it is law that they should avenge their shame: and so it is right to deny before them that their kinsman has not been insulted; if his *sarhaed* is paid to him, the kin is free from shame, and where there is no shame there is no claim.[25]

Insult *(sarhaed)* implies blemish *(mefl)* and *sarhaed* to kin as well as individual, such blemish *(mefl)* can only be removed by *sarhaed* (reparation) or otherwise vengeance *(dial)* will arise; once reparation is made by payment of *sarhaed*, shame *(gwaradwydd)* is removed, and the kin is shamefree *(diwaradwydd)*.

Two of the triads cited above refer to the insult brought about by the infringement of the conventions of relationships between man and woman, and no sections of the law texts as they exist preserve old concepts of honour and shame so well as those which concern woman and marriage. In an age when sexual offences were generally part of the jurisdiction of the church, the sections of the Welsh laws dealing with both marriage and such offences are singularly free from ecclesiastical influence. Terms like *sarhaed* (insult price), *wynebwerth* ("face" price),

[25] Ior §110/19-22.

and *gowyn*[26] (offence payment) are used most often with material connotations and are equated with fixed payments made in compensation for specific offences within marriage. Others like *cywilydd, gwarthrudd* and *gwaradwydd* are used almost exclusively in a conceptual sense, sometimes with no ethical or legal implication. *Sarhaed* is translated in the Latin texts by *iniuria*, and the shame words, *cywilydd, gwarthrudd* and *gwaradwydd* sometimes by the Latin *iniuria*, more often by *"pudor"*, a word which conveys the non-ethical sense somewhat better than English *shame*, which I shall use for convenience. The rules for the exaction of specific payments and the use of abstract terms are bound up with the value placed on preserving the sexual purity of a girl before marriage as one of the assets of kin and lord; the preservation of her chastity and her reputation for chastity within marriage; the deference which she owes her husband and the respect to her person which he owes to her.

In the rules for compensation, in aphorism and triad, there emerges time and again an awareness of what is honourable and conversely what brings shame and of what exactly is the nature of the rôle of both husband and wife. This can be seen at all stages of the woman's life from the onset of the menarche which was regarded by the lawyers as taking place at twelve years; between twelve and fourteen a girl[27] was not expected to bear children and care seems to have been taken at this time to preserve her virginity[28] and to instil in her some idea of the behaviour that was fitting: for, when she was given in marriage, her kin was required to vouch for her virginity and according to the Colan text, her husband could take a surety from her parents *"na wnel hytheu ydau ef kywylyt o'y corff, ac na bo gegus urthau"*,[29] (that she cause him no shame by her body nor be offensive to him). A girl given in marriage as a virgin and discovered to be a *twyllforwyn*[30] merits a greased tail as her *agweddi*, for already, at the giving, surety had been placed on her virginity. One triad attempts to rationalise the three exchanges of property which accompany a marriage of *rhodd* and *estyn* in terms of reparation for the shame *(pudor)* felt by a girl at the loss of her virginity when she is given in marriage, shame felt in the first place at the mere prospect of close contact with a man:

---

[26] Excursus II.
[27] Col §54: Ior §55/4.
[28] Lat B 224.14. *Si filia alicuius vel neptis vel alia quam pater debuerat custodire non custodivit, quod mulier ante stuprata fuerit, reddat et qui rapuit et qui custodire debuit.*
[29] Col §66; Glossary *gwg*; Excursus II.
[30] Lat A §52/25; Lat B 224.3-13; Ior §47/2-5; WML 132.10-19; Bleg 116.29-117. 6 = Lat D 374.26-32; Bleg 61.27-31 = Lat D 342.13-16.

Try kywylyt moruyn: pan deweto y tat 'A uoruyn, neu rodet ty y vr'. Eyl yu pan el y'r guely ar y gur en kyntaf. Trydy yu pan geuoto o'r guely a dyuot y plyth e dynyon. Am rod y telyr amobyr; am y gueryndaut y chowyll; am y chywylyt y aguedy.

The three shames of a girl are: One is that her father tells her, 'I have given you to a husband', the second is, when she first goes to bed to her husband, the third is when she first rises from the bed to the midst of people. For the giving, her *amobr* is paid. For her virginity her *cowyll*; for her shame her *egweddi.*[31]

Failure to save her from abduction and to cherish her for a marriage of *rhodd* and *estyn* was regarded as one of the shames of her kin.

The most extreme violation a girl might suffer was the forcible termination of her virginity by rape, an offence which could also be committed against a married woman but with different consequences, both physical and legal. If a woman, who is a virgin, be raped, her attacker is expected to pay *amobr* to the lord, *egweddi, dilysrwydd* or *diweirdeb*,[32] and *cowyll* to the girl as well as her *sarhaed* or *wynebwerth* and a fine, *dirwy trais* to the king. Three of these payments are identical with the payments involved when a girl is given in marriage, namely the *amobr*, the *cowyll* and the *egweddi*. The explanation for this is that *trais*, according to Charles-Edwards's theory, was perhaps at one stage a legally recognised union. The offensiveness of the action of rape and the dishonour, that it brings, is acknowledged in the exaction of *sarhaed* or *wynebwerth* which is paid to the girl. The *dilysrwydd, dilystod* or *diweirdeb*, if it was a payment, seem to be an acknowledgement of her free state even if the physical condition of virginity is irrestorable. The last payment exacted as compensation for rape is the *dirwy* payable to the king. In the Iorwerth text this is specified as being twelve kine but elsewhere in terms which make it virtually identical with the king's *sarhaed*; according to these texts it consists either of a silver rod, a golden plate and cup or of the silver rod alone.[33] The implication of this rule is that the safe keeping of virgins lay within the king's *nawdd* or protection. They, like some land, are classified as the *diffaith* or waste which belongs to him. *Nawdd* like Irish *snádud* was the ability of individuals to afford protection from all legal processes within a fixed area or fixed period of

---

[31] Col §42. It is significant that the Breton word *enebuarz*, the cognate of Welsh *wynebwerth*, has developed a restricted meaning equivalent to the meaning of Welsh *cowyll*, and is used to gloss *dotatione*, see Loth, 48 RC 331 and also M. Planiol, *Histoire des Institutions de la Bretagne* (Rennes, 1953) ii. 237.

[32] Ior §50/4, where the dirwy is twelve kine.

[33] WML 92.10; Bleg 63.23; Lat A 52/39; B 224.21.

time.[34] Infringement of the king's *nawdd* constituted a *sarhaed* to him. The rape of a married woman is of no concern to the king, for he owes her no special protection. The married woman is under the lordship of her husband. Nor does it attract the payments to the victim which are associated with the creation or termination of marital union, for the woman's union with her husband is unaffected by it. Hence the offence calls for the payment of her *sarhaed* alone to her husband and herself. It is a particularly high *sarhaed*, paid with three augments since such a rape could give rise to kin enmity but we shall return to that later when dealing with *sarhaed* in marriage.

Once given in marriage, both man and wife are expected to maintain certain standards of physical fitness or behaviour. A woman may justifiably leave her husband without losing any of her rights, if he suffer from leprosy, bad breath or impotence.[35] Infringements of the proprieties of behaviour can likewise lead to termination of the union or to the exaction of the payment of compensation or to both. The rules illustrate that the lawyers try to distinguish the infringements by using different technical terms; *sarhaed; wynebwerth* and *gowyn*; and *camlwrw*. These they use for the compensation appropriate to different offences. We have to consider in legal terms:

(a)   offences by a third party against either husband or wife;
(b)   offences by the husband against the wife;
(c)   offences by the wife against the husband.

Offences by a third party are primarily offences against the husband since any physical assault on the husband is regarded as *sarhaed* and any physical assault on the wife is an infringement of his protection and dishonour to him. If she is struck by another man, a compensation equal to half the husband's *sarhaed* is called for.[36] In the case of *galanas, sarhaed* for either husband or wife is paid into the husband's estate. Most of the references to third party insult are, however, found in rules dealing with sexual contact which involve one or other of the partners in marriage.

---

[34] CG *snádud*; cf. Anglo-Saxon *frið*: PM i. 44; the king's peace in early England was not the prerogative of everyone and the *nawdd* of Welsh law involves a limited protection.
[35] Bleg 64.1. *O tri achaws ny chyll gwreic y hegwedi kyt adawho y gwr: o glafri ac eisseu kyt a dryc anadyl* = Lat A §52/54 = Lat B 222.3 = Lat E 471.4 = Lat D 343.28; cf. also the lists of the "teithi" in WML 80.21: *Teithi g6r y6 gallu kyt a g6reic a bot yn gyfan y aelodeu oll. Teithi g6reic y6 dyuot ar6yd etiuedu idi: a bot yn gyfan y holl aelodeu.*
[36] *Si sine causa a viro suo mulier vapulaverit, secundum dignitatem suam ei iniuriam vir suus reddat. Quisquis coniugem alicuius verberaverit, vir eius habebit dimidium sayrhaed.* Lat A §52/44, 45.

Sarhaed (eo nomine) is payable by the husband when he unjustifiably beats his wife; he is justified in beating her if she gives away goods which she is not entitled to give, if he finds her with a man, or if she uses insulting language to him. The measure of the *sarhaed* would be a third of her husband's. If he is unfaithful to her or banishes her from the marriage bed, the compensation is more frequently called *gowyn* or *wynebwerth*[37] and both these names reflect a more archaic terminology. This compensation is specified as being 120d. for the first offence, £1 for the second.[38] The third offence entitled the wife to leave her husband without forfeiting any rights and indeed she was expected to leave him or be branded as a wife without shame (*pudor*). Any blow that she might strike her concubine, even if it results in death, is without redress. Her *wynebwerth* could even be called for after the union had ended if the husband allowed another woman to sleep on the bedclothes retained in accordance with the rules for sharing. This reflects a sanctity of the marital bed also seen in one of the many triads which express social principles rather than legal rules, where expulsion from the marriage bed is regarded as one of the three shames of a wife.[39] In another triad, bringing a mistress into the home is regarded as one of the three things that bring shame to a wife's kin.[40] If a wife be driven from the marital bed for any reason, she is required to raise two witnesses from among the household, a further two if she is driven from the home, and before returning can demand a full *wynebwerth* from her husband.[41]

If the rules for compensation due for offences to the wife on the part of the husband reflect the respect due to the wife, the reparation called

---

[37] The clearest example of an attempt to draw a distinction between *gowyn* and *sarhaed* is found in the commentary on the triad *Tri phrifai gwraig* Ior §51/3. *Sef y6 y sarhaet pob maedu a wnel y g6r arnei. Eithyr am tri pheth, sarhaet y6 idi. Sef y6 y tri pheth hynny y dyly y maedu: am rodi peth ny dylyho y rodi, ac am y chaffel gan 6r, ac am una6 meuel ar y uaraf. Ac os am y chaffel gan vr y maed, ny dyly o diu6yn namyn hynny, kany dylyir diu6yn a dial am un gyflauan. Sef y6 y gouyn: o cheiff y g6r gan wreic arall, talet y g6r idi y treigyl kyntaf chweugeint, a'r eil treigyl punt. Os keiff y tryded* [*weith*], *ysgar a eill heb golli dim o'r eidi.*

[38] Col §1; Bleg 64.3; Lat A §52/60; Lat B 222.14; Lat C 288.16; Lat D 343.31; Lat D adds the clause; *Redwit dicit quod tercio xxx solidos; quarto libera cum toto iure suo abeat. Si pacienter sustineat, de cetero* wynebwerth *non habebit*, which suggests that it is after the third incident that the wife was free to leave her husband.

[39] Lat B 242.33 = Lat E 494.2 *Tres sunt* guarthrud *mulieris; scilicet falsa impositio criminis, id est,* enllib, *et* reith; *et de lecto expelli.*

[40] Lat D 371.28. *Tri chewilyt kenetyl ynt, ac o achaws gwreic y maent: llathrudaw gwreic oe hanuot; eil yw dwyn oe gwr gwreic arall ar y phen yr ty: y trydyt yw y hyspeilaw.* Lat E 475.26 has *Tres sunt iniurie generis ex femina* with *iniuria* corresponding to the *cywilydd* of Lat D.

[41] Lat B 225.8; Lat E 474.2.

for a wife's misdemeanours emphasise the fact that her husband's position is that of her lord. Here again, special emphasis is put on the marital bed. If a wife leaves her husband's bed and fails to allow him his conjugal rights she has to pay him a minor fine or *camlwrw*[42] before she is allowed to return *quia dominus eius est*. Likewise, the uttering of shameful words makes a wife liable to *camlwrw*.[43] *Camlwrw* is the minor fine, specified as consisting of three kine, which is normally paid to the king or territorial lord. The husband could accept this payment of *camlwrw* or take revenge for his wife's behaviour by striking her three times with a rod as long as a man's forearm and as thick as his middle finger on any part of the body except the head.[44] If he took revenge in this way, he could not exact his fine; for revenge and compensation were not allowed for the same offence in Welsh law. The shameful words that a woman was not allowed to utter are specified in another triad: a woman was not allowed to wish a blemish on his beard (to cast aspersions on his virility), wish dirt on his teeth, or call him a cur.[45] Wrongfully giving away property was also a beatable offence, since the kind of property a wife is allowed to part with is specified and determined by the actual status of the husband.[46]

The ultimate shame that a woman could bring on herself and her kin, and the ultimate insult that she could impose on her husband, was to have consort with another man. Even a scandal of this, an *enllib*, was regarded as a *gwarthrudd* (shame) which needed to be refuted by an oath supported by compurgators *(rhaith)*.[47] A *rhaith* of seven women was required by the woman to deny the first scandal, twenty-four the second, and fifty the third.[48] The necessity to raise such a *rhaith* was considered to be a shame in itself. A scandal was confirmed and made a *cadarn enllib* by three things, namely that the woman be seen coming from behind a bush with a man, or beneath the same mantle, and or with a man between her thighs.[49] The wife required a *rhaith* of fifty women to deny the adultery, just as the adulterer required a *rhaith* of fifty men. If the accusation were a valid one, the wife was considered to have commit-

---

[42] Bleg 61.20.
[43] Bleg 61.15; Lat A §52/43: Lat D 341.37: Lat B 223.10.
[44] Bleg 61.17.
[45] Ior §51/3.
[46] Ior §51/6-8.
[47] Lat B 242.32; Lat E 494.2: Ior §55/7.
[48] Bleg 64.25; Ior §55/7; Lat A §52/51; Lat B 222.21; Lat E 471.19.
[49] Col §29; Bleg 111.24-8; WML 127.7-11.

ted a *cyflafan ddybryd*[50] or shameful offence, her husband might reject her, and she lost all her rights. The lawbooks distinguish three degrees of such a *cyflafan: rhoddi cusan* (kiss), *gofysio* (finger) glossed in Lat D as *palatio manuum in vulva,* and *ymrain* (copulate). Kissing and fingering were not punishable if they occurred when playing *rhaffan,*[51] or in *cyfeddach,* or when someone returned from a long journey. The texts disagree as to the actual amounts of compensation due to the husband for these acts. One rule makes full *sarhaed* the compensation for *ymrain* and a quarter *sarhaed* the compensation for *cusanu* and *gofysio.*[52] Other sources make the compensation for *ymrain* a *sarhaed* augmented by a half or two thirds or even three thirds with the additional note that such an action could bring feud between kins *(cenedl elyniaeth)* presumably between the kin of the adulterer and the kin of the husband.[53] This feud could be the *gwreictra* of the *Naw Affaith Galanas* according to the Men of Powys and the *gwreictra* which if it were not settled could be raised as a legal objection to the competence of a witness.

The wife's kin was not completely free from involvement in her adulterous acts since, if the woman wished to deny the charge of a kissing, she needed to be vindicated by an oath of seven people from among the members of her immediate family, *y am tat a mam a brodyr a chuyoryd.*[54] A *rhaith,* in any case, always involved the natal kin of the principal. A woman's association with another man could be of her own free will or against her will. The law texts again offer variant opinions as to the person responsible for paying the *sarhaed* when the wife is the willing party to the adultery. The opinion of lawyer Goronwy ap Moriddig is quoted that, when this happens, the adulterer is not under an obligation to pay the husband's *sarhaed* and that the onus for the payment lies entirely with the wife, who, if she does not pay, is rejected by the husband. Nothing is known of the lawyer Goronwy ap Moriddig[55] and it is hard to believe that originally the adulterer would not have been considered "guilty" of insult towards the husband. The texts are clear as to the

---

[50] Bleg 66.18 *(achaws dybryd)*: Ior §46/5.

[51] LW 581*b* has a note on *gware rhaffan:*
Ludi genus . . . qualis vero non satis liquet: Frequens autem in omnibus fere Codd. occurrit. Versiones Latinae Ludum funicularem vocant, a Rhaff, Funis. Plures sunt id genus ludi rusticis non ignoti: Crediderim hunc esse ludum, quem nos vocamus Anglice Swinging.

[52] Lat A §52/46; Lat B 223.21; Lat E 472.11.

[53] Lat D 345.20; Bleg 66.28. Lat D quotes two rules side by side acknowledging the conflict between them: *sic dicunt quidem: alii vero ut non . . .*

[54] Ior §46/11 (B).

[55] The name Goronwy ap Moriddig occurs in Llyfr Coch Asaph but the context of the reference suggests a later date than that of the lawbooks.

responsibility of the man who forces his attentions on another man's wife, for this brings us to the province of rape and (as we have seen) the rapist is obliged to pay a heavily augmented *sarhaed* to both wife and husband or bear the consequences of feud.[56] Such a rape was also considered an insult to her natal kin.

C. *Galanas*

The rules for compensation within marriage stress the conventions that both man and wife were expected to observe. They also show the persistent if shadowy involvement of a wife's natal kin in her interests. The rules for homicide as presented in the thirteenth-century texts emphasise the ambivalence of her position between two kins. While the *sarhaed* of a married woman is dependent on her husband's status, her *galanas* price is still linked with that of her natal kin and hence, when (as usually happens) in a case of homicide both *galanas* and *sarhaed* are paid, her position in the kin is ambivalent, for the compensation for homicide is paid in two parts. First the *sarhaed* of the dead man is paid by the homicide to an inner family circle of the victim. If he is married, his wife receives a third of this payment. The second payment, the *galanas*, is made and received by a wider kin-group, and the victim's wife takes none of it. The constitution of the wider kin groups in the payment of *galanas*[57] is one of the great complexities of the lawbooks, but it is clear

---

[56] *Supra*, p. 50.
[57] The most important discussions of galanas are: F. W. Maitland, "The Laws of Wales—the Kindred and the Bloodfeud"; *Collected Papers* i. 202-29, first published in *Law Magazine and Review,* August 1881; T. Jones Pierce, "The Laws of Wales —the Kindred and the Bloodfeud," *Medieval Welsh Society,* ed. J. Beverley Smith, (Cardiff, 1972); R. R. Davies, "The Survival of the Bloodfeud in Medieval Wales", (1970) 54 *History,* 338-357. The *galanas* kin is discussed by M. Gwyn Jenkins, "Rhifo Carennydd yng Nghyfreithiau Rhufain, yr Eglwys a Chymru", (1964) 20 BBCS 348-373, where the author attributes the discordant evidence of the law texts to the confusion between two methods of reckoning kinship, the ecclesiastical method and the method of late Roman Law. Dafydd Jenkins offers a corrective to M. Gwyn Jenkins in "Camsyniadau F. W. Maitland: Y Genedl Alanas yng Nghyfraith Hywel" (1967) 22 BBCS 229-336; T. M. Charles-Edwards in "Kinship, Status and the Origins of the Hide" (1973) 56 *Past and Present* 3-33, argues that Anglo-Saxon lineage systems have influenced the pattern of the kin involved in Galanas. My own view does not coincide exactly with that of any of these authorities. It is briefly that the expanded kin of *galanas* settlement and the 2: 1 proportion of paternal and maternal kin participation owes its origin to Anglo-Saxon influence but since the evidence for the extent of the kin in Anglo-Saxon England is extremely tenuous, one cannot say that any specific description of a seven generation group or a nine grade kin derives from an Anglo-Saxon source. The methods of reckoning to the seventh generation probably are indebted to ecclesiastical influence. The phrase *nawfed ach* is possibly an archaic one and can be compared to the *nómad n-ao* of Irish Law. The kin as described in the South Wales law books represents some lawyer's attempt to make an expanded kin group fit in with this archaic phrase.

that the relatives who pay with the homicide are those who will receive payment if he is killed, and that the amounts involved are graduated according to the closeness of the relationship. The kin groups on each side were both the maternal and paternal kins of the killer and the killed, the paternal kin paying or receiving two-thirds and the maternal kin one-third of the sum left after deducting from the full *galanas* price the homicide's liability for one-third. Since the victim was dead, this one-third was conveniently available as a commission for the king for his help in collecting the payment: it is known as the enforcing third *(traean cymell).*[58]

The people involved in composition were those who would normally have been involved in the feud, sometimes called the avengers *(dialwyr).* A woman is not regarded as a natural participant in feud, since she has no spear except her distaff,[59] she receives but does not pay "spear penny", and she contributes to the composition on behalf of any children she has or is likely to have, at half the rate of a male of the same degree of kindred as herself. Through her, her children can claim contribution from the kin. The part played by the maternal kin in the law of *galanas* contrasts strongly with their part in other fields of Welsh law, where the predominant kin group seems to be a four-generation agnatic group.[60] This latter is the group involved in giving a woman in marriage,[61] as it is the group concerned with landholding,[62] though there is an exception to the rule of agnatic landholding in the right of the children of a Welshwoman by an *alltud* to inherit land from her father in certain circumstances.[63]

The four-generation agnatic kin of Wales clearly corresponds with the *derbfine*[64] of Irish law. In Ireland it is the *derbfine* of victim and killer which is involved in feud, paying and receiving the fixed compensation *(éraic)* of seven cumals and the status-variable *enech* price.[65] The maternal kin participates only to the extent of paying or receiving a seventh over and above the *éraic* price, the *cumal aireir*, and one suspects that the kin groups involved in Wales were originally similar. The descriptions of

---

[58] For *traean cymell* see p. 89, *infra.*
[59] Ior §55/8; §53/9; Col §58.
[60] T. M. Charles-Edwards, (1973) cited above.
[61] AL IX.xxx.3, XIV.xlvi.11.
[62] Col §578: Bleg 72.26-8; DwCol §§264-7, etc.
[63] Col §§601, 602.
[64] R. Thurneysen, *Ir. Recht* 16 ff.; D. A. Binchy, "The Linguistic and Historical Value of the Irish Law tracts", John Rhys Memorial Lecture 1943, 31; CLP 223.
[65] *Ir. Recht* 13, §14.

the *galanas* kins in the Welsh texts are fraught with problems. There are at least two distinct textual traditions. The Cyfnerth, Blegywryd, Latin A and D texts refer to the kin as extending to the *nawfed ach* or *nonus gradus*:[66] the Iorwerth and Latin B texts refer to the kins as being descendants in the *seithfed famwys* or *septima generatio*.[67] Both traditions agree that the kin involved in *galanas* is more extensive than that involved in some other legal institutions of medieval Wales, and that the maternal kin plays a prominent role. Four elements in the Welsh pattern of *galanas* bear a strong resemblance to what we know of the regulation of feud in Anglo-Saxon England:

(1) where the woman is always counted as a member of her natal *maegth* in the settlement of feud;[68]

(2) where both paternal and maternal kins were involved in composition, contributing in the proportion 2:1;[69]

(3) where the kin involved was a fairly extensive one, although the surviving evidence does not allow any certainty as to its extent;[70]

(4) where composition for homicide involved more than one payment, the *healsfang* to an inner group of relatives, the *wergeld* to a more extensive kin.[71]

These points of resemblance suggest that the rules regulating *galanas* in Welsh law have been influenced by Anglo-Saxon law and custom, probably during a period when there were reciprocal agreements for composition for homicide between Welsh and Saxon on the English-Welsh border calling for corresponding kin groups.[72] This influence may explain in part the anomalous position of woman in the Welsh law of *galanas*, where her *galanas* links her closely to her natal kin even after marriage and where the maternal kin is deeply involved in the *galanas* of her children, thus forming a strong bond between two different kins for at least one generation.

These rules as represented in the law books invite a series of questions regarding the part a woman plays in a case of killing. What is the procedure:

(1) when a woman kills someone?

---

[66] Bleg 32.1-7; Lat A 122.5; Lat D 334.13.
[67] Ior §108/7; Col §§264-5; Lat B 210.5.
[68] EASL 123, Hn 70.12.
[69] Hn 75.8,9; Hn 76.1a.
[70] T. M. Charles-Edwards. "The Origins of the Hide" (1973) 56 *Past and Present* 3-33, B. Phillpotts, *Kindred and Clan* (Cambridge 1913) 21-7.
[71] Wer 5
[72] "In Dunsaete-land giltige Englische-Wälsche Beziehung", Liebermann i. 374.

(2)   when a woman is killed?
(3)   when a woman's brother kills or is killed?
(4)   when the woman's son kills or is killed?
(5)   when the woman's husband kills or is killed?

(1)   When a woman, married or unmarried, kills someone, her own kin, both maternal and paternal, pays the composition or *galanas*. She herself is responsible for paying the *sarhaed*, with her husband, if any.

(2)   If a woman is killed, her own kin receives the *galanas* and her inner family group the *sarhaed* if she is unmarried; if she is married, the *sarhaed* goes to her husband.

(3)   If the woman's brother kills or is killed, since she is not regarded as a natural avenger, her liability is a limited one. She pays or receives half the amount expected of a male relative in the same degree of kinship, for any children she has or is likely to have. If she has no children and swears she will not have any, she is free from liability.

(4)   If the woman's son kills or is killed, she pays or receives part of the *galanas* along with her husband and her kin contributes or receives one third of the remaining payment. If the son is the offspring of the marriage between a Welshwoman and an alien *(alltud)* the mother's kin is responsible for all liabilities and assets.

(5)   If a woman's husband kills or is killed, the wife pays and receives none of the *galanas* but has one third of his *sarhaed* if he is killed.

To sum up, in *galanas*, as illustrated by the thirteenth century texts, woman is really a transmitter of liabilities and claims, paying and receiving on behalf of her children rather than being an active participator. A woman is not involved in her husband's liabilities or assets in *galanas*, not being reckoned as one of his kin although her children were. The *sarhaed* implied in his killing was considered *sarhaed* to herself and in this the tie of marriage and the change of status implied by the union are a dominant force. Her position in the kin or between kins is ambivalent, with ties of blood and marriage diverging in different directions but converging on her person and serving to link two kins; this link is strengthened by the fact that, for one generation at least, both those kins could be involved in any *galanas* in which her children participated.

The rules relating to *galanas* stress the conduit, non-participant, function of woman in a particular institution. The rules relating to *sarhaed* in the Law of Women give another perspective to her rôle in family and marriage. The law books give us the rules which form the framework of society, to see them operating we have to look elsewhere.

The *Four Branches of the Mabinogi* have proved themselves a rich repository for students of early Welsh Society. The second Branch, the only one of the stories which has a woman's name as its title, shows itself as particularly sensitive to the delicately balanced position of a woman. For the central theme of *Branwen, daughter of Llŷr* is the relationship between two kins and the way in which the infringement of honour determines the course of that relationship which pivots on Branwen herself. The text contains constant echoes of the vocabulary and terminology of those sections of the law books with which we have been concerned.

The first of these comes in the explanation given by Matholwch king of Ireland for his coming to Britain to seek Branwen sister of the king Bendigeidfran as his wife because "he wishes to bind together the Island of the Mighty and Ireland that they be the stronger."[73] These words contain the most explicit expression in Welsh literature of the idea that the role of the wife is that of a link between kins, a peace weaver, the *friðstofe*, a rôle which is a familiar one for the heroines of Germanic and Anglo-Saxon saga. After consultation with his men, Bendigeidfran agrees to give his treasured sister "one of the Three Matriarchs" and the "fairest maiden in the World"[74] (words which are echoed again and again in the following paragraphs) to Matholwch and a time is appointed for the consummation of the union at Aberffraw, the ancient caput of Gwynedd. Before this, the Irish and the Welsh join in a feast where Bendigeidfran and his men sit on one side and Branwen with Matholwch on the other: for although the union has not yet been consummated she has already been given in marriage. On the morrow of the wedding feast there is an incident which echoes a different legal concept. Branwen's half-brother, Efnisien, (the Welsh Bricriu) discovers that his sister has been given in marriage and has slept with Matholwch without his being consulted; "that a girl as good as that one and a sister of mine"[75] should have been handed over in this way is intolerable: "they could not inflict a greater disgrace on me".[76] He reacts by mutilating the horses of Matholwch and his company. This insult shames Matholwch and it astonishes him "that Branwen, daughter of Llŷr, one of the three chief Matriarchs of the Island of Britain, daughter of the king of the Island of

---

[73] PKM 30.19. Y erchi Branwen uerch Lyr y doeth, ac os da genhyt ti, ef a uyn ymrwymaw ynys y Kedeirn ac Iwerdon y gyt, ual y bydynt gadarnach.

[74] PKM 30.29-31.2. A honno oed tryded prif rieni yn yr ynys hon; teccaf morwyn yn y byt oed.

[75] PKM 31.26-28. "Ay yuelly y gwnaethant wy am uorwyn kystal a honno ac yn chwaer y minheu, y rodi heb uyghanyat i?"

[76] PKM 31.28-32.1. "Ny ellynt wy tremic uwy arnaf i."

the Mighty be given to me and should sleep with me, and after that, that I be shamed. And it was strange to me that such a shame was not inflicted before a girl as good as that one was given to me rather than afterwards".[77] Bendigeidfran for his part is on the horns of a dilemma. Efnisien's action is insult to him also as a breach of his protection but he cannot take vengeance on his own half-brother for vengeance within the kin is forbidden. He offers Matholwch compensation in the form, specified in the lawbooks for injuries to animals,[78] and also for the *sarhaed* of the king. The Irish accept the compensation, recognising that if they do not, they "are more likely to suffer greater disgrace than to receive greater compensation".[79]

Branwen goes to Ireland with Matholwch and behaving as befits a queen bestows gifts on all who visit her, "No great man nor noble lady came to visit Branwen save that she gave them a brooch or a ring or a precious royal jewel outstanding to behold."[80] Despite the reconciliation, after Branwen has borne him a son, Matholwch, stirred up by his men to new resentment, expels her from his bed (one of the three shames of a wife and of her kin, according to the lawbooks) and banishes her to the kitchen, there to work and to suffer a daily blow from the butcher—a very obvious example of one kind of *sarhaed*.

Cut off from all other communication with Britain, Branwen spends three years preparing a starling to carry a message to Bendigeidfran who at once, on receiving it, invades Ireland. A frightened Matholwch attempts to make amends by abdicating and offering the kingdom to Gwern, his son, the tangible seal of the union between the two kins, "your nephew, your sister's son, investing him in your presence, in place of the wrong and the harm that has been done to Branwen".[81] The terms are accepted and peace is made. The Irish and Welsh congregate together

---

[77] PKM 32.26-33.4. "Rodi Bronwen uerch Lyr ym, yn tryded prif rieni yr ynys honn, ac yn uerch y urenhin Ynys y Kedeyrn, a chyscu genthi, a gwedy hynny uy gwaradwydaw. A ryued oed genhyf, nat kyn rodi morwyn gystal a honno ym, y gwneit y gwaradwyd a wnelit ym."
This whole passage revolves around the use of the words *gwaradwydd* and *di-waradwydd*.

[78] PKM 33.14-22. A similar mutilation of horses is recorded in the *Vita Cadoci*, A. W. Wade Evans. *Vita Sanctorum Britanniae et Genealogiae*, (Cardiff, 1944), 58, 59.

[79] PKM 33.29-34.2 sef kynghor a uedylyssant, —os gwrthot hynny a wnelynt, bot yn tebygach ganthunt cael kywilid a uei uwy, no chael iawn a uei uwy.

[80] PKM 37.9-13. Ny doey wr mawr, na gwreic da yn Iwerdon, e ym w[e]let a Branwen, ni rodei hi ae cae, ae modrwy, ae teyrndlws cadwedic ydaw, a uei arbennic y welet yn mynet e ymdeith.

[81] PKM 41.9-15. "Ac y mae Matholwch yn rodi brenhinaeth Iwerdon y Wern uab Matholwch, dy nei ditheu, uab dy chwaer, ac yn y ystynnu y'th wyd di, yn lle y cam a'r codyant a wnaethpwyd y Uranwen."

in a special house where the Irish plan a trick, foiled by Efnisien. Discord arises again when Efnisien, seeing the child Gwern playing with Bendigeidfran and his uncles senses yet another slight, takes vengeance by throwing the child into the fire and with that act, the tangible link which unites the people of Matholwch and the kin of Bendigeidfran is destroyed and all hell is let loose. Branwen survives the holocaust to return to Britain and dies heartbroken at the destruction which has come about through her person:

> "Woe, O son of God! Woe is me from my birth!
> The wealth of two kingdoms destroyed because of me."[82]

In a paper on Women in Archaic Society,[83] Jean Poirier summarised certain things which he considered to be common to archaic societies in their attitude to women; among them were the following points:

(1)   Woman bears a fault-bearing role and lives in a condition of perpetual alienation, never completely integrated into her husband's family.

(2)   She never has complete juridical power, being considered by the law as an object of law. She is throughout her life in a position of judicial minority despite the fact that socially speaking she pays an eminent role.

(3)   Woman is impure, dangerous to the group, this danger is the consequence of the inherent servitude of the physiological order of her nature. Preserving her purity is therefore important and virginity a power to be guarded.

(4)   It is important that she fills the function of genetrice and failure to fulfil this function is sanctioned. Marriage, because of this role, is the essential part of a vast social network, the married couple is not separated from society but controlled by the group or kin in which they live.

Some of these attitudes are implicit in the story of Branwen as it is found in the second Branch of the Mabinogi: most of them also seem to me to underlie many of the rules found in the Law of Women, which stress her dependent status, the value placed on her chastity and her ambivalent position between two kins.

---

[82] PKM 45.16-18. "Oy a uab Duw," heb hi, "guae ui o'm ganedigaeth. Da a dwy ynys a diffeithwyt o'm achaws i."

[83] Jean Poirier, "La Statut de la Femme dans les Societés Archaiques", *La Femme, Recueilles de la Societé Jean Bodin XI*, (Bruxelles, 1959), 1ff.

EXCURSUS I:
Tres sunt columpne iuris herwid guyr Powys.[84]

THE text of Latin Redaction B is the unique witness to a set of three enneads which begins with the rubric:

Tres sunt columpne iuris herwid guyr Powys: nau affeith galanas, nau affeith tan, nau affeith lledrat.

We should expect these enneads to correspond to the enneads of the Tair Colofn Cyfraith found in the other Latin and Welsh redactions.[85] There is, indeed, a close relationship between *nau affeith lledrat* of Lat B and the corresponding *naw affaith* in the standard version of the text. There, the *naw affaith* are the nine accessories who aid and abet the principal in cases of theft, arson and homicide. The *nau affeith galanas* and the *nau affeith tan* of the Lat B lists preserve a different meaning of the word *affaith* and offer classifications which have a different legal significance. It is the *nau affeith galanas* which is of interest for the present paper but since a brief examination of the *nau affeith tan* throws some light on the other list and is a help to define the meaning of *affeith*, we shall start by looking at that list; The *nau affeith tan* are:

[1]	*tan geueil*	the fire of a smithy
[2]	*tan y ty nessaf*	the fire of the next house
[3]	*dwyn tan heb wibot*	taking fire without knowledge
[4]	*lad tan*	striking a fire
[5]	*paratoi tyssu*	preparing ------
[6]	*gwascaru moch y tan*	pigs scattering the fire
[7]	*y emdwyn*	carrying it
[8]	*tan yr odin*	the fire of a kiln
[9]	*losgi*	burning

The text is not without its problems. The word *tyssu* does not occur elsewhere and it is difficult to put a precise meaning to phrases like *y emdwyn*. The translation "pigs scattering the fire" is not a syntactically satisfactory one for *gwascaru moch y tan*. The list, however, seems to refer to the things which could be causes of fire, or which represent categories of fire.

Let us now turn to the items in the *Galanas* list. They read:

[1]	*tirdra*	[6]	*gorduy*
[2]	*guereictra*	[7]	*brat*
[3]	*sarhaet*	[8]	*kennadwri y rung bratwyr ay elin*
[4]	*tewessiau*	[9]	*gurthareith*
[5]	*cerh*	[10]	*lad y gelein*

---

[84] The text has been published twice in LTWL 250.35 and AL ii. 881. It deserves a much fuller treatment than I am able to give it within the compass of this excursus.

[85] Ior §104; Bleg 29.26; WML. 37.4.

There are again problems of interpretation in this list. The first and most obvious is that the list as it stands consists of ten not nine items, suggesting that one of the items is an addition to the original ennead. We have no other text to use as a corrective. Most of the terms, are however, known either from other parts of the law text or from the literature; we will look at them in the order in which they occur.

1. *Tirdra*[86] occurs only in the law texts and there mainly in the legal triads as a word referring to an unsettled dispute about land. In one triad,[87] it is listed with *galanas*, (here clearly meaning dispute over homicide), and *gwreictra* as one of three sets of circumstances which could invalidate the competence of a witness. The triad grouping suggests that these three things had some element common to them. The *locus classicus* for a record of dispute over land between kins in early Welsh society outside the law books is the *Surexit Memorandum* of the Lichfield Gospels, where the final words of the settlement, which it records, confirm the establishment of concord between the two kins at the end of a period of animosity or feud.[88]

2. *Guereictra*, "gureictra" is translated in a Latin version of the triad cited above as *abusio uxoris*, one Bleg version of the triad has *godineb* (adultery),[89] instead of *gwreictra*, another Bleg version of the triad replaces it with *kamarueru o un ohonynt wreic y llall*, (one of them abusing the wife of the other), and the Colan text refers to *gwreictra* as an act which belongs to the area of *cenedyl elenyaeth* or kin feud.[89] *Gwreictra* therefore seems to be a case of unsettled kin feud roused by adultery or misuse of a woman.

3. *Sarhaet*, the third item in the list, has been dealt with in the main text of this paper as the compensation for assault and for insult. It was an action which involved the participation of the kin of the victim and the offender and could give rise to kin feud if reparation were not made.

---

[86] H. D. Emanuel had amended the form to *dirdra* on the basis of a note to a triad found in Bleg (234, note to 128.28). I prefer to retain the MS. reading.

[87] cf. Bleg 37.11.
Tri achaws yssyd y lyssu tyston. Vn yw galanas heb ymdiuwyn. Eil yw o vot dadyl am tir yrydunt heb teruynu. Tryded yw kamarueru o vn ohonunt o wreic y llall.
with Bleg 128.25
Ony dichawn ef eu gwrthneu wy yn gyfreithawl, gwedy hynny llysser wynt megys tyston, ae o elynyaeth, ae o odineb, ae o tirtra, megys y dywetpwyt vry yn y llyfyr.
with Col §531
Hyn o llessoet esyt en keureyth Hewel herwyd gueythret: sef ev e rey henny dirdra, a galanas a gureyctra, a'r deu henny en lle un llys, canys gureyctra a henny o genedyl elenyaeth.

[88] Morfydd E. Owen. "Y Cyfreithiau: Natur y Testunau," in Geraint Bowen (ed.), *Y Traddodiad Rhyddiaith yn yr Oesau Canol* (Llandysul, 1974); LL xliii.

[89] See n.81 above.

4. *Tewessiau,* "tywysio" is not a word generally used in the law texts, although familiar enough from the literature where it has the meaning lead or conduct. The renaissance lexicographers sometimes give it a pejorative meaning like *abducere.*[90] We should perhaps bear in mind the fact that this list has one item too many and consider coupling *tewessiau* with the next word in the list namely *cerh.*

5. *Cerh,* "cyrch" is well known from the law texts as a word for assault sometimes found in the phrase *cyrch cyhoeddog*[91] or public assault. For an assault to constitute a *cyrch* it needed to be made by at least nine men. In the thirteenth century lawbooks a *cyrch* is one of the offences for which a double *galanas* is paid by the offender and his kin.[92] If we couple *Tewessiau* and *Cerh* we could understand the pair as meaning to lead an assault, not necessarily an assault which has resulted in a homicide.

6. *Gorduy,* "gorddwy" occurs infrequently in the laws in the phrase *teir bu gorddwy*[93] used for the kine paid by a man who stands by and does nothing, allowing a homicide to be committed. It occurs also in the standard version of the *Tair Colofn Cyfraith* in the compound *porth orddwy,*[94] the term for the accessory to *galanas* who helps the slayer by detaining and holding the victim while he attacks. *Gorddwy* is a fairly common word in the literature for onslaught or oppression: it is the word used in *Culhwch and Olwen* when referring to the forcible abduction of the wife of King Doged, *am rydyallas yg gord6y*[95]—(who captured me by force). Although it is difficult to extract a precise technical meaning for *gorddwy* from the surviving evidence, it is clear that it implies some violent action, an action which is considered in the thirteenth century law texts to belong to the province of *galanas* or homicide.

7. *Brat,* "brad", treachery or treason is coupled with *cynllwyn* or secret killing in the text as an offence for which a double galanas may be exacted unless the traitor is executed;[96] the payment of this composition involves the kin of the traitor.

8. *Kennadwri y rung bratwyr ay elin,* (taking messages between traitors and his enemy) could again be attributed to the province of *brad.* Perhaps it is at this juncture (rather than at 5 and 6) that we see the

[90] Thomas Wiliems, MS. Peniarth 228, s.v. *Abduco.*
[91] WML 46.20.
[92] Bleg 36.6.
[93] Col §278.
[94] Lat E 448.22; Col §249; Ior §104/13.
[95] WM 453.32.
[96] Col §283-7.

expansion in the ennead which increases the number of items to ten and that we should understand 8 as a gloss on 7.

9.   *Gwrthareith* is a unique form and as such difficult to interpret. The prefix *gwrth* adds a negative or opposing sense to the word to which it is prefixed. *Areith*, if that is the second element of the word, means language or speech; if this is so, a possible meaning of the compound might be "defamation". We could alternatively understand the second element as *rhaith*. This word has important cognates in many western European languages, like the German *recht*, Latin *rectus,* and Old Irish *recht*. Its generalised meaning of right or law is seen in the compound *cyfraith* (the usual word for law), and in the negative form *anrhaith*, (the abuse of right, or plunder). In Welsh it is regularly used in the lawbooks for the body of compurgators who support the oath of a principal in various contexts. *Gwrthreith* could mean opposition to a law or opposition to a *rhaith*. The word remains a puzzle.

10.   *Lad y gelein*, the last item in the list, means the killing of the body and takes us once again into the world of the thirteenth century *galanas*.[97]

On the analogy of the *nau affeith tan*, we should expect this list to contain a classification of the nine types or nine causes of *galanas*. If this is so, it cannot be *galanas* in the restricted thirteenth century sense of composition for homicide. We must look for another meaning of the term.

Items 5 *(cerh)*, 6 *(gorduy)*, 7 *(brad)* and 8 *(kennadwri y rung bratwyr ay elin)* belong to the area of galanas and the rules for composition for homicide found in the thirteenth century lawbooks. Items 2 *(gwreictra)* and 3 *(sarhaet)* on some evidence were matters which could give rise to kin feud, item 1 *(tirdra)* is grouped with items 2 and 10 *(lad y gelein)* in some triads as though they have some common feature. The evidence of the *Surexit Memorandum* also suggests that land dispute could be a source of kin animosity.

The original meaning of *galanas* was enmity or kin feud, and the list would seem to contain a classification of the actions that might raise a feud.[98] If this interpretation is correct, it constitutes one of the few pieces of evidence for the feud in early Wales. It is impossible to offer a dating for the text as it stands. Lat B as Charles-Edwards has shown in his discussion of the Naw Cynweddi contains more than one legal fossil. If our ennead is a legal fossil, it is difficult to date. The only orthographic

---

[97] Bleg 82.4 Pwy bynhac a omedho sefyll wrth gyfreith yn llys yg gwyd y brenhin, anreith odef vyd. Eil dyn anreith odef yssyd: fflemawr. Trydyd yw dyn a latho kelein kywlat ac ef.

[98] Bleg 116.1-2; 110.1-5.

forms found in the list which might be considered early are *tewessiau*, *cerh* and *elin*. *Tewessiau* and *cerh* show the use of e for /ə/ and /ï/ but this orthography (though it is a feature of Old Welsh), is not uncommon in Middle Welsh. *Elin* has i for /ï/, *cerh* has again h for /χ/ but that again is a feature of Middle Welsh texts like the Black Book of Chirk, as much as of the Old Welsh Memoranda of the Lichfield Gospels.

EXCURSUS II:
Prifai Gwraig

The triad, pentad or hexad, *prifai gwraig*,[99] raises problems of language. The practical effect of the rules the numerical lists summarise is reasonably clear from reference to other sections of the law texts. The difficulty arises because the lists preserve a number of archaic terms. The way in which these terms are interchangeable suggests that their original significance has been partly if not entirely obscured for the compilers of the thirteenth century texts. These words are often better understood by reference to Irish sources and the history of some of them leads us into the world of primitive feud.

The triad refers to the property to which a wife has exclusive right within marriage. The triad in Ior (G) specifies the *privei* as

y chowyll a'e gouyn a'e sarhaet[100]
her *cowyll*, and her *gowyn* and her *sarhaed*

The amplification of this triad in the same text glosses *sarhaed* and *gowyn* thus:

sef y6 y sarhaet pob maedu a wnel y g6r arnei . . . sef y6 e gouyn o cheiff y g6r gan wreic arall.[101]
sarhaed is every blow which her husband strikes her; her *gowyn* is if she finds her husband with another woman.

The Ior (B) version gives

Tri pryfurey gureyc e chowyll a'e haguedy ae sarhaet.[102]
The three privities of a woman are her *cowyll*, her *agweddi* and her *sarhaed*.

The version of the triad found in Damweiniau Colan reads:

Try pryuey gureyc eu y cowyll ay guardrut ay sarhaet.[103]
The three privities of a woman are her *cowyll* and her *gwarthrudd* and her *sarhaed*.

---

[99] The *prifai* are dealt with by Dafydd Jenkins *infra*, pp. 76, 81-3.
[100] Ior (G) §51/1.
[101] Ior (G) §51/3, 4.
[102] Ior (B) §51/1.
[103] DwCol §180.

where *guardrut* is defined in the same way as *gowyn* in G. The *pimp priuei gureic* found in Lat B and Lat E defines the prifai as:

> *aguedi, amobyr, argyureu, gouin, sarhaet; sextum puelle: scilicet, cowyl.* [104]

A triad found in the Bleg, Cyf and the Latin texts corresponds to the Iorwerth triad but it is introduced by a different key phrase:

> *Tri pheth ny dygir rac gureic kyt gatter am y cham, y chowyll, ae hargyfreu ae h6ynebwerth pan gyttyo y g6r a gureic arall.* [105]

Three things which cannot be taken from a woman though she be left for her wrongdoing, her *cowyll*, her *argyfreu* and her *wynebwerth* when her husband has intercourse with another woman.

We can tabulate the items of the lists in the follow manner:

Ior (B)	Ior (G)	DwCol	Bleg	Lat B, E
1. *cowyll*	1. *couyll*	1. *cowyll*	1. *cowyll*	6. *cowyl*
2. *aguedy*	2. *gouyn*	2. *guardrut*	3. *wynebwerth*	4. *gouin*
3. *sarhaet*	3. *sarhaet*	3. *sarhaet*	2. *argyureu*	5. *sarhaet*
				3. *argyureu*
				1. *aguedi*
				2. *amobyr*

The *wynebwerth* of the Bleg text, corresponds with the *gwarthrudd* and *gowyn* of Col and G—and possibly the *sarhaed* of Ior B. The *pum prifai* shows an attempt to add to the list, items which cannot be properly regarded as *prifai* e.g. *amobr*. Items 3, 4 and 5 of this *pum prifai* list are identical with the G triad. 1, is found in the Ior triad. The items of interest for this excursus are *gowyn/gwarthrudd/wynebwerth* and *sarhaed*. *Gwarthrudd* is a term usually used in moral or social triads and there alternates with words like *cywilydd* and *gwaradwydd*. It is not generally used in the rules for specific payments, where the terms used are *sarhaed, wynebwerth* and *gowyn*, although it is sometimes translated by *iniuria* in the Latin texts. The triads found in Ior and Bleg can be read in conjunction with another clause found in Ior §45/4.

> *Ac os kyn e seythuet wlueden ed edeu hy e gur kubel o henne a kyll, eythyr e kowyll a'e huenepwarth a'e gowyn.* [106]

And if it be before the seventh year, she leave her husband, she will lose the whole of that save her *cowyll* and her *wynebwerth* and her *gowyn*.

The G manuscript reading of the final clause of this text reads:

> *eithyr y chowyll a'e h6ynebwerth.* [107]
> save her *cowyll* and her *wynebwerth*

---

[104] Lat B 243.17; Lat E 494.25.
[105] WML 93.2.
[106] Ior (B) 45/3.
[107] Ior (G) 45/3.

The Chirk Codex version reads:

eythyr e kouyll a'e hunepuurth am e goouyn.[108]
save her *cowyll* and her *wynebwerth* for her *gowyn.*

The Chirk Codex version of the rule suggests that the *wynebwerth* is the composition for the *gowyn* and not a different payment. The Bleg triad cited above suggests that Ior is making a false distinction between *wynebwerth* and *gowyn.* The third item listed in the Ior triad is *sarhaed.* In other sections of the lawbooks the offence specified in the G and Bleg triad as calling for *wynebwerth* or *gowyn* is also called *sarhaed.*[109]

In the Law of Women, the editors of the Iorwerth texts would seem to be trying to use a series of terms in a specialised and restricted meaning. Cross-references suggest that some of these terms were in fact synonymous and that all in fact were some form of *sarhaed.*

J. Lloyd-Jones has described *gowyn*[110] as the verbal noun of a verb *"gowygaf"* which is represented in Welsh by the unique form *"goygwy"* found in the work of the earliest of the Gogynfeirdd. This verb he links with a verb *gwygaf* represented by the form *gwygid.* *Gwygaf* and *gowygaf* are paralleled in Irish by the verbs *fichid* and *fo-fich* though the correspondence between the Irish and Welsh forms is not a simple one. *Fichid* in Old Irish has the meaning fight and *fo-fich* the meaning offend or injure. In the Chirk Codex example of the word *gowyn,* the word has retained the meaning of insult or injure. Two other nouns found in the Law of Women are connected by Lloyd-Jones with *gowygaf* and *gwygaf,* they are *gowg* and *gwg.* Both are used for the offence committed by a woman who after betrothal to one man is found to have had intercourse with another.[111] Col uses the adjective *gegus (gygus)* for such a woman.[112] *Gwg* also occurs in the more generalised sense of a blow particularly clearly evidenced in the triad which has the alternating key phrases:

Tri g6g ni diwygir[113]
The three blows for which reparation is not made
Tri gwth ni diwygir[114] / *Tri hwrd ni diwygir*[115]
The three thrusts for which reparation is not made

---

[108] Chirk Codex 34. 7-9.
[109] Ior §110/10.
[110] Geirfa s.v. *go-ŵyn.*
[111] Bleg 67.21; Lat D 346.19.
[112] Col §66.
[113] WML 137.16.
[114] Lat A 128, Lat B 242, Lat E 494.
[115] Bleg 116.24.

Gowyn as a verbal noun is paralleled by another noun formation found in the laws, the verbal noun *diwyn*,[116] the verb noun of the verb *diwygaf*. This verb is used in the lawbooks for the act of paying compensation or making reparation. It is the act that averts the *gowg, gwg* or *gowyn*. *Diwygaf* has a parallel formation in Irish in the verb *do-fich* meaning to avenge. The verbal noun of *do-fich* is *di-gal* paralleled in Welsh by the noun or verb noun *dial* which means to avenge or vengeance normally retained for the act of pursuit of feud or galanas though there are one or two instances where *dial* is used for the reparation which is made to ward off the feud as in the text of *Saith Esgopty Dyfed*.

The verb used in Old Irish for paying composition is *do-ren*. The noun *díre* from the same root is one of the words used for honour price. In Welsh, the word which corresponds to Irish *díre*, Welsh *dirwy*, has developed the restricted meaning of the compensation or fine paid to the king. We perhaps see the survival of a meaning akin to that of the Irish *díre* in the phrase *difwyn dirwy* used notably when describing the compensation due to the kin when a virgin is raped, a compensation commensurate with the honour price of the king.

These words then which originally from the Irish evidence were connected with insult, feud, reparation have in the hands of the Welsh lawyers of the thirteenth century developed specialised meanings considerably removed from their original function.

MORFYDD E. OWEN

---

[116] All these terms based on variant forms of the root *weik* deserve detailed phonological and morphological analysis. See the items do-fich, fichid, fo-fich, díre, do-ren in *Contributions to a Dictionary of the Irish Language*. This Excursus is much indebted to T. M. Charles-Edwards and Gareth Bevan, both of whom are better qualified than I am to deal with the philological problems.

PROPERTY INTERESTS IN THE CLASSICAL WELSH LAW OF WOMEN

"THE LAW the lawyers know about Is property and land", and in any system the law of marital relations is concerned mainly with rights to property. In law, marriage[1] is a contract which has implications for the status of the contracting parties; most of those implications affect the parties' property rights; and it has been mainly because of those property rights that law has been concerned with marital relations at all. In medieval Wales, though the social conventions were much the same as those of other medieval societies, the basic principles declared in the lawbooks allow for the legal recognition of relationships very far from those conventions. This is, in part at least, the consequence of the fact that the regularity of a marital union had little significance for the inheritance rights of the children of the union. This meant that the circumstances of the formation of the union were of much less legal significance in medieval Wales than in medieval England, where the barons (in the interest of their property rights) insisted on maintaining a stricter law of legitimacy than even the Church required.[2]

The Welsh picture can be most clearly seen if we concentrate on the classical law of thirteenth-century Wales, as it is set out in the lawbooks developed in Gwynedd in the favourable environment created in the first half of that century by the political success of Llywelyn the Great. Most of our information will therefore be taken from the Iorwerth text with occasional references to its variant *Llyfr Colan* and the nearly contemporary collection of case-law, "*Llyfr y Damweiniau*", but attention will of course also be given to the other, less developed and sophisticated, texts by way of contrast and explanation of the lines of development.

---

[1] No exact technical meaning is to be given to the words *marriage* and *married*, unless such a meaning is either in terms indicated or necessarily required by the context. A married woman is presumably a woman with a *mari*, however she came by him.

[2] The resolution of the Merton Parliament of 1236, "Nolumus leges Angliae mutare", meant that it was not until the twentieth century that children born out of wedlock were legitimated in English Law by the marriage of their parents. The first limb of the triad "Tri meib yssyd ny dylyant gyfran o tir y gan eu brodyr" (Bleg 112.3-16) seems to reflect English Law in this matter; the second is likewise quite inconsistent with Welsh Law.

We may begin by describing what social convention (as deduced from hints in the lawbooks) treats as the norm, without thereby implying that normal families were any less rare than normal eyesight. The normal Welshman of the lawbooks was a "free tribesman" (*bonheddig*), who might or might not have ascended to the status of *breyr* (or *uchelwr*)[3] through the death of all his male ancestors. If he was not yet a *breyr*, he would not have come into his inheritance of land, but might have land acquired in other ways, and would certainly be much more than likely to have movable property (for which we can hereafter use the convenient English technical term *chattels*). In the lawbooks' treatment of the property incidents of marital union, the free woman is usually treated as a *breyr*'s daughter, and we may assume that her rights and liabilities in relation to marital property would not be affected by the question whether her father had ascended to the full status of *breyr*, for the distinction between the *breyr* and any other *bonheddig* is one of grade within a single class. We can therefore follow the lawbooks' practice of referring to the *breyr*'s daughter, except where there is special reason not to do so.

Whether *breyr* or mere *bonheddig*, the Welsh freeman is contemplated as the man of some lord, to whom his sons would be commended at the age of fourteen. A son so commended was released from his father's authority, and until he had sons to inherit from him his lord would be his heir. In some respects the position of the villein (*taeog, bilain, aillt*) was similar to that of the freeman: he too would be the man of some lord, but instead of a commendation to that lord at the age of fourteen, the young villein could expect to be recognised (at some appropriate age, probably much lower than would seem natural to the twentieth century) as an adult member of the villein community. As such he would in his own right be entitled to a share in that community's land and subject to its obligations towards the lord, on the same footing as his father.[4]

Who the lord would be, in the thirteenth century, is not easy to say. At an earlier period the lord would be a patron who had provided his man

---

[3] The terms *breyr* and *uchelwr* (sometimes *mab uchelwr*) seem to be exactly synonymous and to imply no more than the status of the *bonheddig* who has no living male ancestor. In the Red Book of Hergest translation of Walter of Henley (2 BBCS 11), *Vchelwyr* translates *franc tenantz* (*Walter of Henley* [etc.], ed. D. Oschinsky, Oxford, 1971, p.312). In modern Welsh *uchelwr* has much more of the sense suggested by the *nobilis* found in the Latin texts, and *breyr* has therefore been chosen for use in the technical medieval sense; this word has come down in the world, since it represents **brogo-rix*, "king of a district", perhaps a Welsh counterpart of the Irish *rí tuaithe*, for whom see Binchy, *Kingship* 5, 14, 15, 31ff.
[4] DwCol §305.

with a fief of cattle;[5] for the villein, and probably for some freemen, the lord might be a mesne lord from whom the man held land very much on the English feudal pattern; but in the thirteenth century many Welshmen must have been in direct homage to their territorial rulers, whether they were local kings of Welsh blood or Norman marcher lords. It is at any rate clear that if no-one else could claim lordship over a particular person, the local ruler (whether he called himself king, lord, or prince) would do so, and in right of that lordship he would be entitled to payment in respect of the daughters of his men.

The Welsh freeman's son ceased to be "at his father's platter" when he was commended to the lord, and his daughter's relation to him changed in a similar way. From puberty at the age of twelve, "even if she does not take a husband, she is entitled to control what is hers, and she is not entitled to be at her father's platter unless he himself wishes it"[6]: no doubt he would usually wish it, at least until it had become clear that she would not be taking a husband and going on to become pregnant after reaching the age of fourteen.[7] If she left her father's platter the woman would apparently be directly subject to her father's lord, but in the normal case her husband would be her lord. This is categorically stated in *Llyfr y Damweiniau*, where the rule is laid down that if a woman speaks shameful words to her husband she is liable to pay him a *camlwrw*, because every woman's husband is her lord: the *camlwrw* was a penalty of three kine payable to the territorial ruler for many kinds of offence,

---

[5] My understanding of the social pattern assumed in the lawbooks owes much to Donald Howells, "The Four Exclusive Possession of a Man", (1973-4) 8/9 *Studia Celtica* 48-67.

[6] Ior §99/4.

[7] This may be the most convenient point to refer to the confusion of the texts over the age at which a woman would be presumed to be past childbearing, which some texts place at 40, others at forty years from 14: Ior §55/4. Wiliam, whose chosen manuscript reads "pedeyr blyned ar dec a deu ugeynt e dele bot en e hyeuegtyt", has the note "not 'fifty-four years' (which is far too long a period) but '[the ages of] fourteen and forty' (between which child-bearing is possible)". This is unacceptable textually, for "the age of fourteen" would require "pedeyr *bluyd* ar dec"; and the reading of MS. *G* (printed in this volume) makes it clear that the passage means that the period of youth lasts from birth through puberty to the age of 54. The medieval Welsh lawyer did not, of course, suppose that every woman would be capable of childbearing to the age of 54: the age is to be regarded as a maximum, and can be compared with those at which English law courts have been willing or unwilling to presume a woman to be past childbearing for purposes of the law of trusts. The presumption has been made for a woman of 49 and refused for a woman of 54: *Stroud's Judicial Dictionary*, 4th ed. by J. S. James (London, 1974) 2099, s.v. *Presumption*. It must however be pointed out that the Iorwerth text elsewhere unequivocally makes the presumption for the purpose of *galanas* at the age of 40: Ior §99/6. Cf. Col §54, which has assimilated the text of Ior §55 to that of Ior §99, and reads "yny uo deugeinmluyt e dyly emduyn, ac ena peidyau, ac odyna nyt a yn llu na bo plant ydy, canis dyogel na bit".

and the woman's offence against her husband is here assimilated to a crime against the state.[8]

The young woman would normally be given to her husband by her father and kindred. It is indeed laid down that if a maiden elopes, her lord and kindred can reclaim her against her will[9]—but the detailed provisions of the lawbooks for "abnormal" cases show that in medieval Wales as in modern Britain the family would often acquiesce in the *fait accompli*. They had every reason to do so, if the rules given by the lawbooks were strictly followed. For according to the next sentence after that just cited, a woman who has once been with a man cannot be reclaimed when she later elopes; hence if the reclaimed daughter had lost her virginity during the first elopement, she had only to elope a second time to be irreclaimable.

It was contemplated that there would be an interval between the giving of the woman (the same technical expression, *rhodd ac estyn*, is used for a lord's grant of land) and the consummation of the union, which would follow a feast (*neithior*). A *neithior* of any importance would be attended by bards, who received a gift of 24d. to share among them, if this was the bride's first *neithior*;[10] a second union had in any case less need of a *neithior*, since one reason for the gathering was to have *neithiorwyr* present to witness to the husband's declaration of his gift to the wife (*cowyll*) and if need arose to testify to the husband's repudiation of the wife as not being a virgin.[11] If the husband did not promptly repudiate her, he was estopped from denying her virginity thereafter.[12] By the morrow of the *neithior* the woman's change of status was complete[13] and the position in relation to the various property rights concerned was clear, though some of the rights did not take immediate effect. Thus we shall see that the *cowyll*, though appropriated to the new wife, was not

---

[8] DwCol §411, cf. §444 and Lat A §52/42.
[9] Ior §50/5, cf. Col §63, Lat A §52/33, Cyfn §73/13a.
[10] WML 33.16-20, Bleg 25.14-16, Ior §40/6, DwCol §§78, 79. Whereas the other texts seem to give the whole gift to the *pencerdd*, DwCol §79 gives it to "the bards", and §78 gives the *pencerdd* "the share of two men, whether he is present or not, if he claims it".
[11] V. *infra*, p. 77.
[12] Ior §47/2.
[13] There were conflicting views about the status of a girl in the interval between the giving of her by her kindred and the consummation of the union: if she then suffered *sarhaed*, "some say that payment is made to her according to her husband's status" (so Ior §55/5); "others say that it is according to her brother's status that payment is made to her, and that she is not a wife until she has been slept with, for a son-in-law is not so called until the morrow": Col §55, 56. The proverbial phrase "cany elwyr dau hyt trannoeth" perhaps suggests the older, traditional, view, which was being displaced in the thirteenth century under the influence of the developing canon law.

transferred to her, and that *agweddi*, though its amount was now determined, might never become payable at all.

The one obligation which involved immediate payment was that of *amobr*,[14] which was owed to the woman's lord. *Amobr* was payable in respect of a woman when she was formally given to a man (even if cohabitation did not follow), or when she entered into open cohabitation (without being formally given), or when she became pregnant.[15] The traditional view has been that *amobr* was payable only once in respect of any one woman, but this view needs closer examination and is the subject of Excursus I appended to this paper. Whether the traditional view is correct or not, it is clear that a payment was certainly expected in some second unions in the thirteenth century, and the practice of the Norman marcher lords was to make the best of both worlds by applying the Welsh rule that *amobr* was payable by the free (whereas the English counterparts *merchet* and *leyrwite* were payable only by villeins) and the English rule that the payment was due for each new marital or extramarital relation, rather than for the original loss of virginity alone.[16]

Like similar payments in other countries, *amobr* has been variously explained. In particular it has been regarded as a commutation of the *ius primae noctis* or *droit de seigneur*, the alleged right of the lord to lie with the subject bride on her wedding night. The better view is that the lord's only right was a right to the payment:[17] *amobr* is itself the *ius primae noctis*, not a commutation of it, and the lord is entitled to it as a fee for his licence to the woman to take a husband, just as he might exact a fee if

---

14 Some of the texts use *gobr* in preference to *amobr*, and the occasional occurrence of *amobr* in those texts suggests borrowing from others which preferred *amobr*. *Amobr* alone seems to be used in later records: the form has the obvious advantage of being unambiguous, whereas *gobr* is used for other fees and also for *bribe*.

15 Ior §51/10, Col §§7, 8.

16 Cf. Davies, *infra*, p. 103.

17 PM i.372, citing Karl Schmidt, *Jus primae noctis* (Freiburg, 1881). The only positive evidence of the existence of the right seems to be that of certain Swiss *Weistümer*, which give a lord or his officer the right to enjoy the bride unless the bridegoom redeems the right by a stated fee. This is probably no more than a dramatic expression of the alleged sanction for non-payment of the fee: see E. Osenbrüggen, *Studien zur deutschen und schweizerischen Rechtsgeschichte* (Schaffhausen, 1868; reprinted 1969) 84ff. Osenbrüggen points out that there is no documentary evidence for the exercise of the right, "denn dergleichen pflegt nicht protokolliert zu werden", *ibid.* 89. If the modern historian tends to a cynical doubt whether a medieval lord felt the need of any legal authority for imposing his sexual favours on a subordinate female, it may nevertheless be true that at a rather later period the exercise was facilitated by the tradition of a legal right. Such a tradition is evidenced for Scotland by the story "The Old Tribute", translated from the Gaelic of Niall Mac-an-Rothaich, Ollamh, by the Hon. Ruaraidh Erskine of Marr in his *The Old Tribute and other pieces* (London, 1929), and for Estonia by the story "The Wedding", in Aino Kallas, *The Old Ship* (translated from the Finnish by Alex Matson; London, 1924).

he allowed a male villein to take orders. In each case the lord is losing an asset and will want compensation.[18]

The Welsh lawbooks, however, show a rationalisation of attitude towards the payment: in the classical law *amobr* is not a fee for permission to take a husband, but a price paid for past protection. This appears from the rules about the persons who may become responsible for the payment. The primary liability seems to be that of the woman herself, for if she elopes and is reclaimed, her father is not required to pay her *amobr*,[19] and it is hard to believe that the lord would forgo the payment—at least in the presumably frequent cases in which the woman was not reclaimed before she had lost her virginity. Elsewhere the principle is laid down that anyone who gives a woman to a man is liable to pay her *amobr*, and as a corollary that if a woman gives herself she must herself pay.[20] The principle is expressed in the alternative: "Whoever gives a woman to a man, it is his duty to pay *amobr* for her, or he shall take sureties from her for its payment"; but it can hardly be supposed that the woman's contractual obligation to the giver would release him if the woman failed to make the payment to the lord. In another text we seem to have good advice rather than a rule of law: "Let no-one give a woman to a man without taking a *mach* for her *gobr* to the lord",[21] and here the implication is perhaps that the *mach* will be taken from the man to whom she is given. That is surely the implication of the advice given to the householder who receives an eloping couple into his house to sleep together: "let the man of the house take a *mach* for her *gobr*, and if he does not take it, let him pay himself."[22]

The rationalisation is even clearer where the lord's claim is based on the woman's loss of virginity by rape. From the archaic point of view it

---

[18] Cf. Davies, *infra*, p. 111. Though in Wales a lord need not usually fear that land would pass into undesirable hands through the woman, this could happen if the woman were given to an alien, whose sons by her could claim to share with her brothers in her father's land. At an earlier period, when personal attachment to the lord was more significant, the lord would want to protect himself against influences which might weaken that attachment. We need to remind ourselves that the relationship of lord and vassal is originally voluntary on both sides throughout its continuance; economic necessity usually prevents the vassal from breaking it off arbitrarily, and while this in time leads to the vassal's losing the right to break it off, it also converts the lord's freedom to bargain for a price for concessions into a duty to grant those concessions for a reasonable (and this soon means a customary) fee. This is the underlying thesis of S. F. C. Milsom's interpretation of the early common law: see especially his *The Legal Framework of English Feudalism* (Cambridge, 1976), and cf. Donald Howells's article cited at n.5 *supra*.
[19] Lat A §52/33.
[20] Ior §48/1.
[21] Cyfn §73/25.
[22] Cyfn §73/26, Ior §48/2.

makes no difference to the lord that she was raped: he has lost the asset of a virgin subject and he must have his compensatory maiden-fee. But in our surviving texts the lord looks to the ravisher for *amobr*, and if he cannot get it from him he must go without, for it was his function to protect the woman from rape and he has failed to perform the function which justified his claim to the fee.[23] This view of the thirteenth-century attitude to *amobr* can find some support in the statement that the king is entitled to the *amobr* of any woman who has no other lord. The "normal" woman has an identifiable lord because her father has a lord, who (as already said) may be the king or some other patron. If the father is a craftsman of some kind, the head of his craft will be his lord for this purpose, so that, for instance, the *pencerdd* is entitled to the *amobr* of his subordinates' daughters.[24] But it may happen that a woman has no lord because she has no father and her mother has no lord: the mother's attempt at filiation has failed, and the mother herself either was in the same position or had found herself in the local society without ever becoming properly attached to it so as to be identified as the client of any particular patron. In such a case the woman's *amobr* is payable to the king, and the proverbial rule that a maiden is "king's waste" is applied to the case.[25] The proverb looks at the matter from the standpoint of the royal profit, but it can also be seen as an application of the principle that the king is the protector of all his subjects.

In relation to the outside world, the payment of *amobr* is the most important economic consequence of marital union. As between the parties, the basic economic principle was that while the union lasted there was community of goods, but not of land: the land was the husband's, for only a few texts speak of a woman's holding land in exceptional circumstances[26] (though she might transmit an inheritance to her sons in certain other cases), and the principle "According to the men of Gwynedd a woman is not entitled to patrimony"[27] seems to have had a general application.

While the union lasted, the chattels of both partners were in the common pool of matrimonial property, though control of particular items would be in the hands of one, as we shall see. If the union broke

---

[23] DwCol §124, Cyfn §73/16, 17. This clearly seems to be an addition to the nucleus of the Cyfnerth text, for it occurs only in MS. *U*.
[24] Cyfn §33/2.
[25] DwCol §§314-16; the mother's status determines the amount of the *amobr*. For affiliation see Excursus II.
[26] Bleg 75.24-5.
[27] Ior §86/1, Col §600.

up, there would seldom be a simple equal division of the whole pool, for one or both of the parties would usually have a prior claim to some of the chattels. Moreover, even the residue left after the satisfaction of such prior claims would be equally shared only if the union had matured fully, by lasting for seven years.

When a union broke up *inter vivos* after less than seven years,[28] the wife took from this residue of the common pool only a fixed amount, called *agweddi*—if she took anything at all. Whether she was to hope for *agweddi* or for half the residue would depend on how long the union had lasted; whether she would get anything from the residue would depend on the circumstances in which the union broke up. It might break up through her fault or without her fault: on the one hand she might have left her husband without good reason or have been rightfully repudiated by him; or on the other hand she might have left him for good reason or been wrongfully repudiated by him, or the separation might have been by agreement.

If the wife was at fault,[29] she was nevertheless entitled to certain items of marital property, which were called her privy things.[30] Though the compilers of some lawbooks had difficulty in forcing their ideas into the frame of the triad, the Iorwerth form seems to give the correct picture: the three privy things are the wife's *cowyll*, her *gowyn*, and her *sarhaed*, which we are told cannot be taken from her for any cause.[31]

Cowyll corresponds to the morning-gift of Germanic society. In the Iorwerth comment on the triad, it is defined as what the girl was given for her virginity,[32] and though this is inadequate as a definition, it is true that only a virgin was entitled to *cowyll*. To complete the definition we must add that the *cowyll* was given (or more accurately promised) to the wife by the husband. The lawbooks specify a tariff for the *cowyll*, based on the status of the wife: in the Iorwerth text £8 for a king's daughter, £1 for a *gwrda*'s daughter, 80d. for a villein's daughter.[33] But these standards

---

[28] What exactly "after less than seven years" meant is not easy to decide, in the light of the various expressions used (see Walters, *infra*, p. 117)—nor necessary to discuss, for the purpose of the present study.

[29] "kyt gatter am y cham", Bleg 119.15-16, WML 93.2-3; "licet ob suam dimitatur culpam", Lat A §52/56; "licet culpa sua a viro suo repudietur", Lat D 376.22-3.

[30] The Welsh word is *prifai*, which (despite the various forms it takes) seems to be best understood as a borrowing of some form of *privé* or *privy*. The triad *Tri phrifai gwraig* also appears as *Tri anghyfarch gwraig*: cf. Howells (article cited at n.5 *supra*).

[31] Ior §51/1: *v. infra* for other versions.

[32] Ior §51/2.

[33] Ior §48/9. Of the variants in the other texts, the most important to notice is that of Cyfn §73/2, which says that land is paid as *cowyll* to a king's daughter, without specifying its value. Here *gwrda* seems to mean *breyr*.

must be understood as applying in the absence of contrary agreement, for the texts clearly contemplate the possibility of bargaining over the amount.[34] Where the wife was given by her relatives, it can be assumed that agreement on the amount would be reached in the presence of the *neithiorwyr*, since in the case of an abducted maiden, her word as to the *cowyll* promised her is conclusive against the man who took her to a place where there were no *neithiorwyr*.[35] Indeed, the Iorwerth text seems to imply that there must be a formal claim to *cowyll* if even the standard amount is to be allotted: the claim must be made before the wife rises from bed on the morrow of the *neithior* and it is in this context that the provision for attesting to the bride's virginity becomes comprehensible.[36] For once she had reached puberty, she was required to establish her virginity by oath, supported by her close relatives, as a basis for her claim to her *cowyll*; this is necessary because the *cowyll* is a privy thing, so that if the bride proves not to be a virgin, the man's repudiation of her will not deprive her of the *cowyll* promised before they went to bed. The duly supported oath is conclusive, so far as the right to *cowyll* is concerned; this is one case in which it is to be expected that the oath will be truthful, since its truth or falsehood will be subject to an immediate test by the *neithiorwyr*, and its falsehood will make those who swore it incompetent as witnesses ever after.[37] We can perhaps picture a ceremony in which the formal declaration of virginity by the bride's party is followed by the man's promise of a defined *cowyll*, all in the presence of the *neithiorwyr*. The publicity thus given to the *cowyll* would parallel that given to the English wife's dower by declaration at the church door.[38]

As the form of the tariff quoted above suggests, the size of the *cowyll* would be expressed in money terms, but it is not to be supposed that money or anything else was in fact physically transferred. The law contemplates rather that certain particular chattels will be designated as making up the *cowyll*: the rule is that the *cowyll* falls into the common pool (so that the wife loses her prior right to it) unless before rising on the

---

[34] Ior §47/2, Col §23. The latter sentence, broadly corresponding to Ior §53/7, adds the condition that the *cowyll* should have been admeasured: "O deruyd rodi moruyn y ur, a meintholy ydy y cowyll . . ." Such bargaining over the amount would be valid under the principle "Amod a dyr ddeddf", "A contract breaks a rule of law": Ior §69/12, Col §140.

[35] Ior §47/1.

[36] Ior §55/3.

[37] "A person can never be made a witness who has sworn falsely in testimony or elsewhere if he admits it or it can be proved against him": Col §529.

[38] PM ii.374-5.

morrow she "uses" it.[39] This she will do by naming the chattels which are to represent it: it is natural to think of the *breyr's* daughter as choosing four particular cows to make up the standard £1, but there is no a priori reason why she should not chose inanimate chattels such as a cauldron or a harp, each worth 60d.[40] There could be an advantage in choosing these, for the wife would not be entitled to claim a replacement for any part of the *cowyll* which had been lost:[41] her right was to such part of the privy things as was still in existence when her claim matured, and harps and cauldrons can be expected to outlive cattle.

We should probably think of *sarhaed* and *gowyn* also as taking the form of specific chattels held in the common pool while the union lasted, for these too were payments from the husband which became due to the wife in circumstances described in another paper.[42] Here it need only be noticed that whereas any legally recognised insult to a single woman would entitle her to receive her *sarhaed* from the offender, a wife received her sarhaed only from her husband, and offensive conduct towards her by a third party would lead to the payment of her husband's *sarhaed* (which was three times as great as hers) to the common pool. The amount of the wife's *sarhaed* varied with her husband's status: the mere *bonheddig's sarhaed* was three kine and three score pence, and his wife's therefore one cow and 20d., the equivalent of 80d., while the villein's wife's *sarhaed* was half as much.[43] But the wife's *gowyn* (payable to her by her husband in compensation for his adultery) did not vary with her status: for the first offence the sum due was 120d., and for the second £1. The third offence entitled the wife to leave the husand without forfeiting any of her rights; she was indeed expected to leave him, for if she condoned his adultery more than three times she was regarded as a shameful wife and could claim nothing. [44]

According to *Llyfr y Damweiniau*, the wife could set aside for her offspring all the goods which she received as her privy things, and if she died

---

[39] Ior §53/7: for the *defnydyo* of MS. *G*, MS. *B* has *dywetto*, "says"; but the different wording of Cyfn §73/23 and Lat A §52/59 make the meaning clear: cf. Col §23 and n.

[40] The mature cow (from her second calf to her fifth) and the mature ox (from its third to its sixth working season) were valued at 60d.: Ior §127/7, §128/3, 4; for harp and cauldron, see Ior §140/19, 21.

[41] Ior §45/2.

[42] Owen, *supra*, p. 51.

[43] Bleg 58.13-22, WML 44.6-22.

[44] Col §67: O deruyd y gureyc dyodef gan y gur y gaffel gan arall hvy no teyr gueyth heb owyn y huynepwerth ydau, ny dyly hy y caffel o hynny allan, canis gureyc kywylydus eu. Cf. Cyfn §73/23a.

the husband had no right to them.[45] It is also made clear that she took them in every case of living separation, as we have already seen. If she was at fault in separating from her husband, she took nothing more, but fault might be negatived in several ways. The husband's triple adultery has already been mentioned; unjustified repudiation by the husband would likewise leave the wife with her full rights;[46] and the wife was also justified in leaving if the husband was leprous or of stinking breath, or if he could not copulate with her.[47] Finally it can be assumed (though it is nowhere clearly stated) that the partners could separate by agreement and that if they did so the wife would have her full rights, unless the agreement provided otherwise.

This means that she would take a part of the residue of the common pool, and if the separation came before the union had matured by the lapse of seven years, that part would be the *agweddi* appropriate to her status and to the circumstances in which the union was created. If the wife's status was high enough and she had been given by her kindred to a poor enough man, her *agweddi* might well give her more than half the residue, but in most cases it is to be expected that she would take less than half. The *agweddi* of a king's daughter was £24, that of a *gwrda*'s daughter £3, and that of a villein's daughter £1: it will be realised that these sums represent 96, twelve and four standard cows or oxen respectively.[48]

The assumption that the *agweddi* should be thought of in terms of cattle receives strong support from the lawbooks' presentation of the *agweddi* payable on the termination of a union not established in the conventional way. The *agweddi* of a woman who eloped was three bullocks whose horns were as long as their ears.[49] According to the Iorwerth text, if a man slept three nights with a woman and then wished to be rid of her, he must pay her a bullock worth 20d., another worth 30d., and another worth 60d., and this may have come to very much the

---

[45] DwCol §183: Pob peth o'r daaoed a dewedassam ny uchot e gaffael, e gureyc a eyll dody e daoed hynny ar neylltu ydy y epyl, a pan escaro ac ef ny dyly rannu ac ef a ced boet maru nys dely ef.

[46] This is implied by the references to the privy things as remaining with the wife if she is justifiably repudiated.

[47] Ior §45/4, Cyfn §73/15b, Lat A §52/54.

[48] Ior §48/9; Cyfn §73/2a, 5, agrees with Ior, but §73/7a gives the villein's daughter £1½, which parallels the rule for *sarhaed* cited above. To think of the *agweddi* in terms of cattle immediately suggests the possibility of parallels with the bride-wealth arrangements studied by anthropologists in twentieth-century Africa.

[49] Ior §48/3: though the entitlement is not here specifically called *agweddi*, the wording of §48/7 implies that it ranked as *agweddi*.

same total, though the name *agweddi* is not applied to the payment.[50] *Llyfr y Damweiniau* seems to deal with the case more logically, and assimilates it to elopement in respect both of the payment due and of the effect on the woman's status: "If it happens that men suppose that the status of a woman who elopes and a woman who is slept with for more than three nights does not follow their husband's status because their kindred did not give them, and they suppose that their status is according to their kindred and their *sarhaed* according to their brothers' status: law says that after becoming *agweddïol* by him, she cannot leave him unless she is willing to lose her *agweddi*, and that he cannot send her away unless he is willing to pay her *agweddi* (and the *agweddi* of each of those two women is three bullocks with horns as long as their ears), and therefore law says that those women are entitled to have their status and their *sarhaed* according to their husbands' status."[51] It is not quite easy to see what difference there is between elopement and sleeping together for three nights: the point of the distinction may be that a night or two's casual cohabitation had no economic consequences, whereas a third night gave the wife a right to compensation and a fourth night established the relationship as an elopement, on the same footing as that of a couple who had from the first intended to have a continuing relationship.

The transient relationship of three nights gave the woman the right to a reduced *agweddi*, and here we perhaps have an example of a legalistic attitude which would assert as a general principle that any woman was entitled to an *agweddi* of some sort when she was dismissed. Such an attitude would explain the use of the word *agweddi* in one of the lawbooks for the mocking payment made to the "false maiden", the girl given to a man as a virgin and found to be "corrupted". She was given the opportunity to hold a bullock by its greased tail: if she succeeded, she took it as her *agweddi*, according to the Blegywryd text.[52] However, this is not consistent with the rule that a woman rightfully repudiated lost her *agweddi*, and we may have here a misinterpretation of the Latin word *dos*. The Latin Redaction D, from which the Blegywryd text is believed to have been translated, has the Welsh word, spelt *egweti*,[53] but the

---

[50] "Bullocks with horns as long as their ears" are the subject of an as yet unpublished study by Mr. J. G. T. Sheringham, which he has kindly allowed me to see. He shows that if similar to modern Welsh black cattle they would be yearlings; according to Ior §127 their value would then be from 12d. to 18d.

[51] DwCol §471.

[52] Bleg 61.27-31.

[53] Lat D 342.16.

earlier Latin Redactions A and B both have *pro dote*.[54] Now as it was put in Glanvill,[55] *dos duobus modis dicitur*, in medieval England and on the Continent,[56] and (as we must conclude from the Latin texts of Welsh law) in Wales too. In the traditional Roman law sense *dos* was *dowry*, the property given with the bride by her family. In England it was more often *dower*, the share of the husband's property which the wife took for her lifetime on his death, and which had probably been assured to her at the marriage. In the Latin texts from Wales, *dos* is certainly used on occasion for *agweddi*,[57] and perhaps for *cowyll* (which is not exactly *dos* in either of the English senses, for it is paid by the husband to the wife);[58] it may also be used for *argyfrau*, which is the property (*animalia* in the Latin) brought by the wife from her family, i.e. her dowry.[59] So in the "greased-tail" rule, *dos* may have been used for *argyfrau* and incorrectly re-translated into Welsh: *argyfrau* is the word used in *Ior*.[60]

According to all the texts except *Ior,* the privy things of the wife included her *argyfrau*.[61] In most of the texts, the inclusion of *argyfrau* means the exclusion of *sarhaed*, which is certainly wrong; the difficulty of compressing the material into a triad is avoided at one point in Latin Redaction B by swelling the triad to a pentad or hexad: "The five privy things of a woman: namely, *agweddi, amobr, argyfrau, gowyn, sarhaed*; a sixth of a maiden: namely, *cowyll*".[62] If the word *argyfrau* was rightly used in the context discussed in the last paragraph, there was at least one case in which the woman did not take her *argyfrau* when repudiated, and that is of course a sufficient disproof of the alleged rule. It may nevertheless be possible to resolve the apparent conflicts between the various rules.

We must start with the fact that there is no indication of any legal right to *argyfrau*, but in the "normal" case we can assume that the bride would be given a dowry by her family, and perhaps that the husband

---

[54] Lat A 52/30, Lat B 224.13.
[55] Glanvill vi.1, vii.1 (ed. Hall, pp.58ff, 69ff.).
[56] Vinogradoff, *Roman Law in Medieval Europe* 23.
[57] Lat A §52/1.
[58] Lat A §51/7.
[59] Lat A §52/56; Cyfn §73a/17b.
[60] Ior §47/5. The variants on the rule are examined and compared with a Swedish parallel in E. Anners and D. Jenkins, "A Swedish Borrowing . . . ?", (1962) 1 WHR 325-33. R. E. Megarry, *Miscellany-at-Law* (London, 1955), 157 n.2, asks "whether tying a knot in the bull's tail was an illegal practice".
[61] Cyfn §73/15c, Lat A §52/56, Bleg 119.15.
[62] Lat B 243.17-18 cf. also Lat E 494. *Pimp priuei* [MS. Pimt riuei] *gureic*: scilicet, *aguedi, amobyr, argyureu, gouin, sarhaet*; sextum puelle: scilicet, *cowyl*. At 222.6-9 Lat B has a version of the triad closely corresponding to that of Lat A.

would expect her to bring with her enough to cover the *agweddi* if that should become payable.[63] This would be very necessary if a woman of high status were given to a poor man. The normality of bargaining for a dowry is indicated by the provision that if goods are promised with a bride, and a single penny of the amount promised is not delivered, the man can repudiate the bride but gets none of the goods.[64] Since this provision has been interpreted as meaning that the man keeps all the goods, it is desirable to emphasise that such an interpretation strains the grammar of all versions of the provision.[65]

It is also inconsistent with what seems to be the most satisfactory interpretation of the next sentence of the texts, which sentence reads "There is no need of a *mach* for goods which come as endowment with a woman".[66] We might have expected the words to be "there is no right to a *mach*", and the actual wording supports the view that the rule is an archaic one whose significance had been forgotten by the thirteenth century. Now Dr. Donald Howells has very convincingly argued that when a patron-lord provided his client-man with cattle, no *mach* to warrant the client's right to the cattle would be given, because the client had no such right: the cattle were deposited with him, but the permanent right to them (to call that right *ownership* would beg many questions)

---

[63] Cf. Col p.45. Charles-Edwards (*supra*, pp. 28-9) seems to assume that the bride always brought with her a definable share of her father's chattels, namely half the amount to which her brother would be entitled on inheriting at the father's death. To take a concrete example, if the bride had three sisters and two brothers, whose father had sixteen cows, she would bring two cows with her: for simplicity we can neglect other chattels. There is some support for this view in the statement at Bleg 75.19-22, "Megys y mae brawt yn etiued dylyedawc o tref y tat, velly y mae y chwaer yn etiued dylyedawc o'e gwadawl, trwy yr hwn y kaffo hi wr priawt dylyedawc o tir": "As the brother is an heir entitled to land patrimony, so the sister is an heir entitled to her endowment, through which she may get a *priod* husband entitled to land." But the brother is of course an heir entitled also to a share of the father's chattels, and the statement just quoted need mean no more than that the sister has a legal right to receive the endowment (*gwaddol*) on her father's death, and that this future interest can buy her a husband. The reference to specifying goods to accompany the bride (Ior §54/8) suggests that the amount of the *argyfrau* was a matter for bargaining, and it is easy to see, by considering an extreme case, that there cannot have been a universal rule: if a sonless widower gave his only daughter in marriage, would she take all his chattels as *argyfrau*? In such a context as this (as Mr. Dafydd Walters reminded me) an English property lawyer would murmur the words *advancement* and *hotchpot*. The calculation of the bride's share would be more complicated if her father had a wife living, and even more complicated if that wife were not past childbearing.

[64] Ior §54/8, Col §49.

[65] V.C. II.i.70 translates "and she cannot reclaim any of her property", but *reclaim* would be more appropriate as a translation of *aduc*, which most manuscripts have for the *d6c* of our MS. G.

[66] Ior §54/9, Col §50. The word here translated *endowment* is *cynhysgaeth*, which does not seem to be used as a technical term.

remained in the lord.[67] He could re-claim them at any time, and the absence of a *mach* ensured that the client could not set up a legal objection to the claim. In just the same way, the bride's kindred provided the *argyfrau*, and gave no *mach*, because they would want to be free to reclaim the cattle if the circumstances seem to warrant it. On this view the *argyfrau* is not one of the wife's privy things, but on a separation where the wife is at fault the husband may nevertheless lose the *argyfrau* because the kindred can lay claim to the cattle as being theirs. In Roman-law terms they can use the procedure of *vindicatio*; in Welsh-law terms they can proceed to *damdwng*, a procedure usually mentioned in the lawbooks in the context of theft, but equally appropriate to the circumstances under consideration here.

This interpretation also explains the lawbooks' other rules about *argyfrau*. Any claim the wife may have to the *argyfrau* when the union ends is only to so much of the original gift as is still identifiable in specie;[68] she is therefore advised to keep the gift unconsumed until the end of the maturing period of seven years, for if she allows the gift to be used she can claim no compensation for what teeth and side have consumed.[69] The texts imply that after the seventh year the *argyfrau* falls into the common pool: in theory, the kindred could still claim any identifiable item of the original gift, but it is unlikely that in practice many cattle would then survive, or be worth claiming if they did survive.[70] In the absence of records of litigation there is no basis even for guessing how often man and wife in practice treated all their possessions as an indivisible whole from the start, but it will do no harm to remind ourselves again that the rules set out in lawbooks of every kind (and most of all, perhaps, in books of lawyers' law like the Welsh ones) more often deal with exceptional than with normal cases.[71]

It has already been emphasised that after continuing for seven years the most casually-inaugurated union was treated as matured and had the same legal implications as the normal union of social convention, in which the bride was formally given by her kindred. We need not here

---

[67] Howells, 8/9 *Studia Celtica* 59.
[68] Ior §45/2.
[69] Ior §48/4, 5.
[70] If milking heifers were among the gift, they would be past their prime after the fifth year of the union: see n.40 *supra*.
[71] As a modern illustration we may take the textbooks' interest in the effect of identical offers by the two parties and of an attempted revocation by telephone of a posted acceptance of an offer, in the English law of contract. Neither problem has come before a court for solution—nor is either at all likely to do so.

examine the exact limits of this seven-year period, which may have ended as early as the fourth day of the seventh year;[72] what concerns us is that after that period had elapsed, the common pool of chattels would be shared equally between the spouses if the union broke up. As already indicated, the wife's privy things were first taken out of the pool, and we might expect to find the husband's privy things being likewise reserved to him, but there is no triad of a husband's privy things. It is provided that if status gives the husband more, he should make his claim before sharing begins, and there is a triad or tetrad of the exclusive possessions of a man which seems to offer a parallel to the wife's privy things.[73] As Donald Howells points out, however, the parallel is imperfect, for most of the items named do not come into the marital property pool: they are chattels which cannot be claimed by anyone else, not because the husband has a special right to them but because even he has them only on sufferance from his patron-lord.[74] The correct parallel, that is, is with the wife's *argyfrau*, which may be withdrawn from the pool by the kindred who gave it without a *mach* to warrant it. Only one item in the male triad or tetrad is taken from the common pool: this is the husband's *wynebwerth*, which like the wife's is a payment in respect of adultery.

When living partners separate, they share the chattels as instructed by the law texts. The rules are no doubt meant to ensure that both parties are reasonably provided for, in default of agreement, though it is not easy to understand why the two stones of the quern, for instance, should be separated. Howells notes that though there are detailed rules for the sharing of the minor livestock, there is no mention of neat cattle, and suggests that this is because there would seldom be free cattle which could form part of the common pool: normally neat cattle would be reclaimable as a fief provided by the patron. In point of fact, the Latin A version of the *schema* allots all the cattle to the husband; this is consistent with Howells's argument, and also with the view that the whole of the *schema* is archaic and may be many centuries older than the classical manuscripts in which it appears.[75] The husband would take the cattle, at the earliest period, because they were really his lord's; if the wife's kin could after so long a time identify any cattle as part of the wife's *argyfrau*, they could claim them, but otherwise the husband took all. For

---

[72] See n.28 *supra*.
[73] Ior §55/14, 15, where the three exclusive possessions of a woman are identified as her three privy things, without naming them.
[74] Howells, 8/9 *Studia Celtica* 59.
[75] *Ibid.* 62; Lat A §52/6.

later stages of development we can perhaps assume equal sharing of cattle forming part of the common pool.

When the marital property was to be shared because one of the partners was dying, the rules which gave specific chattels to one or other did not apply, but the dying partner, with the parish priest, made the division and the healthy partner chose one of the two shares. The dying partner could then dispose of his/her share, and was in some danger of precipitating a family quarrel. For though he was in a position to express his will, his clear right to bequeath goods was limited to debts and *daered*, and if he bequeathed anything more his son could "break" the bequest—at the price of being called an uncouth or savage son.[76] The expression *mab anwar*, here translated in its modern sense, is believed to be a survival from common Celtic social ethics, in which the "un-warm" son was contrasted with the *mab gwâr* (in modern Welsh suggesting courtesy or civilised behaviour), whose warmth was made available to his parents in old age.[77]

The provisions of the previous paragraph would apply only where the dying partner had warning of the approach of death, but presumably they would apply even if death came during the first seven years of the union. This we are specifically told for separation by death (rather than "by life and death"):[78] where death was sudden, the allocation of specific chattels would no doubt apply, and this means that the children would inherit the dead partner's share. It will be realised that there was no question of sharing land or giving it by will: the wife would have no land, and the husband's interest in land was in effect a life interest, so that his sons would take equal shares in the land on his death.[79] The position of the widow could, it seems, be difficult, for we are told that she was allowed to remain in the matrimonial home for nine days after her husband's death and should then leave "after the last penny" (of her chattels), but we are not told where she was to go.[80] The English widow took her dower as an interest in land, which could seriously embarrass her son (and sometimes his son and even his son's son) but at least ensured that she had where to lay her head.

We can only hope that the Welsh widow found her children *gwâr*

---

[76] Ior §45/7, 8.
[77] D. A. Binchy, "Some Celtic Legal Terms", (1955) 3 *Celtica* 228-31.
[78] Ior §45/5.
[79] For discussion of the law of inheritance and disposal of land, see D. Jenkins, "A Lawyer looks at Welsh land law", (1967) TC 236ff., and especially 239ff.
[80] Ior §51/9.

enough to provide a home for her. She had one bargaining counter, in the share of her husband's chattels which she could bring with her. This would almost always be more than the share which any child took, for only if there was no bequest of *daered* and only one child would the whole of the husband's share go to the same inheritor. Daughters as well as sons shared in their father's chattels, but a daughter's share was only half a son's. The right of a child to receive its father's property did not depend on the circumstances of its begetting, though proof of entitlement was easier for what English lawyers of the thirteenth century would have regarded as legitimate children. It must be remembered that neither ecclesiastical nor secular law in medieval England regarded a religious ceremony as essential to the validity of a marriage: the commitment of the parties to each other was what created the union, and a religious ceremony was of legal importance as providing notorious evidence of a commitment which might otherwise be very difficult to prove.[81] In Wales the corresponding evidence would be provided by the secular *neithior* or the mere gift of the bride by her kindred, and it is consistent with this that the first of the three ways in which a child becomes an undeniable member of his father's kindred is by being begotten in the legal bed and reared at the father's expense for a year and a day. It was thus possible for a husband to repudiate his wife's child at any time during its first year of life; on the other hand, if a man contributed to the maintenance of a child "even if it be a child of bush and brake", it thereby became undeniable. Finally, a child was also undeniable if duly affiliated by its mother according to the formal rules, in the "mother church".[82]

To round this study off, we can look at the property implications of rape, which can be interpreted as a logical application of the principles which we have examined. This application is concisely set out in each of our texts, and all the variants are clearly related to each other.[83]

In the first place rape was open cohabitation which entitled the woman's lord to *amobr*, if the ravisher admitted the act or it was proved against him, though (as we have already seen) if the woman could not identify her ravisher the lord had no claim.[84] The rule for payment by the ravisher makes no distinction between virgin and non-virgin in respect of his liability to pay *amobr*; at another point of the tractate, however, we

[81] PM ii.369-77.
[82] DwCol §§152-4. For the procedure on affiliation, see Excursus II, *infra*.
[83] Ior §50/4, Cyfn §73/14, Lat A §52/35; cf. Bleg 63.23 = Lat D 343.19.
[84] *Supra*, pp. 74-5.

are told that *amobr* was not payable for a married woman who was raped.[85]

Again, rape was a union which had come to an end, without fault on the woman's part, and she was entitled to take property from it. It had not lasted seven years, so her claim was for *agweddi*, and in *Ior* to *agweddi* "according to the greatest amount to which she may be entitled": this we can probably interpret as meaning that she would get the full legal *agweddi* appropriate to her status. Her ravisher would hardly be allowed to plead his own wrong in proof that she was not given by her kindred. If she was a virgin, the loss of her virginity in the union would entitle her to *cowyll*, and here again the ravisher cannot plead his wrong to show that she did not make a claim to *cowyll*, or that she did not identify particular chattels: she seems to be entitled to the maximum *cowyll* as to the maximum *agweddi*.[86] A third payment, given her by all the texts, seems to be in some sense a price paid for the woman's chastity: this is her *dilysrwydd* or *dilystod*. This (originally abstract) noun is derived from the noun *llys*, meaning objection;[87] the *dilys* is that to which no objection can be raised, with the result that when a man has taken a second wife the first (from whom he had parted) is thereafter *dilys*: no objection can be raised to her taking another husband, and the former husband cannot re-claim her even if his experience with the second wife reveals her previously unappreciated virtues.[88] An unchaste wife would clearly be open to objection from her husband; if her unchastity was involuntary, this could form the basis of a claim to compensation from her ravisher, but the texts give us no hint of how that compensation should be assessed.

The violence of rape, quite apart from its sexual factor, had legal implications both private and public. Like any other assault, it was an insult to the victim, so that *prima facie* we should expect *sarhaed* to be payable to her. The Cyfnerth and Blegywryd texts indeed name *sarhaed*, and Latin A *iniuria*; the Iorwerth text, perhaps influenced by its use of *sarhaed* for the husband's payment to his wife for improperly beating

---

[85] Ior §54/6; see Excursus I, *infra*.

[86] This interpretation involves the assumption that the words "os morwyn uyd" apply only to the *cowyll* (which is supported by Cyfn §73/14), whereas the words "yn y ueint u6yhaf y dylyo" apply to both *cowyll* and *agweddi*.

[87] The word *llys* is used for the grounds of objection to a witness: proved perjury (as noticed at n.37 *supra*) is a *llys*.

[88] Ior §52/4, §46/4. *Dilysrwydd* is also used in the Law of Women in a sense very different from the present, but quite easily reconcilable with it: in Ior §54/9 the *dilysrwydd* for which no *mach* is given is the validity of the title (or "immunity from claim") to the property in question: *supra* at n.67.

her, gives the victim her *wynebwerth*. And since sexual intercourse with a man's wife was *sarhaed* to him,[89] it quite logically adds a provision omitted by the other text, that if his victim is married the ravisher must pay her husband his augmented *sarhaed*.

The public law consequence of the violence of rape is that a *dirwy* is payable to the king.[90] According to the Iorwerth text, this is a standard *dirwy* of twelve kine; the other texts do not specify the amount of the *dirwy* at this point, but elsewhere, in the context of the triad on *dirwy*, they explain that the *dirwy* for *trais* (which may there include robbery as well as rape) takes the form of the rod and cup which are paid to the king as *sarhaed*.[91] In that particular passage the spirit of the lawbooks is indeed far from the juristic sophistication of the classical law.

EXCURSUS I

Was *amobr* payable only once?

The alleged rule that *amobr* was payable only once in her lifetime in respect of any particular woman seems to find support in a number of passages in the classical lawbooks. The most positive of these is probably that in *Llyfr y Damweiniau*:[92]

> A woman never pays but one *amobr* by law, and that she pays according to the status of the land from which she derives . . .

In the next section there seems to be a corollary to this passage:

> Whoever rapes a woman let him pay her *amobr* since a woman pays only one *amobr* . . .

but the various manuscript versions are confusing, and the passage seems to contradict the rule stated in the main text of the Law of Women, found in some of those manuscripts:[93]

> If a married woman [*gwraig wriog*] is raped, there is no obligation to pay *amobr* for she herself paid it when she married [*pan urha6ys*].

---

[89] Ior §110/10.
[90] In Cyfn, Bleg, and Lat A the *dirwy* is payable to the *arglwydd/dominus*: the wording rather suggests that the same lord receives both *dirwy* and *amobr*.
[91] Bleg 43.31 (= Lat D 338.10), WML 123.17.
[92] AL IV.ii.18 (in a lacuna in DwCol).
[93] Ior §54/6, cf. Col §48.

The principle is also invoked in the statement of the law on payment of *amobr* in respect of a bride whose allegiance may have changed; if *amobr* was paid to the former lord, the new lord cannot claim it for three reasons of which the first is[94]

> because there is only a right of one *amobr* from a woman.

There is also a passage found in the Iorwerth text of the Law of Women:[95]

> Every woman is entitled to go the way she will, for she is not entitled to be car-returning and there is no right to anything from her except her *amobr: and one* amobr *at that, for a woman has no* ebediw *save her* amobr; *therefore, as a man is bound to pay only one* ebediw, *so likewise a woman is bound to pay only one* amobr, *for she has no* ebediw *save her* amobr

—where the italicised clauses are missing from MS. *B*, and may be an addition in the other branch of the manuscript tradition, for they do not appear in MS. *G*, and the emphasis in *Col's* version of this passage is different.

It is a single clause in the Col version which provides the starting point for the suggested interpretation of the rule. *Col* has[96]

> A woman is free to go the way she will, for there is no constraint on her save her *amobr*. A man is bound to pay only one *ebediw*, unless he has two land-holdings under two lords; and so also a woman for her *amobr*.

It can therefore be argued that what the lawbooks are concerned about is the identification of the lord to whom the *amobr* is payable, and that when they declare that only one *amobr* is due, they mean that it will be paid only once in respect of any particular occasion. This is the only sensible meaning of the rule that a man pays only one *ebediw:* we need no lawbook to tell us that a payment due on death can arise only once. The proviso in *Col*, however, shows the general rule for *ebediw* being modified as the relative economic importance of land and livestock changes. The modification suggests also a change in the significance of lordship or patronage, from a relation in which the fief (whether in livestock or land) was the price of the vassal's faithful adherence to the lord to one in which the interests of both lord and man were primarily economic. The compiler of *Col* plainly saw no reason why a man should not hold land of two lords, but (though there is no *a priori* reason why a

---

[94] DwCol §424.
[95] Ior §52/5.
[96] Col §§26, 27.

man should not be provided with cattle by two lords) the obstacles to the establishment of two simultaneous fidelity relationships involving the same vassal are also plain.

If we now look at the texts from this standpoint, we shall see that the statements of the alleged rule all come from the classical period, when the lord-man relationship was coming to be more and more based on land. It was then important to ensure that there should not be claims to *amobr* from two persons, each having some title to be regarded as the lord of the woman's father. That seems to be the point of the rule in *Llyfr y Damweiniau* that a woman pays one *amobr* "according to the status of the land from which she derives":[97] if her father had two holdings from different lords, it would usually be easy enough to identify the holding from which she "derived".

There could be doubt about the lord who was entitled to a virgin's *amobr*; there could be none where a second union was in question. It is repeatedly declared that a woman was free to go where she liked, and that she had no right to return to her kindred; hence no-one could claim her *amobr* in right of his lordship over her father, and the claim must be made in relation to her residence.[98]

EXCURSUS II

Affiliation and Rearing

As has been continually emphasised, it was not "legitimacy" of birth but acceptance by the father which determined the status of a child in Welsh law:

> The law of the church says that no one is entitled to patrimony [*tref tat*] save the father's eldest son by the proper wife [*o'r wreyc pryaut*]. The law of Hywel adjudges it to the youngest son as to the eldest, and judges that the father's sin and his illegality should not be set against the son for his patrimony.[99]

As these sentences show, the main significance of the principles for the male child was in relation to the inheritance of land; for the female, acceptance by the father meant the right to be "at his platter", and the

---

[97] *Supra*: Aneurin Owen's translation, "the land upon which she was born" is not literal enough to be justifiable.
[98] Cyfn §73/13c, Lat A §52/34, Col §65.
[99] Ior §87/5, 6. For *gwraig briod* see the Glossary. The proposition of §87/5 is less a statement of canon law than of English common law.

obligation to pay *amobr* to the father's lord rather than to the mother's lord or (in the absence of any other claimant) to the king. The amount payable would depend on the status of the father, but if the girl was not accepted or deemed to have been accepted by a father, on the status of the mother.

Nevertheless, a presumption operated in favour of the children of a regular union. For the first of the three circumstances which prevented a kin-group from disowning a son was that he had been begotten in the "legal bed" and reared at the man's expense for a year and a day.[100] We are not told what made the bed legal: if we could agree on the meaning of *priodas* and *gwraig briod*, we might interpret the legal bed in a corresponding way. The presumption of acceptance is not a very strong one: it can be rebutted by repudiation during the year or by mere failure to maintain the child for that period.

Maintenance of the child was a necessary condition if the child was born in what we may call regular wedlock; in other circumstances it was a sufficient condition. To give goods for rearing the child was the second limb of the triad already cited, even if the child was that of a woman of bush and brake:[101] it was not, we may suppose, necessary that the goods should correspond to the standards set out for a year's rearing in order to raise the presumption. These standards are stated at two points: on the one hand there is a statement of what is to be provided for a wife who is pregnant when the union ends, on the other a bare statement, in a floating fragment of the Cyfnerth text, of the legal substance of a year's rearing.[102]

The third possible qualification is formal acceptance "in the mother church as law says", for which the procedure is given in detail in the Iorwerth text. Subject naturally to the presumptions already discussed, the alleged father need do nothing until a formal assertion of paternity has been made by the mother. This she does by bringing the child[103] to the church "in which his [the father's] burying-place is"[104] and there swearing on the altar and its relics "to God first and to that altar and to the good relics that are on it and to the son's baptism 'that no father

---

[100] DwCol §152.
[101] DwCol §153. It is not clear whether the woman of bush and brake is different from the whore (*putain*) or whether the expression is merely a euphemism.
[102] Ior §49/3, Cyfn §44/5.
[103] Ior §100/2. The Welsh text has *mab*, which in this context must be taken as meaning a child of either sex.
[104] "er egluys e bo y uydua endy": the obvious temptation is to translate *y uydua* by "his family vault". If the father was an alien, the church was that in which he received holy water and mass bread: Ior §100/4.

created this child in the heart of a woman save'—(such and such man, by his name)—in my heart''. The wording of the mother's oath makes it clear why she was allowed only one attempt at affiliation: if this oath were twice sworn, against different men, it must necessarily be false on at least one of the two occasions—and we have other evidence that Welsh law was sensitive to the enormity of mutually inconsistent oaths.[105]

When the mother has sworn to the child's paternity, ''it is proper for the father to do one of two things: either to take the child legally or to deny him legally'', and at this point the text passes at once to the procedure for denial, by the father's swearing ''to God first and to that altar and to the good relics that are on it and to the man who separated him from the creation of father and mother, that he never created that child in the heart of a woman and that there is no drop of his blood in him but from Adam''.[106] We are not told of any formality appropriate to acceptance by the father; but ''if there is no father'' (presumably because he is dead, though his banishment would also give occasion for the substitute procedure), the child could be received by the *pencenedl*[107] as one of seven ''of the best men of the kindred'', by ''taking the child's hands between his own hands and giving him a kiss, for a kiss is sign of kinship, and then putting the child's right hand in the hand of the oldest of the other men, who should give him a kiss'' and so pass him on to each of the others. If there was no *pencenedl* twenty-one of the best men of the kindred (fifty, according to the men of Powys) were needed, and the procedure was initiated by ''the man who is in the place of the lord'' by putting the child's hand into that of the oldest of the kinsmen. Though it was no doubt in the lord's interest that a child should be affiliated, his representative would not give the sign of kinship.[108]

From the triad in *Llyfr y Damweiniau* it seems that in the classical law formal affiliation was possible only in this church ceremony, but a triad in the Cyfnerth text records a more archaic procedure with more sinister language. The second and third limbs of the triad deal with acceptance by the *pencenedl* or the fifty kinsmen; the first limb provides for affiliation by a pregnant woman of bush and brake. She is to call her parish priest to her and swear to him, ''Let me bear a snake from this pregnancy if any father created it in a mother but the man to whom I bring it.''[109]

DAFYDD JENKINS

[105] DwCol §129.
[106] Ior §100/5, 6.
[107] What the office of *pencenedl* implied is not known with certainty: see the Glossary.
[108] Ior §103/1-4.
[109] WML 129.6-16.

THE STATUS OF WOMEN AND THE PRACTICE OF MARRIAGE IN LATE-MEDIEVAL WALES

THE STATUS of women and the character and consequences of the marriage bond are issues which are central to the study of any society.[1] Yet they are also issues which by their very nature are often only indirectly illuminated by contemporary historical evidence, especially for the medieval period. Nowhere is this more obviously so than in late-medieval Wales. The historian can turn to two major categories of sources: the texts of native Welsh law, *Cyfraith Hywel*, and the records, more especially the court rolls, of the Principality and Marcher lordships of Wales in the late-medieval (post-1284) period. Both categories of evidence have their shortcomings and are in any case so different in character as not to be easily compatible with one another.

The texts of *Cyfraith Hywel* present the historian of late-medieval Wales with so many and such unfamiliar problems that he is sorely tempted to dismiss the law-texts as valid source-material for his studies. In the first place, it is well-known that the texts of *Cyfraith Hywel* contain, pell-mell, tractates and individual *dicta* drawn from widely differing periods and contexts. Such chronological uncertainty is the despair of the historian. That is why he often regards the study of Welsh law as, strictly speaking, pre-historic, best left to the ingenuity of linguistic experts, social anthropologists and antiquarian-minded lawyers. Furthermore, there is the added objection that between the neat, clear-cut theorems of the legal texts, even where they can be approximately dated, and current social practice there may well be a considerable gulf. The law-texts are concerned with the ideal and the static; they make few concessions to the untidiness of human activities or to the impact of social change. They were written by law-men for law-men and are thereby more concerned to display the subtlety of legal argument rather than to provide an insight into actual social situations. A passage from the law-texts themselves

---

[1] I have left this paper largely in the form in which it was delivered at the Conference on Welsh Medieval Law in 1974. Such an *apologia* is issued not so much to explain its colloquial style but rather to emphasise that it is no more than an exploratory draft and one which is much concerned with defining the problems and shortcomings of the evidence. All references to unpublished documents relate, unless otherwise stated, to material at the Public Record Office, London.

may serve to illustrate the point: more than one text dwells on the rights of an estranged husband, overcome with memories of former marital bliss, to reclaim his former wife if he caught her with one foot in and one foot out of her intended second husband's bed.[2] Interesting as is the argument as an example of the sophisticated legal casuistry of native Welsh lawyers, it has about it that air of unreality which hardly fosters confidence in the validity of the law-texts as a guide to the central issues of social custom. Such indeed they were not meant to be: they were, it must be repeated, lawyers' manuals, not guidebooks for social observers. Yet whatever their shortcomings and pitfalls as historical source-material, the historian neglects the legal texts at his peril. So long as he recalls their character and purpose, they can serve him well. Above all, they can instruct him in the ethos and presuppositions of native Welsh medieval society in a way in which his conventional sources, often the by-product of an English colonial administration, singularly fail to do so. He for his own part can liberate the textual expert from some of the con-stricting fundamentalism of textual studies of the laws, by showing how and how far *Cyfraith Hywel* was operated and modified in late medieval Wales. We will never square our conventional historical evidence com-pletely with the legal and textual studies of the law-texts, for they are based on different *genres* of material and often relate to different periods. That, however, is no reason for being unwilling to learn from both sources.

In terms of conventional sources for the study of marriage in the late-medieval period, the Welsh historian suffers from one obvious disadvan-tage. He lacks those records of ecclesiastical courts which English historians have relied upon so heavily in order to gain an insight into the practices and conventions of medieval marriage. Since the Church's jurisdiction in formal marriage litigation was as clearly established in Wales as in other parts of Western Christendom, he is thereby denied a major source for the study of marriage customs. Instead he has to rely largely on the records, mainly the court rolls, of the secular lords of later-medieval Wales and on such glimpses as they provide him of the status of women and the nature of the matrimonial bond.

Since this paper will be based largely on evidence drawn from these court rolls, it is as well to recognise clearly at the outset the limitations of these records, and indeed of all "public" records, for the study of marriage customs. Marriage and the negotiations which preceded it were essentially private affairs, entered into by two persons or at most two

[2] Ior § 46/4, Bleg 66. 9-13.

families. Marriage and its attendant problems did not, therefore, in normal circumstances come within the purview of secular lordship and it has therefore left but few traces in the records of lordship, the major documentary source for the historian of late-medieval Wales. "Private" records relating to marriage are equally difficult to come by. Marriage contracts, as we shall see, were certainly concluded, though many of them were probably witnessed orally rather than committed to writing. It is not until the late fifteenth-sixteenth centuries that written marriage contracts begin to survive in Wales and then only for the wealthier native families. In these circumstances, the historian has to rely largely on the records of such marital disputes as were brought to the attention of the seignorial courts and such incidental light as they throw on the marriage customs of native Welsh society.

But here again a major caveat needs to be borne in mind in assessing the evidence. Disputes relating to marriage and to the implementation of marriage contracts were likely to be terminated not in the seignorial or royal courts, but through an agreement concluded by the parties concerned and/or by the appointment of mutually acceptable arbitrators.[3] Historians are now beginning to realise what an important rôle such extra-curial arbitrations played in the socio-legal mechanism of late medieval society: the peace of the king and the decision of the lord's court were often only last-resort options, and often expensive options at that, in the pursuit of the settling of disputes. Nowhere was this more obviously so than in late-medieval Wales where the dimensions of incomprehension and distrust between the law-keepers and the law-breakers in terms of language, legal approach, and social presuppositions were an added incentive for extra-curial decisions. Cases relating to land, to assault, and to *galanas* or homicide-payments, we know, were so decided by extra-curial arbitration, only occasionally confirmed by a court decision; and in cases of contract and debt the verdict often lay with the witnesses of the contract, *amodwyr*.[4] Such also was the case with regard to marriage contracts. Two examples from the court rolls themselves may serve to illustrate this point: when Iorwerth ap Madog ab

---

[3] Cf. R. H. Helmholz, *Marriage Litigation in Medieval England* (Cambridge, 1974), 31: "The court records show the tenacity of the belief that people could regulate their own matrimonial affairs without the assistance or the interference of the church".

[4] See for example E. D. Jones, "Rhannu Tir Rhys ab Elise", (1943) 3 NLWJ 23-8; J. Wynn, *History of the Gwydir Family*, ed. J. Ballinger (Cardiff, 1927), 18 (cases relating to land); R. R. Davies, "The Survival of the Bloodfeud in Medieval Wales", (1969) 54 *History* 338-58 at pp. 354-5 (*galanas*—arbitration); *idem*, "The Law of the March", (1970) 5 WHR 1-31 at p. 18 (extra-curial settlement of assault cases). For *amodwyr* see 5 WHR 17 and n. 63.

Einion of Wrexham quarrelled with his step-father about the conditions of the divorce between his mother and step-father, it was decided that the case should be settled by the pledges of the divorce-contract.[5] In Dyffryn Clwyd in 1354 four men were appointed to make an agreement (*concordia*) between Hywel ap Dafydd Hen and his father-in-law, Cynwrig the Fuller (*Pannwr*), about the disputed question of the marriage portion of Hywel's wife. Should the agreement so concluded be broken, the offender was to pay a fine of £3, of which £2 went to the innocent party and £1 to the lord.[6] The case may be interpreted as showing the lord as the upholder and ultimate financial beneficiary of the private agreements of his tenants; but it may also be used as a reminder to ourselves that the terms of marriage agreements and the settlement of marriage problems, financial and otherwise, generally lay well beyond the reach of our court rolls.

What then can we learn from the court rolls about the law of women in late medieval Wales? The answer is alarmingly clear: very little, and that spasmodically and always indirectly. The cases relating to the law of women which appear on the court rolls may be divided into two very broad groups. To the first category belong the civil actions between private parties. These never deal directly with the marriage contract or the divorce agreement as such; but rather with the consequences of such contracts and agreements. That is, they are mainly pleas of debt and contract. For example, we learn something about the character of marriage-portions (*maritagia*) from the court rolls because of the actions of debt brought to recover such portions; but it is difficult to generalise on the basis of such cases for they are only the subject of court actions where the more obvious instruments of persuasion, arbitration and threat have failed. The second category of cases are those where the lord's interest, normally his financial interest, was at stake. The most obvious of such cases and among the most fruitful in terms of information are those relating to *amobr*, the virginity fine due to the lord for the sexual lapses or marriage—for the Welsh law and Marcher custom took a truly Pauline view of the purposes of matrimony—of the women of his lordship. The theoretical basis of the claim to *amobr* lay in the assumption that the lord was the protector, the champion, of the virginity of his womenfolk; but protection as so often soon degenerated into a racket and a sordid and profitable racket at that. It was also a worthwhile racket for the historian, for the lapsed ladies of Wales were ingenious and

---

[5] Court Rolls (S.C.2) 226/18, m. 11 (1345).
[6] S.C.2/218/4, m. 8v.

illuminating in the legal arguments they produced to escape the penalty for their promiscuity. On occasion, of course, the wishes of private parties and the financial interests of the lord coincided. We have already seen how in marriage contracts and agreements it was not unusual to stipulate a fine for breach of contract and to ear-mark a proportion of that fine—normally a third or a half—for the lord, by way of recognition of his help in enforcing the contract.[7] In such a fashion—and the analogy with the practice of the compelling third (*traean cymell*) in the case of *galanas* is an obvious one[8]—some of the private matrimonial affairs of Welshmen come briefly within our view.

But only briefly; for, without labouring the point too much, it is imperative to realise that the law of women was essentially personal, familial and largely extra-curial. Furthermore by the later middle ages, most of the aspects of marriage were firmly within the ambit of canon law and of the jurisdiction of the ecclesiastical courts.[9] Ecclesiastical reformers such as Gerald of Wales and Archbishop Peckham, it is true, inveighed against the sexual permissiveness and marital improprieties of the Welsh and were outraged by their flagrant flouting of the law of the Church on the institution of marriage. Their remarks have often (and rightly) been quoted as evidence of the reluctance of the Welsh and the Irish to conform to current ecclesiastical orthodoxy in a crucial area of social custom,[10] but their polemical and *parti-pris* nature is often

---

[7] See above n. 6. In a similar case in 1359-60 it was recorded that a marriage agreement carried a penalty clause of £4, half of which was payable to the lord and half to the injured party: S.C.2/218/7, m. 16v.; 218/8, m. 12.

[8] For *traean cymell* in the law texts and court rolls see (1969) 54 *History* 345-6.

[9] For canon law learning on marriage, A. Esmein, *Le mariage en droit canonique* (Paris, 1891) remains the standard work. Recent brief introductions are provided by G. le Bras, "Le Mariage dans la théologie et le droit de l'église du XIe au XIIIe siècle", (1968) 11 *Cahiers de civilisation médiévale*, 191-202; J. L. Barton, "Nullity of Marriage and Illegitimacy in the England of the Middle Ages" in *Legal History Studies 1972* (ed. D. Jenkins: Cardiff, 1975), 28-49, and C. N. L. Brooke, *Marriage in Christian History* (Cambridge, 1978). The evidence on marriage litigation in English ecclesiastical courts is admirably considered in R. A. Helmholz's book (see n. 3) and in M. M. Sheehan, "The Formation and Stability of Marriage in Fourteenth-Century England: Evidence of an Ely Register", (1971) 33 *Medieval Studies* 228-63.

[10] Already in the late-eleventh century Archbishop Lanfranc attacked the practices of the Irish whereby men "marry within their own kindred or that of their deceased wives; others desert their wives as and when they please; they even traffic them for other men's wives in exchange": Margaret Gibson, *Lanfranc* (Oxford, 1978), 123. In another letter, quite probably prompted by this one, Pope Gregory VII claimed that "Many of them [viz. the 'Scots'] not only abandon but even sell their wives": *The Epistolae Vagantes of Pope Gregory VII*, ed. H. E. J. Cowdrey (Oxford, 1972), no. 1. References to Welsh marriage customs in the writings of Gerald of Wales and the letters of Archbishop Peckham are well known; rather less well known is the prohibition (probably in 1175) of the Welsh from marrying within prohibited degrees or changing their wives: *Councils and Ecclesiastical Documents Relating to Great Britain and Ireland*, ed. A. W. Haddan and W. Stubbs (Oxford, 1869-78), i. 382.

overlooked. The Welsh were by no means alone in finding it difficult to square their marriage practices with the idealised view of the sacrament of marriage proclaimed by the Church; while, on the other hand, there is evidence, however scrappy, of the ways in which the teachings of the Church on such issues as consanguinity were in fact being increasingly accepted as the norm in late-medieval Wales. This growing if reluctant acceptance of the teaching and jurisdiction of the Church in the field of marriage is crucial to an understanding of our sources: it serves to explain their silence on much that relates to marriage (for the reason that such issues were the concern of the church courts); it also helps to explain some of the discrepancies between the evidence of the law-texts and the court rolls on the question of marriage practice. The former, in essence if not in their surviving manuscript form, largely predate the articulation of the Church's teaching and the growing acceptance of the jurisdiction of its courts; the latter belong to a period during which Welsh custom was being increasingly subsumed within the Church's law and teaching on marriage.

Two further caveats need to be entered regarding the evidence from which this note-book on the law of women in late medieval Wales is compiled. One relates to the geography of the evidence and thereby to the applicability of the conclusions. It is from the north-eastern March that the vast majority of our cases are drawn. That this should be so is in large measure a matter of archival accident: no area in Wales has such a wealth of court records as the north-east, primarily of course the court-rolls of Dyffryn Clwyd but also in lesser measure those of Bromfield and Yale, Caus, and Clun. But there is also a more historically and legally defensible reason for choosing this region for our study. The more I study the records of this district and compare them with those of other parts of Wales (including the Principality proper) the more convinced I become that it was an area of unusual legal and social conservatism. It is here that we can study most clearly some of the most distinctive features of Welsh society, particularly as they affected the status of women, most notably the organisation of society into patrilineages for land-inheritance purposes, the firm insistence that land could only be transmitted by and through males, the corollary that women were excluded not only from inheritance but also from a dower-share in their husband's land.[11] These basic tenets, which elsewhere had been modified in greater or lesser

---

[11] For a consideration of some of these issues in the light of the evidence of the court rolls see R. R. Davies, *Lordship and Society in the March of Wales 1284-1400* (Oxford, 1978), Part IV.

degree, were still cardinal in the legal practice of the north-eastern March or at least parts of it. That is why in a preliminary atlas of the legal geography of late-medieval Wales, the area needs to be placed alongside parts of the southern Principality—to which Professor T. Jones Pierce and Mr. J. Beverley Smith have drawn our attention[12]—as a district where Welsh law proved peculiarly resilient.

So much about the geography of our sources. Our final preliminary word needs to be said about their language. One of the problems that faces the historian attempting to determine the degree of survival of Welsh law and terminology in the late medieval period is the fact that his records, often compiled by an English-speaking clerk, were written in Latin and often based on formularies for the composition of court records current in England. In certain spheres—notably those of land law and *galanas*—the Welsh terminology so obviously lacked a Latin equivalent that the clerks were reduced to using vernacular terms. On other occasions the Welsh phrase was so gutturally and inscrutably native that it defied translation: such was the case with *brwydr gyfaddef, barn y diddim, damdwng,* and *tremyg*.[13] The use of such terminology is as least a minimal indication to the historian that the vocabulary and probably the substance of native law survived in these spheres of social custom. In the case of the law of women, however, there was an internationally-acceptable vocabulary which, even if it did not correspond precisely to Welsh usage and Welsh institutions, was sufficiently close to be used in the court records.[14] Key-words in the legal texts such as *gowyn, cowyll, agweddi* and *wynebwerth* do not, as far as I know, ever appear in the court rolls. Their disappearance may be due to the fact that blanket Latin terms such as *dos* and *maritagium* lay too conveniently to hand; but it is more likely, in my opinion, that by the fourteenth century the words themselves and the social institutions which they described had become archaic. That this was so is suggested by the fact that an occasional Welsh phrase associated with the law of women still survived: thus in a case in Dyffryn Clwyd in 1366 the collectors of *amobr* proved the married status of a woman by saying that she was a wife *"trwy rodd ac estyn a thâl cynhysgaeth"* (i.e. by gift and investiture and by payment of

---

[12] See in particular T. Jones Pierce, "The Law of Wales—the Last Phase", (1963) TC 7-32, and J. B. Smith, "Einion Offeiriad", (1964) 20 BBCS.

[13] For these phrases and their use see R. R. Davies, "The Twilight of Welsh Law", (1966) 51 *History* 143-164 at pp. 160-1.

[14] It is worth observing that canon lawyers allowed that the precise intent of vernacular phrases might be crucial in marriage litigation, notably in determining the character of consent in a marriage contract: Helmholz, *Marriage Litigation,* 38.

marriage portion).[15] Indeed the word *cynhysgaeth* (which is not often used in the law-texts,[16] where the corresponding term appears to be *argyfrau*) is an example of the way that Welsh socio-legal terminology evolves in the later middle ages, for *cynhysgaeth* both in official documents and literary texts henceforth appears as the accepted term for the Latin *maritagium*.[17] It is also a reminder to us that we must not seek to place the evidence of the late-medieval court rolls too firmly or too rigidly within the theoretical framework of the law texts. Between the earliest manuscripts of the Laws and the earliest records of the court there is a gap of at least a century and a half and in substantive terms the chronological hiatus must be even wider. Not even the most conservative legal system is likely to remain static for such a period, least of all given the momentous political and legal changes in Wales, Britain, and Western Europe in the twelfth and thirteenth centuries.

After such an inexcusably long introduction, it is time to turn to the evidence. One feature stands out immediately. It was vital to know in the March whether a woman enjoyed Welsh or English status, for from this distinction flowed a whole host of important consequences. I have dwelt upon this distinction elsewhere;[18] but its importance needs to be underscored again in the present context. On the question of land inheritance the distinction was eminently clear: a woman of English status had the right to succeed to land in the event of the absence of a nearer male relative; a woman of Welsh status could *not* inherit land nor could a title to land be inherited through the female line. The evidence from Bromfield and Yale is particularly clear in this respect. "The lord", so declared the authoritative Survey of 1391, "wishes . . . that inheritance shall remain partible among the same male heirs, as used to be the custom".[19] When this custom began to be circumvented in the fifteenth century the significant phrase "Welsh custom to the contrary as used from ancient time notwithstanding" was appended to deeds of enfeoff-

---

[15] S.C.2/219/3, m. 18v.

[16] For examples of its use in the Laws see Col § 49-50.

[17] Examples of the use of the word *cynhysgaeth* in the records of the late medieval period are many, e.g., S.C.2/219/5, m. 19v. ('de proficuo de Kenenesket uxoris sui', 1368); B.L. Add. MS. 46, 846, f. 78 ("y cenhysceth a roes ei thylwyth e hun iddi": late-fifteenth-century legal memoranda); J. Gwynfor Jones, "The Wynn Family and the Estate of Gwydir" (University of Wales, Ph.D. thesis, 1974, p. 48, for a reference to "gwartheg cynhysgaeth" in the will of John Wyn ap Maredudd d. 1559). For reference to *cynhysgaeth* in literary texts see *Geiriadur Prifysgol Cymru sub verbo*.

[18] *Lordship and Society in the March of Wales*, 306-318.

[19] B.L. Add. M.S. 10,013, f. 7. The petition of the Welshmen of the lordship for the right of female succession in the event of the failure of male heirs of the body was not granted: *ibid.*, f. 170.

ment allowing daughters to succeed in the absence of male heirs.[20] The same rule with regard to succession through and by males was likewise firmly adhered to in Dyffryn Clwyd;[21] but elsewhere in the March, both north and south, and in the Principality it was apparently often relaxed especially where there were no direct male heirs.[22] This is a theme which deserves separate and thorough investigation but it is clear that Welsh custom as it was strictly applied in Bromfield and Yale and Dyffryn Clwyd had the most profound influence on the status of women. In a society where title to land depends on membership of a patrilineage and is restricted to the male members of a four-generation agnatic group, the woman has strictly speaking no rôle to play other than as the bearer of male offspring. In terms of the descent and distribution of the major source of wealth, she is a non-person. She cannot, by definition, be an "heiress" and her attractions as a wife must depend on her own charms and on the moveable goods she brings with her as a marriage portion. Whether this means that, paradoxically, in such a society women are more likely to be esteemed as women rather than as heiresses, actual or potential, is an intriguing issue; but it may explain why Welsh medieval history, though it has an occasional Amazonian heroine, has none of those heiresses whose fortunes and fate are such a prominent feature of the territorial politics of medieval England.

Nor does it have dowagers, for women were not only debarred from inheriting land but also from receiving dower in land by their husbands to be enjoyed after their partners' death. Here the contrast between *Cyfraith Hywel* and the common law of England by the thirteenth century was complete; so also was the contrast between Marcher practice and most English customary law. It was a contrast, as will be recalled, which Edward I sought to remove in the Statute of Rhuddlan: "whereas women in Wales have hitherto not been dowered by their husbands, the king permits that henceforth they shall be dowered". His provision was not without effect, for in areas such as Anglesey and Flintshire in the

[20] NLW Peniarth MS. 404. f. 97-98 (1425), f. 125 (1458).
[21] Thus when two daughters petitioned in 1421 for permission to succeed to their father's land, they admitted that "as daughters they could not by Welsh law hold or possess land hereditarily": S.C.2/221/10, m. 37. Likewise on another occasion two sisters who had recovered land by the assize of mort d'ancestor subsequently lost it because the land was held by Welsh tenure and "therefore no female could have any hereditary right to it", S.C.2/221/9, m. 28v.
[22] Even some of the law texts conceded the right of daughters to succeed in the event of the absence of male heirs: Bleg 75. 24-5. The whole question of the inheritance practices of late-medieval Wales deserves the kind of detailed consideration which Jean Yver has given to the customary inheritance practices of early-modern France: *Essai de géographie coutumière* (Paris, 1966).

fourteenth and fifteenth centuries we find Welsh widows leasing their dower lands.[23] Not so, however, in the north-eastern Marcher lordships; there the lords insisted on upholding ancient Welsh practice. "The land . . . is Welsh land and is held by Welsh tenure. Therefore she cannot have dower assigned from it."[24] Such was the argument advanced in court in Dyffryn Clwyd in 1398 and frequently repeated by other litigants. It was an argument which went unchallenged. It was even more definitively expressed in the revised version of the Statute of Wales with which the Earl of Arundel prefaced his massive Extent of Bromfield and Yale in 1391.[25] The passage is worth quoting in full: "On land held by Welsh tenure, that is *gafael*, a wife ought not to be dowered from the inheritance of her husband, according to the practice of these parts. However, if her husband holds land by knight service or by charter or by English tenure, then let her be dowered according to the practice of such tenures. A Welsh woman ought to receive a third of the goods and chattels of which her husband dies in possession, namely land held by him in mortgage"—and I may here interject that it was accepted that a woman had the right to succeed to *tir prid* lands as they were not inherited family lands and that the husband indeed had the right to devise them by will[26] —"and his moveable goods, if a child of the union was still alive. If no child survives, then the widow is to receive half of the moveable goods, provided that she has not cohabited with another man during her husband's lifetime and has remained unreconciled to her husband before his death. In that case she forfeits all claims." It is a passage which deserves closer study: some will find in it echoes of English law, particularly in the last clause which largely restates chapter 34 of Westminster II (1285); others will find the clause relating to half the goods reminiscent of the provision of Welsh law that in the case of separation by death the goods of husband and wife ought to be equally shared.[27] For us, however, the main significance of the passage lies in the fact that the legal archaism of the March enables us to highlight the

---

[23] See for example, University College of North Wales (U.C.N.W.) Mostyn Collection 2468 (Flintshire, 1337), 774 (Anglesey, 1389); John Rylands Library 1659 (Flintshire, 1419). Furthermore the right of Welsh wives to be dowered in land and tenements either before or after marriage was said on one occasion to be "the custom of Wales" (*consuetudo Wallie*): *Calendar of Inquisitions Miscellaneous*, i. 330, no. 1095.

[24] S.C.2/220/12 m. 10v.

[25] B.L. Add. MS. 10,013, f. 5v.

[26] For *prid* see Llinos Smith, "The Gage and the Land Market in Late Medieval Wales", (1976) 29 *Economic History Review* (2nd ser.) 537-50. For an example of the transfer of *prid*-land by marriage see S.C.2/219/2, m. 16 (1365) and by will U.C.N.W. Penrhyn Collection, 14 (1431).

[27] PM ii.405; Bleg 61. 5-6; Lat A 51/4; Cyfn 73/9a.

profound distinction in the status of women in relation to land according to English common law and Welsh law in the age of Bracton and Iorwerth ap Madog. It is not merely a contrast of legal significance, for the rights, or the absence of rights, of women to land are among the most important determinants of the social and economic landsçape of rural society and of the movement of territorial wealth.

One of the other consequences which flowed from the Welsh legal status of a woman was the obligation to pay *amobr* on her behalf. Welsh women paid *amobr* for their sexual delicts and upon marriage; English women did not. *Amobr* will rear its head again in this paper; but at this juncture I must at least not shirk the issue of what decided the racial status of a woman and thereby the obligation to pay *amobr* on her behalf. It was an issue which worried contemporaries a great deal; but on the whole they took the line that land tenure was the simplest determinant of racial status.[28] We can illustrate this no better than by a case which was heard in the presence of the lord of Dyffryn Clwyd himself.[29] The immediate issue was one of distraint: the *amobr*-collectors claimed the payment of *amobr* from Adda ab Adda Ddu and as he refused to pay they took two of his plough-oxen in distraint. That, by the way, is a reminder to us of how catastrophic to a man's livelihood official distraint could be. The claim of the *amobr*-collectors was based on the fact that Adda had taken Dyddgu ferch Heilin Foel, widow of Ieuan ap Dafydd Goch, to wife. Adda did not deny the fact. His claim to exemption from *amobr*—which at the rate of 7*s*. 6*d*. or 10*s*. a time was no mean imposition—was based on the argument that Dyddgu after the death of her father and of her first husband had succeeded to her father's *English* lands as the true heir and had paid *English* dues for them. She was therefore exempt from all burdens (*servitute*) due upon her in respect of the status of her first husband. The argument was accepted and the case of the *amobr*-collectors was dismissed. The case was not necessarily a test case; but its implications were clear and generally accepted. Racial status was largely determined by land tenure; and status (*braint*) based on land tenure might prevail over that based on marital bonds. That being so, it comes as no surprise to learn in another case that a wife claimed exemption from *amobr* because her father had once held land which had

---

[28] Other criteria could also be involved. The woman who was the occasion of the *amobr*-demand had to be born in the lordship, her father had to be one of the lord's tenants, and her marriage had to have been celebrated in the lordship: S.C.2/218/4, m. 7, m. 8v. (1354); 218/7, m. 22 (1359). It was claimed that *amobr* was not payable in cases of rape, *ibid.*, m. 14.

[29] S.C.2/218/2, m. 12; 218/3, m. 14 (1351-2).

formerly been held by English tenure; that really was too blatant an attempt to acquire English privileges on the most specious basis.[30] Once the Welsh status of a woman had been determined, then her chances of avoiding payment of *amobr* were slim. In the area of the technicalities of *amobr*, Welsh law remained supreme. So at least we learn from the Dyffryn Clwyd evidence, for there all issues relating to *amobr* were referred to the decision of the Welsh *ynad* (*judex Wallicus*).[31] The implication is obvious: in one major area, and that an area where the lord was financially involved, the Welsh law of women was still in current usage and was expounded by men proficient in *Cyfraith Hywel*.

So much for the racial status of a woman and its implications. What of her marital status? Now it is well known that in Europe as a whole marriage was often regarded as a contract rather than a sacrament, in spite of the desperate attempts of the church and of canon lawyers to persuade to the contrary. Wales was no exception. Indeed the whole tenor of the Welsh law was to assume that any cohabitation of man and woman by mutual consent created a legal union wherein the woman had the *de jure* status of a wife.[32] In the fourteenth century, we may believe that many, probably most, marriages were solemnised in the parish church;[33] but that this was not always so is admirably illustrated by a case of 1359. Two women were at law regarding fifteen pieces of bluet cloth; their arguments were both subtle and, one suspects, bitchy. The defendant claimed that she ought not to reply as she was married (*co-operta est per maritum*). Not so, said the plaintiff, since the marriage had not been solemnised *in facie ecclesie*. Maybe so, was the counter-reply; but there had been a marriage contract (*contractus matrimoni*) between them, as a

---

[30] S.C.2/218/7, m. 14v. (1357). The case of the *amobr* collectors was that the defendant and her husband acknowledged that she was the daughter of Gronw ap Madog Llwyd and that Madog Llwyd father of the said Gronw was a Welsh proprietor (*priodor Wallicus*). She could not therefore claim any English liberties except by producing a seignorial charter which specifically granted her such liberties. The case shows how closely interwoven were the issue of liability for *amobr* and that of the definition of racial status.

[31] Cf. (1966) 51 *History* 155 and n. 68. The following is an illustrative entry: "Adhuc loquela inter Bleth' Duy querentem et Eignon ap Ken' Lloyt defendentem in placito inivste detencionis unius bovis . . . Postea Judex Wallicus, inspecto processu secunde Curie precedentis, consideravit quod predicta Duthgy solveret Ammobr": S.C.2/218/6, m. 17 (1358).

[32] The situation was not dissimilar in England. The statistics for the diocese of Ely reveal that seventy per cent of matrimonial cases related to 'private' marriages, contracted other than at the parish church, M. M. Sheehan, "The Formation and Stability of Marriage", (1971) 33 *Medieval Studies* 249-50.

[33] Thus we hear in 1373 of a marriage solemnised in Llangynhafal church: S.C.2/219/9, m. 10 (1373).

result of which the lord had collected his *amobr*. So she was married and she placed her case in the judgement of the Welsh *ynad*.[34] The case has many facets to it, not least the payment of *amobr* as proof of marriage and the way that Welsh law is invoked; but what is particularly relevant to us is the way that the marriage-contract is regarded as sufficient proof of marriage in itself without a subsequent ecclesiastical ceremony. It reminds us forcibly of the homilies of the sixteenth century which inveighed against the practice of regarding trothplighting, hand fasting and the making of a contract as in themselves establishing the state of matrimony.[35]

One reason for fighting shy of a church ceremony was not so much public blushes as the expense. One item in the expense account was the fee claimed by the officiating cleric. It was known as the tithe of investiture, *degwm rhoddi*.[36] The phrase reminds us that, though an ecclesiastical ceremony was unnecessary, formal investiture of the bride—*rhodd ac estyn*, the very words used with regard to land also— was essential if the family (*cenedl*) of the husband were to avow their responsibilities with respect of marriage. We may refer to a case which we have already quoted: when Dafydd ap Dafydd Fychan was challenged to pay *amobr* because of the adultery of his wife, he claimed (quite reasonably it may appear to us) that she was not his wife. The *amobr*-collectors, however, retorted that she was indeed his wife by gift and investiture and by payment of her marriage portion and that therefore he was responsible for paying *amobr* on her behalf until they were legally divorced.[37] Likewise a chaplain who had given a woman in marriage could find himself held responsible for paying *amobr* on her behalf;[38] whereas a daughter who married secretly (*yn llathlud*) could not expect a marriage portion from her father nor, according to the Laws, was he responsible for paying *amobr* on her behalf.[39] That is, whereas marriage was one of the easiest of states to enter into in Welsh law, nevertheless

---

[34] S.C.2/218/7, m. 15v.
[35] Excerpts from these homilies are quoted in G. G. Homans, *English Villagers of the Thirteenth Century* (Cambridge, Mass., 1941), 164. For the question of "prenuptial concubinage" in peasant societies see Jack Goody, *Production and Reproduction. A Comparative Study of the Domestic Domain* (Cambridge, 1976), 43-48.
[36] S.C.2/219/3, m. 15v. (1366).
[37] S.C.2/219/3, m. 18v.: "predicta Wervill' est uxor dicti Dd' per Rothe et Estyn et talle Kenennysketh per quod dictus Dd' tenetur solvere amobr' pro predicta Wervill cum deliquerit donec divorsium inter ipsos legitime perficietur".
[38] S.C.2/217/6, m. 19 (1341).
[39] Col § 64; for illustrative cases S.C.2/217/10, m. 19-19v. (1341).

the nature of that entry, especially the publicity of the act and the sanction of the family, was not without its legal consequences.[40]

Since marriage was so lightly undertaken, that great gulf between the offspring of legal and illegal union, between legitimate and illegitimate children, which dominates English law was largely absent in Welsh law and custom. This is an issue which can only be attended to briefly here in so far as it concerns the law of women. The horror with which contemporary churchmen regarded the Welsh attitudes to illegitimate offspring is well known; it has generally been explained in terms of the sexual permissiveness of the Welsh. Nothing could be further from the truth. Prior to marital union, the husband expected, indeed demanded, his partner to be a wise and careful virgin. Likewise within marriage, Welsh law insists on a high standard of marital behaviour: for a wife even to kiss another man was a serious offence (*cyflafan ddybryd*) which merited an insult-payment (*sarhaed*).[41] The explanation of the apparently cavalier attitude towards so-called illegitimate offspring lies elsewhere. It lies in good part in the ease with which marital union was concluded and the almost equal ease with which it was dissolved. In a situation in which marriage was, in ecclesiastical and legal terms, a rather formless institution, it was not surprising that a man (or woman) should have children by more than one union. We are only likely to hear of them when their claim to the paternal or family land was either allowed or debarred and a formal record made of the arrangements. Thus when Madog Ddu ap Madog ab Adda devised his lands in Maelor Gymraeg in 1321 he gave them to one son fathered (*procreatus*) by him from Lleucu and to four sons likewise fathered (*procreati*) by him from Angharad.[42] He did not designate one group of sons as legitimate nor brand the other as illegitimate; nor did he comment on the status of the women who had borne his sons; nor did he apparently have a sense that he was publicly admitting his sexual lapses. Rather was he proclaiming that he had sons by two unions, both of which might or might not be regarded as marriages. (For what constitutes a marriage and transforms a partner into a wife is largely a matter of social definition and legal custom.) He was also and most importantly proclaiming that he was accepting the male offspring by both unions as rightful heirs to his lands. Welsh law would have upheld his right to do so, even if he had decreed that only one of his two unions was

---

[40] Cf. PM ii.375 for a discussion of the legal implications of the publicity of the marriage act.
[41] Ior § 46/5, 8.
[42] Clwyd Record Office, Trevor-Roper Collection, no. 4.

a true marriage and only one set of his sons legitimate. The practice of *cynnwys* as it appears in late-medieval court rolls and extents accepted that sons born out of wedlock could be avowed by their fathers as their own and thereby admitted as rightful heirs to their fathers' lands.[43]

This essentially permissive and compassionate attitude towards off-spring born of several unions—and it is an attitude which is directly or indirectly reflected in seignorial documents from very different parts of Wales—is highly significant in any consideration of the Welsh attitude towards the status of marriage. But there is more to it than that, for it also reflects on the status of women in Welsh society. In a strictly unilineal society, the rôle of the partner who has no claim to inherit or to transmit land is no more, strictly speaking, than that of a mate from whom children are begotten. She may be described as a wife and a mother and may enjoy the affection and devotion of her husband and children; but in terms of lineage and inheritance she is no more than the bearer, *procreatrix*. That description is comparable to the term occasionally used by social anthropologists in their analyses of unilineal societies in Africa; interestingly enough, it occasionally figures in the documentation of late-medieval Wales. Thus when Ieuan Goch ab Einion Goch of Caerwys gave a quarter-burgage to Gwladus ferch Madog ap Dafydd in 1390 he described her *not* as his mother but as his *procreatrix*.[44] The term may appear derogatory, even insulting; yet it is no exaggeration to say that in terms of inheritance in an unilineal society it was the status of the son, not that of the mother, which was crucial. Another deed of 1378 from Gronant in Flintshire may illustrate the point further.[45] The grantor was one William son of Walter; the grantee was the grantor's son and was described as "Robert son of Gwenllian daughter of Philip by me (viz. William son of Walter) conceived (*procreato*) of the said Gwenllian". The father gave to his son all his lands in Gronant with reversion, for lack of legitimate heirs, to "William

---

[43] The rule of *cynnwys* as it operated in pre-Conquest Wales was clearly expounded by a jury in the lordship of Maelor Gymraeg in 1344: "a tempore quo pater alicuius recepit filium pro puero suo quod idem filius ante conquestum percipiet partem suam hereditatis patris sui, non obstante bastardia; et aliter non": B.L. Add. MS. 10,013, f. 172v. In Clun in 1338 a jury of twenty-four declared that legitimate sons and daughters should share the paternal inheritance proportionally with the bastard: Shropshire Record Office, 552/1/8, m. 3. The rule of *cynnwys* was upheld in north-east Wales after the conquest but with the proviso that a seignorial licence was essential: *The Extent of Chirkland*, ed. G. P. Jones (Liverpool, 1933), 61; B.L. Add. MS. 10,013, f. 7 ("Bastardi non habeant de cetero hereditates et eciam . . . non habeant propartes cum legitimis nomine conwois sine licencia domini distincte et aperte capte et optenta").

[44] U.C.N.W. Mostyn Collection, 2007 (1390).

[45] Clwyd Record Office, Mostyn of Talacre Collection, 247.

son of Gwenllian daughter of Owen conceived by the same Robert of the said Gwenllian''. The grant is notable in several respects: both father and son had sons apparently born out of wedlock and both wished to respect the rights of those sons to the paternal lands. The sons so born interestingly enough bear their mothers' names, for, as the Flemish proverb has it, ''no one is a bastard through his mother''. In both cases it is the acceptance of the paternity of the son rather than the status of the mother which is crucial. Neither Robert nor William was called a bastard, yet the very fact that both in land deeds bore their mother's lineage together with the references to ''legitimate heirs'' shows that attitudes were changing. Respect for ecclesiastically-recognised marriages was gradually ousting the practice of more casual (though equally solemn) unions of former days, and as a corollary a sharper and ultimately damaging distinction was drawn between the offspring of formally-approved marriages and unsanctioned, illicit unions. The rights of bastards were becoming a matter for parental choice or, as was stated in the Cydweli charter of liberties of 1356, might only be exercised in the event of the failure of legitimate heirs.[46] Changing attitudes on questions of legitimacy implied, of course, changing attitudes on the issue of marriage. On both issues Welsh habits were dying hard; but they were certainly dying.

Our digression into the field of legitimacy has taken us beyond marriage; but we must revert to the institution of marriage itself. There was, or at least there could be, more to marriage than the union of two persons and the legal obligations that flowed from the union. Marriage normally involved a contract, oral or written; and in that respect the law of women and the law of contract overlapped. We know little or nothing directly about the content of these contracts; but we can make a fair guess from the indirect evidence of the court rolls. The major item in them was the size of the *maritagium* and the terms for its payment; non-payment of the marriage portion was far and away the most common reason for citing the contract in court.[47] The marriage contract would also normally stipulate the penalty for the breach or non-fulfillment of the contract. As with all contracts in medieval Welsh law, the presence of witnesses was important. The wedding guests were there not only to enjoy the junketings but, in a very real sense, to witness the marriage. It

---

[46] Duchy of Lancaster Miscellaneous Books (D.L. 42) 16 f. 43v.—f. 45v.
[47] Cf. R. H. Helmholz, *Marriage Litigation*, 26: "Matrimonial litigation in medieval England was dominated throughout by the suit brought to establish and to enforce a marriage contract."

was a social function which might have legal consequences. It was to the wedding guests (*neithiorwyr*) that the outraged bridegroom was to appeal and to report if he found that his wife was no virgin.[48] How important a rôle they might be asked to fulfill is admirably illustrated by a case of 1343 from Dyffryn Clwyd. When Madog ap Gruffudd and his wife Dyddgu separated, the question as to who was responsible for the breakdown of the marriage was an important one, for according to the original marriage contract the guilty party was to pay 30*s.* to the innocent party and 30*s.* to the lord. What is important in the present context, however, is that the decision as to guilt was left to twelve witnesses (*fidejussores*) who had been present at the marriage.[49]

There was more to the contract than promises and penalties for breaking them; there was also an actual exchange of moveable goods or of ready cash by way of a marriage portion to the bridegroom. The *maritagium* was paid normally by the father or brother of the bride. It often took the form of animals and stock: two cows in one case; sixteen sheep in another; one cow, one horse, one ox in another; one cow and 3*s.* 9*d.* in another.[50] On other occasions household goods, clothes or bed linen, were given;[51] but more frequent were outright cash gifts, the largest of which known to me is one of £12 granted by a brother to his sister.[52] The range of *maritagia* would no doubt be greater if our evidence was fuller: we hear, for example, of a father giving a house and an orchard with his daughter and of a brother who not only gave £3 in cash and a gift of corn to his sister on her marriage but who also promised to plough for her.[53] Such information as we have on marriage-portions, or *tâl cynhysgaeth* as they were known in Welsh, suggests that they formed a not inconsiderable drain on the moveable wealth of Welsh peasants. The drain was in one way all the greater, for law strictly prohibited Welshmen from alienating hereditary land to solve the problem of marital gifts and to provide a competence for their daughters. It was a society in which the affection of father for daughter was strictly circumscribed by the overriding need to preserve the integrity of the patrilineage lands.

---

[48] Ior § 47/3.
[49] S.C.2/217/8, m. 9.
[50] S.C.2/216/4, m. 24 (1323); 220/10, m. 1 (1390); 217/7, m. 15 (1342); 217/6, m. 19v. (1341).
[51] S.C.2/218/4, m. 8v. (marriage gift included "ij lintheamea, ij bolster' ij curthpan et ij robas pro diebus festivarum", 1354).
[52] S.C.2/219/3, m. 7v. (1366).
[53] S.C.2/219/4, m. 21 (1367); 217/6, m. 28 (1341).

Financially embarrassing the marriage portion might be, but it was a *sine qua non* for most matches. Indeed the giving or withholding of the marriage portion could be regarded as a test of the validity of a marriage.[54] When John fitz Nicholas fitz Geoffrey of Ruthin found that his prospective wife had made off with another man and had also taken the goods which her mother had given her in free marriage, he very justifiably regarded himself as liberated from his marriage-contract in spite of the attempts of his prospective in-laws to keep him to it.[55] *Per contra*, a father who had not given his daughter a marriage-portion could regard that fact as evidence that he had not sanctioned the marriage of the daughter.[56] Over the marriage-portion itself the wife appears to have had certain rights: this is suggested by the law-texts and supported by the court rolls. In 1376 Dafydd ab Iorwerth ap Cadwgan was found guilty of breaking a contract with his late wife regarding £4 worth of common goods, the condition of the contract being that he would not alienate any part of his wife's share of the goods until a separation (*divorcium*) had been agreed between them.[57] The case does not necessarily refer to the marriage-portion; but it suggests clearly that within marriage, or at least pending a separation, a wife could have specified legal rights over a proportion of the joint property. Particularly, we suspect, over any property she herself may have brought with her. Our suspicion is strengthened not only by the case we have already quoted of a mother who gave her daughter half of her (i.e. the mother's) property in free marriage but also by a passing reference in the list of the goods of a deceased man to 26*s*. 8*d*. "of the profit on his mother's *cynhysgaeth*".[58]

And so we pass naturally to the status of the wife in marriage. All that emerges from the court rolls is confirmation of the obvious legal tenet that for most purposes a wife's status was related to that of her husband rather than to that of her family. The issue arose normally over the vexed question of *amobr*, not so much in respect of payment at first marriage (for there the obligation clearly rested with the woman's family)[59] but in the event of a subsequent marriage. A certain Gwerfyl in Dyffryn Clwyd

---

[54] Cf. W. Ullmann, *Medieval Papalism*, (1949), 63 n. 1: "Older canonistic learning, following feudal sentiment, decreed that no matrimony was contracted and no sacrament created, unless dowry was given." See also Helmholz, *Marriage Litigation*, 47-57.

[55] S.C.2/218/7, m. 16v.; 218/8, m. 12 (1359-60).

[56] S.C.2/217/10, m. 19v. (1345).

[57] S.C.2/219/11, m. 21v.

[58] S.C.2/219/5, m. 19v. (1368).

[59] Indeed it was specifically asserted that the first *amobr* was legally exactable on the father's inheritance and payable by any *uchelwr* (Welsh free tenant) who gave his daughter in marriage: S.C.2/218/7, m. 14v. (1359); 222/5, m. 14v. (1446).

was twice married: she claimed that she held English land and was therefore of English status. Not so, however; for her first husband was Welsh
and she remained of the same status as he was in his lifetime until she
remarried and was therefore liable to pay *amobr*. The same argument
was repeated in a case of 1366.[60] Four years later the jurors of Bromfield
and Yale added a refinement: a woman who had been legally separated
from her second husband (an unfree tenant) reverted to the status she
enjoyed as the wife of her first husband (a free tenant).[61]

A great deal may be sifted from the documents about the rights of
women *vis à vis* moveable property and over the necessity for a husband
to secure the consent of his wife in the devising of any land he held *jure
uxoris*; but it is very difficult to make of it a coherent body of law,
especially since the status of the woman—whether she was married, a
widow or a spinster, English or Welsh—is rarely specified. That is why
we are driven back once more to the question of *amobr*, for it was
around this issue that the law of women most readily encrusted. *Amobr*
was one of the most oppressive and objectionable dues of late-medieval
Wales; an obvious barometer of its unpopularity is that in the land-glut
that succeeded the Black Death, tenants occasionally won the concession
that they might hold their land free of the obligation to pay *amobr* on
behalf of their womenfolk.[62] Paradoxically it gave women a certain
status in the courts which might otherwise have been denied to them. For
it appears that, at least on occasion, a jury of women might be empanell-
ed to determine whether a woman had or had not committed the sexual
offence that warranted the payment of *amobr*.[63] They, I assume, might
be regarded as being in no way interested or at least directly involved
parties. It is a practice, incidentally, not unknown in England.[64] *Amobr*
was levied for sexual offences as well as for marriage[65] and clearly it
could become a grave financial embarrassment for a family unfortunate
enough to have a daughter of lax morals. In several of the Marcher lord-

---

[60] S.C.2/218/7 m. 17 (1359); 219/4, m. 3v. This latter case is a particularly noteworthy
example of the conundrums posed by the question of defining a woman's racial status
when that issue was compounded by two marriages and subsequent widowhood.
[61] B.L. Add. MS. 10,013, f. 174.
[62] *Lordship and Society in the March of Wales*, 449-54.
[63] S.C.2/219/3, m. 16—16v. (1366).
[64] PM ii. 395.
[65] *Amobr* may be compared with *merchet* which has recently been the subject of a detailed
study by Eleanor Searle, "Merchet in Medieval England", (1979) 82 *Past and Present*
3-43. However, one of Professor Searle's central contentions—that "merchet had the
function of controlling manorial land tenure and inheritance" (p. 6)—does not apply to
amobr and could not do so in a society where land was transmitted by and through
males.

ships—Denbigh, Maelor Gymraeg, and Clun among them—and in the Principality the solution was to have her declared a common prostitute (*meretrix et incontinentis*). She might be handed a white rod as an emblem of her hopeless state.[66] It was a state which was, of course, recognised in Welsh law; but what is perhaps most interesting is that in Bromfield the justification for the practice is said to be "so that her family should not henceforth be charged with *amobr*" (*ne amplius parentele eorum calumpnientur de amobr*). For better-behaved ladies, marriage was the normal occasion for the exaction of *amobr* and on that occasion the due fell on the father or near male relatives. What with marriage-portion, a wedding-feast for the *neithiorwyr*, a *degwm rhoddi* for the parson, and an *amobr* for the lord, a wedding in late medieval Wales must have appeared often as a financial catastrophe. The only way in which the obligation could be shifted was by the rule that the payment of *amobr* was a due that fell on the father's land, not on his person. Hence whoever held the land was dunned for the *amobr*. Out of several cases which prove this argument one may be chosen: when Tangwystl ferch Einion was found guilty of adultery one-third of her *amobr* was exacted from the man who held a lease of one-third of the father's land.[67] In view of the fact that the sins of a lessor's daughter might be visited on the lessee, the campaign to exonerate land from *amobr* was a very understandable one. Once married, the father and his land were free of all responsibility for *amobr* and it was then the innocent husband who had to pay for the lapses of his errant wife.[68]

Such a wife was clearly a liability and the sooner she was jettisoned the better. And so we come to the ultimate stage in the *cursus matrimonii*: the separation or more specifically what I may call the separation *inter vivos*. Divorce (*divorcium*) was the word that contemporaries used: construed in the modern sense it is a word which would offend the susceptibilities of the canon lawyers of the twelfth and thirteenth centuries. We must, I think, give them some offence, for while it is true that the word *divorcium* was used for separation as well as divorce,[69] there can be no doubt that marriages were terminated. Furthermore they were not

---

[66] For this practice see *Lordship and Society in the March of Wales*, 137, and (1966) 51 *History* 155. The use of the white rod also prevailed in Clun: Shropshire Record Office 552/1/1 (1329).

[67] S.C.2/218/4, m. 11 (1354). For other cases see S.C.2/218/7, m. 14 (1359); 218/4, m. 11v.

[68] S.C.2/219/3, m. 18v. See above n. 37.

[69] That is, for a divorce *a mensa et thoro* (i.e., separation) as opposed to a divorce *a vinculo* (dissolution of marriage). The latter allowed the parties to remarry; the former only permitted them to live apart.

necessarily terminated for canonical reasons and the partners certainly then regarded themselves as free to enter into new marriage contracts.[70] Several facts suggest that divorces were not very difficult to come by and that they were regarded as the termination of a contract, not the annulment of a sacrament. The reason for divorce, the *casus divorcii*, is rarely within the competence of the secular court; but it may, as in England, appear as a subsidiary issue in a plea of contract.[71] Thus the marriage of one Ithel ab Ieuan Sais was terminated after three years by the adultery of his wife: we know it to be so because his father-in-law tried, rather ungraciously, to recover the marriage portion.[72] In another case that has already been quoted twelve witnesses present at the marriage were asked to adjudge which party was guilty of giving grounds for divorce:[73] it was a request which in its substance, procedure and the competence of the courts ran clean contrary to canon law. What the divorce-rate was we shall never know; but that separation was regarded as a distinct possibility is suggested by the contingency clauses written into marriage agreements about such an eventuality. We know little about the precise terms of separation and certainly have none of the luxuriant details that the law-texts provide on the division of goods. Nevertheless there is a clear hint on more than one occasion that the marriage-portion of the wife was in some measure recoverable. In one case the separating partners had agreed that the wife should receive £1 "in respect of the goods given to her by her friends" (*pro bonis per amicos eiusdem sibi illatis*).[74] In another divorce, the bride's father, who had given the couple and the heirs of their body half a burgage as a marriage portion, now divided that half-burgage into two quarters, one for the husband and one for his estranged and errant wife, but for their lives only, with reversion to himself and his own heirs.[75] In the case of moveable goods the arrangements were doubtless more complex, for those goods were, in a way that land was not, joint property. When Ithel ab Ieuan Sais and his wife were separated "such goods as had not been consumed (*non devastata*) were to be divided between them in the usual fashion" (*modo debito*).[76]

---

[70] For the concept of "self-divorce" (as opposed to an ecclesiastically-sanctioned divorce) see Helmholz, *Marriage Litigation*, 59 *et seq* and Jean Scammell, "Freedom and Marriage in Medieval England", (1974) 27 *Economic History Review* (2nd ser.) 523-38, esp. 532-3.
[71] PM ii. 380-83.
[72] S.C.2/216/14, m. 23v. (1334).
[73] S.C.2/217/8, m. 9; see above n. 49.
[74] S.C.2/216/4, m. 15 (1323).
[75] S.C.2/217/8, m. 9 (1343).
[76] S.C.2/216/14, m. 23v. (1334).

Modo debito: that little phrase is an apt comment on these cases with which I have troubled you. Once we threaten to penetrate into the area of marital customs and habits in any detail, our court rolls fail us. We have always to be satisfied with externals and accidentals, with the occasional and fortuitous rays of light which cases of contract, debt and *amobr* cast on the practice of marriage and on the status of women. Even if we could assume (which we cannot) that marriage customs were uniform and changing at an uniform pace throughout Wales in the fourteenth and fifteenth centuries, it would be difficult indeed to construct a coherent body of marriage custom from the cases, overwhelmingly from north-east Wales, which have been quoted in this paper. Yet fragmentary and unsatisfactory as is the evidence, it allows of certain broad conclusions.

It is clear that the corpus of the "law of women" (*cyfraith gwragedd*) as it is found in the redactions of the law texts and as it has been explained in other essays in this volume was undergoing a period of profound change in the late-medieval period. Some of the terms and practices of the native law are still visible in the crabbed and cryptic entries of the court rolls; but more striking is the total disappearance of much of the native legal terminology and the conjuring of new terms to apply to and to reflect a changing body of custom and practice. Above all, the international law and norms of the church and the jurisdiction of its courts were slowly but profoundly altering the way in which the concepts of marriage and legitimacy were regarded. These changes were in turn encouraged and accelerated by the influx, both conscious and indirect, of English legal habits with their emphasis on inheritance by and through women, on the dower-rights of widows, on the practices of jointure and of marriage-portions in real estate, on the exclusive rights of legitimate heirs and on the ostracized status of bastards. The *Corpus Juris Canonici* on the one hand and the Statute of Wales on the other announced social norms and legal prohibitions which could only profoundly change the native Welsh "law of women" and with it many of the basic assumptions on which the Welsh social order was based. That change is assuredly, if dimly, perceived in our records and is but one chapter in the transformation of Welsh society in the later middle ages.

R. R. DAVIES

THE EUROPEAN CONTEXT OF THE WELSH LAW OF MATRIMONIAL PROPERTY

THE PURPOSE of this paper is to demonstrate that the medieval Welsh law of marriage, and of the property rights and transfers to which it gave rise, can be set in the context of a general European legal tradition. The legal definition of monogamy endorses the observations of social anthropologists: marriage is a social rather than a cultural institution,[1] i.e. a marriage affects the community as well as the spouses, by bringing about actual or potential changes in family relationships, property distribution and (where there are children of the union) changes affecting the size of the community and consequently the balance between its collective ability to work, to house, feed and defend its members, and so on, and is not merely a private matter which the community need not or should not regard.

A. *Monogamy: meaning of "marriage"*

Where monogamous unions are normative,[2] as they are in *Cyfraith Hywel*, the word "marriage" stands for two things: (1) the juristic act which confers a change of status on the spouses, from being single to being married; or more accurately in the context of archaic law,[3] the legal recognition of a union whether or not the formalities prescribed by law or custom have been observed; and (2) the continuation of that new status and of the rights it confers and the duties it imposes on the spouses. Some legal systems use a separate technical term for this relationship: in English law it came to be called *coverture*. In German the act of marrying is *Trauung* (fam. *Hochzeit*; and cf. verb *heiraten*) as distinct

---

[1] Cf. E. E. Evans-Pritchard, *Social Anthropology* (BBC Lectures, London, 1951) 16-17.
[2] Polygamy, concubinage etc. are discussed briefly below, p.120 and n.27.
[3] "Archaic" is used here as intermediate in the series "primitive-archaic-modern", where "primitive" means pre-literate or nearly so, and "archaic" means lacking certain social and economic integers regarded as essential characteristics of modern society. Cf. the present author's paper delivered at the Fifth Colloquium on Welsh Medieval Law, Bangor, April 1979. An amplified version of that paper, which deals with land law, inheritance and the property consequences of marriage in *Cyfraith Hywel*, is to appear shortly as one of a series of monographs intended to present the Colloquium's proceedings to a wider public. References in these notes to "Walters" are to this monograph.

from the consequent status, *Stand der Ehe*; in French, *le mariage, les noces* as distinct from *l'état de mariage*.[4] This status is not always regarded as being conferred in full at the outset of the "marriage" in the first sense of the word. In some systems, including the Germanic law of the Frankish period[5] and systems influenced by pre-Tridentine Western Canon Law,[6] the stages by which full married status was achieved were expressed by distinguishing betrothal (*verlobung* in Frankish law, *desponsatio* or *sponsalia per verba de futuro* in Canon law) from the composite actions of marriage and consummation, i.e. the nuptials (*trauung; exponsalia* or *sponsalia per verba de praesenti, subsequente copula*) though it would be to misunderstand the subtlety of this earlier law to think of betrothed couples as in all cases free to change their minds (assuming that it was their consent, rather than that of their guardians, which effected the betrothal[7]). There might be three stages: (i) betrothal, (ii) public or notorious demonstration, by ceremony or subsequent conduct, of the spouses' intention to regard themselves and be regarded as married and (iii) subsequent consummation. Furthermore where, as in republican Roman law, more than one kind of marriage was recognised, the precise status which marriage conferred on the spouses and their children depended on the choice of form. Both sets of characteristics, the recognition that there are stages in the progression towards full married status and the existence of two basic types of marriage, are recognised in *Cyfraith Hywel*. There are only incidental references to betrothal, as in Bleg 119.11-14 and Col §§42-45, viz. the triad dealing with the three so-called shames of a maiden, the first being when her father tells her he has betrothed her to a man. (The words *cywilydd* and *gwarthrudd*,[8] literally "disgrace", "shame", should

---

[4] Scots law and other systems influenced by Romano-Canonical law use the phrase "stante matrimonio". In Roman law, the verb to describe H's marriage of W is *in matrimonio duco*; for W's marriage to H it is *nubo*; the giving in marriage of the woman by her paterfamilias is *in matrimonium colloco*. Formal English (e.g. in the 1662 Book of Common Prayer) likewise distinguishes "to marry" (H to W) "to be married to" (W to H) and "to give/be given in marriage" (W's father etc. to H).

[5] Hübner, 597 (§91.I.2.B in German text and Eng. tr.); Brissaud, 93ff. (§101ff.); Calisse, 549ff. (§324ff.).

[6] i.e. prior to the decree *Tametsi* of the Council of Trent, 1563; text in Denzinger/Schönmetzer, *Enchiridion Symbolorum* . . ., 36th ed. (Barcelona, 1976) 417-8 (new canons on matrimony, 415ff.).

[7] Hübner, 599 (§91.I.2.B.a) and cf. 602 (§91.I.2.B.b).

[8] for *cywilydd* in various contexts, cf. Bleg 111.20, 119.8; Col §§42, 45, 66; for *gwarthrudd*, cf. Bleg 116.3; DwCol §§148, 169-71, 180, 181. Latin D 376.17 uses the word *pudor*. For the interval between the "giving to a man" and the marriage-feast and wedding night, cp. Jenkins *supra* p.72.

perhaps be understood in an amoral sense, rather as "disparage" in English legal texts merely states the fact of an unequal union. The Welsh words proclaim the fact of lost innocence and recognise the arrival of puberty or nubility; they do not lower the status of the girl, they just assert a change in it.)

In *Cyfraith Hywel* marriage in the sense of nuptials or *Trauung* might arise in one of two basic ways. The normal way was assumed to be the gift of the girl by her kindred, or her *sib* (to maintain the Germanic parallel): marriage *o rodd cenedl*.[9] The abnormal case was for a girl or woman to elope, or be abducted and subsequently decide to remain with her abductor: *llathlud*.[10] In this second case the laws distinguished between a maiden[11] (*morwyn*, Latin *puella*, i.e. a *merch*, a girl, who is a virgin) whom her kindred can compel to return home, and a woman[12] (*gwraig*, Latin *mulier*) who may decide her own fate.

Once she has entered into the married state, by whichever means,[13] the wife's status is measured by reference to the length of time she has been married. For the first seven years[14] (that is, long enough for a girl married at or shortly after 12 to have borne children) she is described as being *adan ei hagweddi*; that is to say, if an event occurs of a kind which the law contemplates, which ends the union in fact or entitles her to treat it as ended, she becomes entitled to a share in the pool of movables common to herself and her husband. That share is expressed in the laws in

---

[9] Bleg 60.23 (*kymer gwr wreic o rod kenedyl*); cf. McAll *supra*, pp.9-10, 17-18; Jenkins *supra*, p.72. *Sib* is the term now widely used by anthropologists, but, to maintain historical accuracy, the word was *sippea* or *sippa* in OHG, *sippe* in MHG.

[10] Bleg 63.3 (*llathrut heb gyghor y chenedyl*); see nn. 11 & 12, *infra*. Caradas, concubinage or unlawful connexion, is not discussed here: cf. McAll *supra*, p.16. For the linguistic connections of *llathlud* and the alternative form *llathrudd* see the Glossary.

[11] Bleg 63.3-9; Lat B 221.31ff.; D 343.4ff.; E 470.29ff. For the control of girls before marriage, before and after puberty, see Jenkins *supra* p.71 and McAll, *supra* pp.7-10.

[12] Bleg. 63.7 et s; Lat A §52/34; B 221.35; D 343.7.

[13] Cf. Jenkins, *supra*, p.85.

[14] The text in Bleg is not entirely clear; 64.30-65.2 says that where a woman is married *o rodd cenedl* her husband must vouch for her *gwadawl* (*gwaddol* in ModW) during the first seven years. Jenkins points out that the parent text of Bleg (Lat D 334.15) has *sub dote* for *gwadawl*, which argues a mistranslation, so that in this case *gwadawl* means *agweddi*. The exact *terminus ad quem* of the wife's time *adan ei hagweddi* is also confused. Bleg says *Or byd rodyeit ar wreic y wr, bit y gwr dan y gwadawl* [i.e. *agweddi*] *hyt ympen y seith mlyned; ac o cheiff hi teir nos o'r seithuet vlwydyn, hanher y holl da a geiff y wreic pan yscarhont* (64.30-65.2) (". . . if she reaches the third night of the seventh year . . ."). Literally this means a total of six years and three nights, whereas in general all the texts, not just Bleg, refer to a seven year period (cf. Jenkins, *supra* p.76 n.28, but detailed examination of the manuscripts is required before the point can be settled, if then. Jenkins also remarks that the very confusion may be evidence that by the thirteenth century the subject had become of no practical significance anyway.

terms of a fixed sum of money,[15] varying with her father's status and the circumstances of the union. This is her *agweddi*,[16] which is not so much a deferred endowment as a security for non-desertion. Where the union arose other than by gift of kindred the *agweddi* was reduced, though according to Bleg "the men of the South" (in contrast with the men of Gwynedd) had formerly allowed an eloping wife the same *agweddi* as one married by gift of kindred.[17] Subject to this earlier exception, a woman not married by gift of kindred was entitled to a smaller amount in the event of separation. Some lawyers called this lesser sum *agweddi* also, while others perhaps regarded only the full sum as deserving that name, and there may be some significance in the fact that the reduced amounts are fixed in terms of cattle, whereas the standard "legal *agweddïau*" are

---

[15] The fixed sums in the legal texts do not preclude the possibility of a contractual alternative payment; cf. Bleg 114.28-29, a triad which reads "Three thing which break [i.e. dispense with, permit departure from] the [written] law—contract (*amot*) reasonable custom (*defawt gyfiawn*) and death"; cf. "Amod a dyrr ddeddf", Ior §69/12, Col §140. Unless written law is expressed in unambiguously imperative terms, brooking no alternative, it is generally the case that prescribed duties like payments can be varied by the agreement of the parties, or by *defod gyfiawn*. Similarly in Germanic law of the later middle ages there was the brocard "Willkür bricht Stadtrecht, Stadtrecht bricht Landrecht, Landrecht bricht gemein Recht"—"Arbitrary power breaks Town law, borough custom; Town law breaks local state law; local state law breaks common law", and cf. Hans-Rudolf Hagemann, "Gedinge bricht Landrecht", (1970) 87 ZRG 114 (so that the local and particular rule always overrides the more general); cf. the Ordinance of 1495 setting up the Reichskammergericht, which marked the formal reception of the glossators' Roman law as the common law of the German Empire, in which the court was ordered to adjudicate in accordance with that law, "and such customs of inferior jurisdictions *as are pleaded*, if they are fair, tolerable and proper": the customs overrode the common law, subject to this qualification, if pleaded (cf. Sohm, *Institutes of Roman Law*, 3rd Eng., tr. of 12th Ger. ed., tr. J. C. Ledlie (Oxford 1907), 152; Hübner, 20; Vinogradoff, RLME, c.5. Cf. Jenkins, *supra,*p.77, citing Col §23.

[16] The legal amounts are given in Bleg as £14 for a King's daughter (67.14, cf. Lat D 346.2-3) £7 for the daughters of certain royal officers (Bleg 12.31, 21.25, 49.14-15), £3 for a free man's daughter and £1½ for a villein's daughter (Bleg 60.24-5 and 27). See Jenkins *supra* p.79 for the equation between these amounts and standard cattle values at five shillings per animal. Bleg 60.23-61.1 further states that in the case of desertion by the husband after marriage *o rodd cenedl*, in addition to *agweddi* quantified as above, the husband must pay *cowyll* and *amobr* to his wife: £1½ and 60d respectively if she is free-born, 120d and 24d if unfree; and from Bleg 67.11-13 we learn that the *cowyll* of the king's daughter is land, as much as her husband metes out, and her *amobr* £6. But the corresponding Latin texts only specify payment of *agweddi* in these circumstances (A §51/1; B 221.6; D.341.22, E 470.7). The reference to *amobr* in Bleg may well be mistaken. The Cyfnerth text (§73/5-7) *infra*, from the Bodorgan MS., corresponds with WML 89.25-90.4 (from MS. *V*) as well as with the passage cited from Bleg. However, in MS. *W* (WML 91.1-3) we read: ". . . talet y heguedi idi. Os merch breyr uyd teir punt uyd y heguedi. Punt a hanher yn y chowyll. wheugeint yn y gobyr." This seems to be the intended sense, and I am grateful to Professor Jenkins for drawing my attention to it. For *agweddi* in general see Walters, .13(3)(b); for the root of *cynyweddi*, *dyweddi* and *agweddi* cf. E. Benveniste, *Le vocabulaire des institutions indo-européennes*, 1. *économie, parenté, société*, (Paris, 1969) 240.

[17] Bleg 63.13 (Lat D 343.12).

expressed as sums of money.[18]

If, however, it endured for seven years,[19] the union can be characterised as *priodas* (without coming to a conclusion about its precise earlier status); and the semantic connexion between the two senses of *priod*—"married" and "one's own property" may be significant. If the spouses thereafter separate the wife is entitled to "half" the common movables, measured not by simple division but by the allocation to each spouse of specific items.[20]

The comparisons to be made here include a number of distinctions found in Roman law between marriages of different kinds, principally between marriage with and without *manus*, the latter having largely replaced the former by the end of the Republic,[21] though what is comparable in the Welsh and Roman law is the recognition of plurality of marriage forms each with differing personal and proprietary consequences, using "proprietary" loosely.

The etymological and conceptual links between *manus* and OHG *munt* (Latinised as *mundium*) are also significant.[22] In Germanic law, legitimate (i.e. legally-recognised) sexual unions were differentiated from other unions, a distinction not to be ignored in a society which in its early days recognised polygamy.[23] Abduction, *frauenraub*, could lead to marriage, as in Welsh law,[24] as could gifts to "purchase" a wife from her kindred (*frauenkauf*), in the presence of neighbours who were primarily members of the *sib* of one or other spouse, like the Welsh *neithiorwyr* (wedding-guests) who were also *cyfneseifiaid* (kindred)[25] and who likewise stayed on after the feast to await evidence, albeit indirect, of the consummation of the marriage.

---

[18] Ior §48/7 implies that the eloping wife was entitled to *agweddi*; the same text specifies the three legal *agweddïau*: §48/9.

[19] Subject to what has been said in n.14, *supra*.

[20] Bleg 64.30-65.32; Lat A §51/2, §52/2ff; B.221.8; D 341.24 & E 470.8.

[21] Gaius, Institutes I.108 et s. (*manus*); cf. Justinian, Institutes, 1.9 & 10; Sohm, *Institutes of Roman Law* (*supra*, n.15) §92-94; Schulz, *Classical Roman Law* (Oxford, 1951) c.3; Buckland, *Textbook of Roman Law*, 3rd ed. rev'd Stein (Cambridge, 1963) c.3 esp. paras XLI to XLIII.

[22] Hübner, 585-6 (§90.I).

[23] ibid. 588 (§90.II).

[24] ibid. 593 (§91.I.1.A.). A contemporary European example of marriage by ceremonial capture has been recorded from observation of the North Greek nomadic herdsmen, the *Sarakatsanoi*; see J. K. Campbell, *Honour, Family & Patronage—a study of institutions and moral values in the Sarakatsán community* (Oxford, 1964); Angelika Chatzemichale, *Sarakatsanoi* (Athens, 1957) and cf. P. L. Fermor: *Roumeli—travels in Northern Greece* (London, 1966), c.1 at 3-27 (esp. 26-7) and 45-6.

[25] Hübner, 594 et s. (para. 91.I.1.B), 596-7 (para 91.2.A). For the similar position in non-Roman Italy after 476 AD, cf. Calisse, 549ff. (§§324-8), 555ff. (§§329, 331) for imperfect and morganatic marriages.

B. *The Anthropological context*

While a thorough comparative study of the relations between marriage and property would require consideration of systems of kinship and alliance, the varieties of guardianship of persons and property under patriarchal and matriarchal family government, and the relationship between notions of common property and inheritance in the joint undivided household and individual acquisition and disposition *inter vivos*, or by testament, nevertheless much of the law of marriage and the property transfers or claims to which it may give rise can be treated in relative isolation from extended family structures without undue distortion.[26]

Social anthropologists employ a variety of methods for the preliminary classification of marriage laws and customs, particularly in primitive or traditional societies. Three of these classes can be established by asking the following questions: (i) Does the society under scrutiny adhere to monogamy, or does it recognise concurrent or consecutive polygamy;[27] and is the distinction blurred by the recognition, albeit tacit, of concubinage or other irregular unions not capable of maturing into full marriage? (ii) Does the society limit the choice of partner to those outside the extended family (exogamy) or conversely to those, apart from kindred in the first and second degrees, and probably all ascendants and descendants in the direct line, within it (endogamy), rather than leave the choice wholly unrestricted? Kinship patterns, the status of children, and the destiny of property in succession, are closely affected by determinants like these. (iii) Do the modes of marriage recognised in the society fall within recognisable patterns? These are frequently classified along the lines of marriage by *capture* (in exogamous societies); by *exchange* (e.g. sister for sister); by *gift* from wife's family to husband (but the wife herself is pre-eminently the gift[28]); by *purchase* by the husband from the wife's family; or by *right*, e.g. where a man's right to marry a female

---

[26] For the doubtless desirable comprehensive approach, the starting point must be Lévi-Strauss, *Les Structures élémentaires de la Parenté*, 1949, (Eng. tr. of 2nd (1967) ed., by Bell, Sturmer & Meedham as *The Elementary Structures of Kinship*, London, 1969): the work is dedicated to the American anthropologist of Welsh extraction, Lewis H. Morgan whose fundamental studies, *Systems of Consanguinity* and *Ancient Society* were published in 1869 and 1877 respectively. As an illustration of a relevant anthropological treatment of descent including its legal elements, cp. "The Patrilineal Principle in Early Teutonic Kinship" by H. H. Meinhard in *Studies in Social Anthropology . . . in memory of E. E. Evans-Pritchard*, ed. Beattie & Lienhardt (Oxford 1975) 1.

[27] using this term loosely to cover polygyny and polyandry; cf. R. Fox, *Kinship & Marriage* (Harmondsworth, 1967) index s.vv.

[28] Lévi-Strauss, *Elementary Structures of Kinship* (supra, n.26), 65.

cousin, or to reject her before another can marry her, is recognised.[29] The list is not exhaustive, but the first, third and fourth modes (capture, gift, and purchase) are present in *Cyfraith Hywel*, though since our texts show the laws in a developed, if still archaic, form, it is not surprising to find that these categories of bride-acquisition overlap.

C. *Forms of divorce*

As with the word *marriage*, "divorce" can be made to do duty for a variety of ways in which (apart from death, real or presumed) a marriage comes to an end. Again as with marriage, divorce may be a juristic act performed by the spouses or by legal authority, or it may come about *de facto*, the legal order recognising actual breakdown. (I wish to stress that it is archaic law that is under consideration. Modern divorce law, often conflating an unspecified morality with policy, is less easy to analyse in these terms.) Facts which precipitate the termination of the union may include the discovery that the original union was null, on physical, dissensual, or religious grounds as well as on the more obviously legal ones (e.g. that there is a prior living undivorced spouse) as well as behaviour inconsistent with acceptance by a spouse of the duties which law and custom in that society lay upon those who are married. Death, actual or presumptive, may be added to this second group, since it ends the marriage in fact. The elaboration of the grounds of nullity in Western European legal systems, medieval and modern, is largely due to the Church, and the Welsh laws are almost silent as to any ecclesiastical influence on marriage;[30] but divorce as a juristic act effected by either or both spouses, either for fault or by consent, is clearly stated.[31]

D. *Marriage and the transfer of property*

So much for the context. I now propose to concentrate on the money or property element in marriage in the Welsh laws, under the four headings (1) the wife as property; (2) bride-purchase by the husband; (3) bride-gift and *dos*; and (4) endowment of one spouse taking effect upon the death of the other.

---

[29] *Ibid.* 398-9, and see generally Lewis, index, s.v. marriage.

[30] Cf. e.g. the passage in Ior §87, which McAll discusses *supra,* pp.16-17. The non-intrusion of Canon law into thirteenth-century manuscripts of the Welsh laws is a striking characteristic, in contrast with many other European written laws of even date.

[31] I have attempted an account of divorce as regulated in certain texts of Cyfraith Hywel, with the references, in Walters, .13(4).

(1) *Wife as property*

Many primitive and archaic systems of law treat women as items of movable property, perhaps the most valuable item (so long, that is, as the sexual balance is maintained, or when there are fewer women than men). Indeed modern systems of law have been slow to remove obligatory male guardianship of the person and the property of females, and only in the nineteenth and twentieth centuries in England and Wales, Scotland, France, and Germany have women achieved or retrieved more or less equal legal status with men. It is obviously significant in terms of family patterns to discover a point in time or an epoch after which women can dispose of themselves in marriage. With the recognition of marriage by *llathlud* where the girl eloped, this point had clearly been passed by the time of our texts of *Cyfraith Hywel*.

(2) *Bride-purchase*

A bride could in some societies be acquired by the would-be husband performing work for the bride's family, as Jacob laboured twice seven years, for the unloved Leah and the beloved Rachel.[32] This service may be commuted to or made alternate with a "bride-price" (or "bride-wealth" as some anthropologists prefer to call it), again paid by or on behalf of the husband to the father or family of the bride.[33] Payment may be in money or kind, depending on the state of the society's economy, and payment by instalments may be acceptable.[34] This payment is what comes to be called a *donatio ante nuptias* when custom requires payment in full before delivery, the *traditio* or *coemptio*, of the bride (like any simple sale and delivery), later renamed *donatio propter nuptias* when it is recognised that payment may take place before, at or after marriage,[35] showing some shift away from a strictly mercantile attitude. Whatever its name, this *donatio* must be distinguished from the *dower* or *tertia pars* which was a present right to future enjoyment of part of her husband's property (usually his lands) which a wife acquired, by contract, custom or statute, on marriage in some legal systems. It is discussed in para (4), *infra*.

---

[32] Genesis xxix.15-30.
[33] cf. Lewis, 248ff.
[34] Lewis, 252.
[35] The Scottish legal text, Regiam Majestatem (c.1305), a native compilation drawing on Roman and Canon law and on Glanvill for its sources, makes this distinction specifically in c.15 §1: "Olim dicebatur donatio ante nuptias hodie propter nuptias. Et quia hodie fit ante et post nuptias, ideo merito donatio propter nuptias nuncupatur." (Skene's text, ed. Lord President Cooper, Edinburgh 1947: 11 Stair Society 118.)

In Welsh law we have to consider in this context *agweddi* and *cowyll*. *Agweddi* has been discussed above as the wife's share in the common stock if the union ended in certain circumstances before the end of seven years: it was a potential right only, and if the union lasted seven years the wife's entitlement on its termination was not *agweddi* but a "half" of the common pool, which was made up of movables of all kinds (including livestock), but did not include land. *Cowyll*, on the other hand, was a *prifai* of the wife, an unconditional property right which (once duly established[36]) she did not lose even if her husband's desertion or dismissal of her was justified by her fault. Its other special characteristic was that only a bride who was virgin (or whose lack of that quality was not protested by her husband) could claim *cowyll*.[37] If duly claimed, *cowyll* became her separate property, *parapherna* to use the Southern European term, like her *argyfrau* (Latin, *animalia*), the property which she brought with her upon marriage.[38]

The close parallel with cowyll is the *donum matutinum*, "morning gift" (*morgengifu, morgengabe* etc.) of Germanic law,[39] though without some of the special variations of that institution, e.g. where it was no more than a pension in return for a morganatic marriage. Italian barbarian law also had the institution of *mefio* or *meta*, a wedding-day gift by husband to wife, the content and purpose of which would have been agreed at betrothal. So great and valuable did these gifts tend to be in some cases that the Laws of Liutprand laid down maximum amounts.[40] *Morgengabe* in contrast was payable, as the name implies, on the morning following the wedding-night. Its payment and the publicity attending it (the presence of the family) ended the husband's right to repudiate a non-virgin bride. In Lombardic law its amount became limited to a quarter of the husband's property whereas under Frankish law it was one-third. The amount was reduced progressively by subsequent legislation to one-eighth.[41] It has been suggested that *mefio*, (cf. *wittum*,

---

[36] As a *prifai* (an unconditional property right of which not even her own fault could deprive her) *cowyll* had however to be specifically appropriated by the bride who, before rising after the wedding-night, should make her claim to it; failure to do so meant that the property which would otherwise constitute her *cowyll* would be held by both spouses in common. Cf. Bleg 64.8-10.

[37] Ior §45/2, §50/4; cf. the distinction between the *prifai gwraig* in Lat B 243.17ff. and the additional *prifai* "puelle", *cowyll*.

[38] For a more detailed account see Jenkins, *supra* pp.68-70, 73-5 arguing that *argyfrau* formed part of the common pool of movables once the marriage endured beyond 7 years, and Walters .13(3)(c).

[39] Hübner, 625 et s. (§94.II.3 et s.); Brissaud, 754-5 (§521), 760 (§525); Calisse, 574-5.

[40] Calisse, 572.

[41] Calisse, 574.

douaire) represented a settlement made by husband on wife, whereas the payment to her father or other guardian was a purchase of *mundium* over her.[42] Of course later medieval feudal law often sees the control of the wife's property, at least during marriage, pass from her to her husband as guardian, she resuming some control, not necessarily over her own original property, at his death. Such considerations naturally affect the practical consequences of gifts by husband to wife at marriage. However, the position in *Cyfraith Hywel* has not reached the point where at marriage (in the absence of a special contract) the wife loses nearly all property rights to her husband. Rather, so far as household movables are concerned, there seems to be community of property, as the elaborate rules for distribution in the event of *ysgar* or separation after seven years witness;[43] and as to immovables, this is not the place to consider the complex nature of land ownership. Again *mefio, wittum, douaire* in the sense of a gift made or enforceably promised at marriage, should be distinguished from dower in the sense of a widow's claim, not to property conditionally donated to her at marriage, but to a part, usually a third, of her husband's property, eventually just his lands, as recompense for past labour and to support her widowhood: the *tertia pars collaborationis* of Frankish law and ultimately of English common law dower: cf. (4) *infra*.

We may summarise the wife's entitlement in *Cyfraith Hywel* to *donationes propter nuptias* by saying that for the first seven years of marriage she might (at need, i.e. if the appropriate circumstances arose) and if not at fault herself, claim her *agweddi* (in a modified form in North Wales if married by *llathlud*), and that thereafter she could take her legal share if the spouses separated whatever the cause. Her *cowyll*, once claimed, she could always appropriate, but perhaps it is unrealistic to think of that happening except at separation.

In societies which we may characterise as "feudal" in that some sort of personal relationship of vassal and superior, lord and man, is pervasive, a further payment may be legally prescribed when a girl is married, to which the lord of the girl's father is entitled. Under the names *leyrewite* (in the case of irregular union) and *merchet* at the lower end of the social scale, and "marriage", i.e. payment to the lord for permission for a free vassal to marry, at its upper end, such payments were a commonplace of pre- and post-conquest English law, where *merchet* and "marriage" were

---

[42] Calisse, 572.
[43] Bleg 64.30-65.32; Ior §44/3-19; Lat A §52 "de separacione"; B 225.10-39; Jenkins, *supra* pp.78-83; Walters .13(3).

also regarded as the price of the superior's consent to the marriage of a vassal's daughter. A similar pattern appears in continental feudal law.[44] The lord's consent is connected with proprietary and personal right: the value of the fief was diminished by the loss of an unmarried woman (who at marriage might well pass under alien lordship) unless compensation were paid to the lord, and the lord in any case owed duties of protection to all his vassals since he was in a real sense their guardian.

At different epochs, the lord is either clearly guardian of all those women not *sui juris* (MHG *selbmündic* or—*ec*), i.e. not in the *mundium* or wardship of husband, father or other male agnate; or he is regarded as enjoying a species of *mundium* over all his vassals. When it is remembered that the earlier we trace these institutions, the more likely it is that the person exercising the *mundium*, the "lord" or superior of the more developed feudal law, is himself the senior male agnate, the more understandable these payments become, and closer to other payments (*donationes propter nuptias* in general) made at marriage by a man to the family of his wife.

The giving or withholding of consent by the lord is not invariably connected with the right to receive this payment; Lombardic law actually punished a *mundoald* (guardian) who capriciously refused his consent,[45] whereas many modern systems retain an unquestionable right in the guardian of a minor to give or withhold consent to the minor's marriage[46] but would regard a bargain to purchase that consent as *contra bonos mores*.[47]

The name for such payments in *Cyfraith Hywel* is *amobr*. Those bound to pay it and in what circumstances, its amount according to status, its alleged connexion with the so-called *droit de seigneur* and so on have all been sufficiently discussed in this volume[48] and elsewhere[49] recently, and will not be considered further save in the context of other payments due on the occasion of marriage in the Welsh laws.

---

[44] Brissaud, 118 & nn. 3-5 and 119 n.1 (§114.a.); Hübner, 677 (§100); Calisse, 276 (20 solidi payable to woman's guardian for failure to obtain consent to marriage, to buy off the feud, in Lombardic law), 284 (*guidrigild*—cf. wergild—equivalent to that of woman's nearest male agnate payable if her husband, having married her without her family's consent, slay her).

[45] Calisse, 540 and n.5.

[46] Cf. current text of French Civil Code, art. 148 (amended 1927) and case-law in Recueil Dalloz 1908.2.73 and 1951.532.

[47] French Civil Code, art.6, 1131, 1133, etc.

[48] Jenkins, *supra* 73-5 and Excursus I.

[49] Walters, .13(2).

(3) *Dos and maritagium: contribution from the wife's side*

Although *dos* is generally treated as a mark of the Roman legal tradition and the systems both to which Rome was indebted and which are derived from it, contributions by or on behalf of the wife made at marriage to help equip a new household or to provide a capital base from which that help can be produced, are also found in many European customary legal systems, side by side with the husband's endowment (immediate or potential) of his wife. Indeed a conscious linking of these two reciprocal payments can sometimes be detected. In Athenian law the φερνή provided by the wife's guardian (her father or nearest male agnate) as her dotal contribution, while it was administered during marriage by her husband, remained her separate property (προίξ), and to guarantee its integrity (since at divorce it reverted wholly to her control and at her death went to her heirs) she enjoyed a hypothec equivalent to its value over her husband's property, her ἀποτίμημα. Property given to a woman at marriage as specific gifts to her, ἀνακαλυπτήρια, and probably other classes of paraphernal property which she brought with her for her personal use at marriage, or which she afterwards acquired, were her separate property, as indeed were her husband's his, against which she had no claim at his death.[50] The Roman law of *dos* is too well known—or at least too accessible—to need restating here. Legislation progressively extending the definition and the protection of dotal property[51] and the developed pre-Justinianic rules were incorporated into the *Codex Theodosianus* and are also found in the compilation known as *Pauli Sententiae*, and were thence absorbed into Vulgar Roman law in the West until, by the early thirteenth century, law books like the *Exceptiones Petri* abandoned citations from the *Codex Theodosianus* and from the Breviary of Alaric in favour of the recovered texts of Justinian's *Corpus Iuris*.[52]

---

[50] See generally J. W. Jones, *Law & Legal Theory of the Greeks*, Oxford 1956; A. R. W. Harrison, *The Law of Athens—family and property*, 1969; W. K. Lacey, *The Family in Classical Greece*, London, 1968; D. M. MacDowell, *The Law in Classical Greece*, London 1978. L. Beauchet, *Histoire du droit privé de la République Athénienne*, 1969.

[51] *L. Iulia de fundo dotali*, cf. Gaius 2.63; D.24.3.66.pr. extending that *lex; SC Velleianum*, temp. Nero, cp. D.16.1.2, as a further reinforcement.

[52] The Western development prior to the 13th cent. was from *C. Theod.* via the Breviary of Alaric (*Lex Romana Visigothorum*) through the *Summa Trecensis* and *Lo Codi*; cf. Vinogradoff, RLME c.1 "The Decay of Roman Law" and the sources listed at 41-2; and for the *Exceptiones Petri*, c.2 "The Revival of Jurisprudence" and sources listed at 69-70. Cf. also Brissaud, 801ff. (§550). The Justinianic additions to the sources on *dos* include *Constitutiones* of A.D. 529, 530 and 537 which between them gave the wife a Greek-style hypothecary action to recover her *dos*, made all her immovable property inalienable and, in the Novel 61 (A.D. 537) gave her a right to demand the restitution of her *dos* where it was imperilled e.g. by her husband's maladministration.

In the customary law systems there is a considerable diversity of schemes by which a contribution might be made by the father, or if dead the brothers, or indeed some other donor, along with the wife at marriage, to which the name *maritagium*, or a variant, *liberum maritagium* or frankmarriage, is given in English law,[53] and *faderfium*,[54] *aussteuer*, or *heimsteuer*[55] in Germanic law. The latter was essentially no more than personal clothing and ornaments at first, but was extended at length to all property, as the wife's capacity to inherit became allowed, as early as the seventh century in Lombardic law. Calisse describes *faderfio* as originally a trousseau rather than a marriage portion, although it later extended to any property of any amount, and notes that by its payment the girl lost (or perhaps, had satisfied) any claim against the property of her family of origin.

A conscious connection between *maritagium* and endowment of the wife by her husband, as well as recognition of the confusing use of *dos* to describe both, is found not only in the late twelfth-century Glanvill in England, but in a borrowed version in the early fourteenth-century Scottish law book *Regiam Majestatem*:

> Dos duobus modis dicitur. Dicitur enim dos vulgariter id quod liber homo dat sponsae suae ad ostium ecclesiae tempore desponsationis . . . si non nominat [dotem], tertia pars liberi tenementi sui viri quod habuit tempore desponsationis intelligitur sibi pertinere . . .[56] In alia acceptatione accipitur dos secundum leges Romanas, secundum quas proprie appellatur dos id quod cum muliere datur viro, quod vulgariter dicitur maritagium . . . ["tocher" in Scots] . . . potest itaque quilibet liber homo terram habens quandam partem terrae suae dare cum filia sua vel cum qualibet alia muliere in maritagium, sive heredem habeat sive non.[57]

Evidence of such gifts in *Cyfraith Hywel* is slight. In Bleg. 64.30-31 we read that after marriage *o rodd cenedl* the husband had to guarantee his wife's *gwaddol*, "endowment", for the first seven years (cp. n.14, *supra*). This may be a synonym for *agweddi*, or it may be intended to cover all the property of the wife, including *argyfrau* and *cowyll* which she brought with her or received from her husband at marriage. But any parallel with *maritagium*, if one is discernible, is shadowy, although T. P. Ellis suggested that *gwaddol* also meant an unmarried daughter's right to a share in her father's movables as *dos* or *maritagium* so that she

---

[53] Cf. PM ii, 15 et s., 291-2, 420 n; Plucknett, *Legislation* 125-128; A. W. B. Simpson, *Introduction to the History of the Land Law*, (Oxford, 1961) 60-64.
[54] Brissaud, 755 (§522); Calisse, 573-4.
[55] Hübner, 624 (§94.II.1).
[56] Reg. Maj. (ed. cit. *supra*, n.35) c.16, 120-1; cp. Glanvill vi.1. (Hall 58-9).
[57] Reg. Maj. c.18, 131; cf. Glanvill viii.1. (Hall 69).

would not go to her marriage empty-handed.[58] It has been suggested[59] that generally *maritagium* could be used to compensate the husband for disparity where the wife came from a lower caste or class than his own. Certainly in the middle ages and after a moral duty was recognised, under which the well-to-do were urged to give or bequeath money to aid "the marriage of poor maids".[60]

(4) *Dower: payment to the wife from the husband's side*

The restricted description of dower given in the rubric above is intended to emphasise that in the earlier medieval period, the Germanic type of dower was a true gift to the wife, albeit sometimes conditional, which was enforceably promised if not actually transferred at or immediately after the marriage. It was made by or on behalf of the husband and its amount could be settled by agreement (e.g. at betrothal, where that was a recognised preliminary to consummated marriage) although fixed amounts for dower, or maxima, frequently appear in the written laws and custumals. Whatever its primitive connexions with bride-price and *pretium virginitatis*, it early became a regular species of *donatio propter nuptias* providing for a separate endowment of the wife upon separation or widowhood, distinct from any provision which her family of origin or her husband's heirs might otherwise have been constrained to make for her by law or custom, and in this respect is connected with the transfer of the *mund* or guardianship of her from her father or nearest male agnate to her husband.[61]

The quite separate notion that dower was an inevitable consequence of marriage (at least where there was dowerable property) that could always be claimed by a widow even where no formal gift or promise of dower had been made at marriage (itself a possibility hard to reconcile with the texts of earlier medieval law) belongs to a later epoch so accustomed to the gift that it was prepared to imply it in all cases; and it would be anachronistic to discuss it in relation to European laws around the time, or at the state of evolution, of *Cyfraith Hywel*,[62] except to distinguish it clearly from endowment at marriage.

---

[58] *Welsh Tribal Law*, i.402.
[59] Lewis, 251.
[60] The duty is commended e.g. in Langland's "Piers Plowman" (Bk.VII, in Truth's letter to the Merchants) and is repeated in the Preamble to the Statute of Charitable Uses of 1601 (43 Eliz I c.4).
[61] e.g. in Beaumanoir, *Coutumes de Beauvaisis*, 13th cent., (ed. Salmon; Paris 1899, 2 vols.) the provisions on *douaire* are put in the context of *garde:* c.13 & 15.
[62] Cp. F. Joüon des Longrais, *La conception anglaise de la Saisine*, Paris 1924 (argument summarised in English by Plucknett in (1927) 40 *Harvard Law Review* 921-5) esp. Pt. III, "Etude spéciale d'une saisine de franc tènement: la saisine de douaire" at 315-441.

Dower of this later kind is a claim by the widow against part of the late *husband's* property; indeed she frequently forfeited it if she remarried or was otherwise incontinent,[63] a loss which could scarcely be justified if she already had title to it dating from her wedding, whatever legal sophistries the medieval lawyers might produce about implied conditional gifts.[64] Such a dower is quite distinct from property, technically already hers, which the widow reduces into possession at or within a stated period[65] of her husband's death, and which formed part of her estate if she predeceased her husband, giving him analogous rights to a life estate in her lands.[66]

The first kind of dower, with which we are concerned, is then property to which the wife has had a title since her marriage, even if the gift was conditional. A common characteristic of this dower is that it corresponds to or is a substitute for a right of succession, which a wife would not otherwise enjoy against her husband's separate property, since she is not his heir in the technical sense,[67] so that her dower is provision for her widowhood, without which she would be the pensioner of the true heir (if he were well-disposed) or left unprovided for. As guardianship of her had been transferred from within her family of origin at her marriage (cf. n.61, *supra*) she would when widowed have no claim against them. Hence the great importance of adequate dower, settled at marriage. Widowhood was not the only circumstance which actualised dower, however; there are examples of it being enjoyed upon separation *inter vivos*.[68]

---

[63] In the language of the English writs of dower, it was said to be enjoyable only *dum casta*.

[64] Cp. Glanvill, vi; vii. 1-2, 18 (Hall 58-74, 92-4); Bracton f.92 (Woodbine/Thorne ii. 265ff.) & cf. Plucknett, *Legislation*, c.5 and Milsom, *Historical Foundations of the Common Law* (London, 1969) c.8.

[65] i.e. the "quarantine", forty days after her husband's death.

[66] In Normandy and Scotland as well as England, a widower enjoyed a life estate (by operation of law, never by contract) called "curtesy", "courtesy", *curialitas* in all the lands of his deceased wife provided a living child had been born to them: Coutume de Normandie art. 382, 391 (in Berault's reformed ed., Rouen 1620, but the text is ancient); for Scotland, Reg. Maj. c.58; for England, Glanvill vii. 18 para 3. For Lombardic and Frankish law in Italy, cf. Calisse, 623-4.

[67] Thus in Normandy, where there was no community between spouses, and where *douaire* represented the primary property right of a widow, it could be said "s'est à titre d'héritiers, et non à titre de communes, que les femmes en Normandie prennent part aux meubles et conquêts": Merlin, *Répertoire universel et raisonné de jurisprudence*, 4th ed. (Paris, 1812) ii.548, s.v. *Communauté*.

[68] As, of course, in *Cyfraith Hywel: agweddi* is invariably taken only by a separated wife within seven years of marriage, and *cowyll*, as a *prifai*, is hers however the marriage ends, even where it is by her fault.

The exact nature of the wife's title to dower, upon, during and after marriage[69] depends upon the state of the contemporary law concerning joint and separate property, and whether some kind of community[70] of movables was recognised (in which it is joint use, or use for the common good, which signifies more than the title to each movable, particularly where consumable goods and perishables, *res fungibiles*, are in question), and where land is still regarded largely as a non-personal asset, not available for disposition outside the rules of inheritance and the feudal relationship. In later medieval law and beyond, when the husband was regarded as having acquired by marriage not only the guardianship of his wife's person but extensive control of her property, it makes little sense to speak of the wife's title during marriage to property, or of gifts (other than by way of dower or parapherna) to her even from her husband, since effectively he would retain control of it all.[71] This probably accounts for the second sense of dower, *supra*, where questions of title are simplified if the widow's claim is against her late husband's property.

One English source earlier than Glanvill may be mentioned in conclusion, the so-called *Leges Henrici Primi*,[72] c.1115 but composed from pre-Conquest sources, English and continental. The texts on "dower" are interesting in that they recognise a number of different kinds of property, e.g. from the *Consuetudo Westsexe*:

> Si sponsa virum suum supervixerit, dotem et maritationem suam cartarum instrumentis vel testium exhibitionibus ei traditam perpetualiter habeat et morgangivam suam et tertiam partem de omni collaboratione sua preter vestes et lectum suum.[73]

The West Saxon widow, according to this text, therefore got her dowry (her husband's gift *ante nuptias*); her *maritagium* (perhaps settled on the

---

[69] cf. n.63 *supra* (loss of dower upon re-marriage or other incontinence).
[70] cf. Jenkins, *supra* 78-9, 83-6; Walters, .13(3), and see Beaumanoir, ed. cit. n.61 *supra*, c.22, §622 (compaignie par mariage). *Compaignie* (*companagium*, "sharing bread") is a synonym for *communauté*.
[71] In England, Scotland, and the Duchy of Normandy (in contrast with the rest of the French *pays coutumiers* where community at least of movables prevailed), except for certain town-dwellers and merchants who were subject to their own customs (for which cf. M. Bateson, *Borough Customs* ii, (1906, 21 SS), this control grew until, in the absence of a contrary antenuptial marriage settlement, it amounted to absolute ownership of her movables and the sole right to the rents from her lands. In the *pays coutumiers* other than Normandy, this control was expressed in some species of *compaignie* or *communauté* (*supra*, n.70), since the husband alone administered that community. For Germanic law cf. Hübner, 621 et s., 626 et s. (§94.I & III.1); Calisse, 571-2, 602-3 (again linking guardianship of person with that of ward/wife's property).
[72] ed. L. J. Downer, Oxford, 1972.
[73] *ibid.* c.70. 22 (pp.224-5) and n. at 386.

spouses by her husband's father[74]), evidenced in writing or before witnesses; her *morgengabe*; her *tertia pars collaborationis*,[75] i.e. one-third of the common stock of movables; in addition to her clothing and bed. The Germanic and Welsh parallels are striking. Downer (n.72, *supra*) compares this with the much more restricted reference to dower in Henry I's Coronation Charter of 1100, cc. 3, 4,[76] and traces much of the text to the Lex Ribuaria, c.37. 1, 2, c.48; but it is well-known that the *Leges Henrici Primi* must be treated with caution, particularly if we try to identify the subjects to whom they purport to be addressed.[77]

From these generalisations based upon known rules of early European medieval law, it is clear that in *Cyfraith Hywel, agweddi* is not so much a form of husband-to-wife endowment as a security to be realised in the event of the marriage failing within seven years. A second species of pro-vision for the wife upon separation after seven years or more of marriage or the prior death of her husband is the share she obtains in the division of movables; and that the gift which most closely resembles dower, in the post-nuptial form of *morgengabe*, is *cowyll*, though this will consist of movables, not land (except as noted *supra*, n.16) and as it is a *prifai* of hers, she takes it whatever the grounds of separation, even her own fault, and does not forfeit it by subsequent re-marriage or irregular connexion, provided only that she stated her claim by indicating the purposes to which her *cowyll* was to be dedicated before rising for the first time from the marriage bed.[78]

D. B. WALTERS

---

[74] But "dotem et maritationem" may be one thing, a single antenuptial gift.
[75] cf. *Monumenta Germaniae Historica*, Leges V, Marcolfo, Formularies II.7, where this phrase appears as descriptive of a widow's rights.
[76] Text in Stubbs' *Charters*, 9th ed. (Oxford, 1913) 116, 118.
[77] Other comparable texts not discussed by Downer include the Leges Visigothorum of Recceswind (654) and Erwig (681), text in *Monumenta Germaniae Historica*, Leges (Quarto series), I—Leges nationum Germanicum, Leges Visigothorum (ed. Zeumer), 1902, esp. *de donationibus*, i.e. from husband to wife at marriage, s.307 et s., at 17 et s.; *Lex Visigothorum* Bk III *(de ordine conjugali), de dispositionibus nuptiarum*, s.3 at 124; ibid. *de quantitate rerum conscribende dotis*, 126; ibid., IV.2, *de successionibus* s.11 (p.177), s.14 (p.182), s.16 (p.183), this last concerning the widow's claim to her husband's post-nuptial acquisitions.
[78] *Supra*, 16-17 and nn.38-40 *(cowyll)*; 17-19 and nn. 42-46 *(morgengabe, mefio)*.

TEXTS OF THE TRACTATE ON THE
LAW OF WOMEN

THREE versions of the tractate on the Law of Women are printed here with English translations: the Welsh versions from the "Cyfnerth" and "Iorwerth" texts (Aneurin Owen's "Gwentian Code" and "Venedotian Code" respectively), and the Latin version from the oldest extant manuscript which contains the tractate. The Latin version (Lat A) can be taken as representing the "Blegywryd" text (Owen's "Dimetian Code"), since that has been shown to derive from the Latin Redaction D,[1] which has much in common with Lat A. As it is generally accepted that the order "Cyfnerth", "Blegywryd", "Iorwerth" represents a rising order of sophistication,[2] that order has been followed here; the relation of the texts to each other is discussed by Dr. Charles-Edwards below.

I. THE "CYFNERTH" TEXT
edited and translated by Dafydd Jenkins

THE irregular numbering of the sentences of the text here printed needs explanation and indeed apology. It derives from the scheme adopted by the editor as a working tool in an attempt to edit the Cyfnerth text from its surviving manuscripts in such a way as to show the relation of the manuscripts and to make possible a tentative reconstruction of their archetype. That attempt now seems very unlikely to succeed, but the numbering scheme, which makes exact reference easy, has been used. It is based on the division of the text of MS. *U* (the shortest of the manuscripts) into chapters numbered consecutively; since the chapters are defined by the manuscript's rubrics (occasionally by coloured initials only), they vary greatly in length. Within each chapter, the sentences found in MS. *U* are numbered consecutively, and each sentence not found in MS. *U* is identified by adding a letter to the number of the "primary" sentence which it follows in the "senior" manuscript in which it occurs. Thus §73/2a is a sentence which is not in MS. *U* but in MS. *W* follows §73/2 (i.e. the second sentence of the chapter in MS. *U*.)

---

[1] H. D. Emanuel, "Llyfr Blegywryd a Llawysgrif Rawlinson 821", (1960) 19 BBCS 23-8; English translation at CLP 163-70.

[2] T. Jones Pierce, (1952) 3 *University of Birmingham Historical Journal* 124-5, reprinted in *Medieval Welsh Society* (ed. J. B. Smith, Cardiff, 1972) 295-6.

The manuscript sources, in order of "seniority", are:[3]

U: N.L.W. Peniarth 37 (pp. 81-84). This is the *Morg.* of William Maurice's *Deddfgrawn* or *Corpus Hoelianum*,[4] and is a small-paged manuscript attributed by Gwenogvryn Evans (*Rep.* i.371) to the late thirteenth century, but more probably of the early fourteenth century; it is in the same hand as the "Iorwerth" MS. *G* (printed below) and Peniarth MS. 45, which contains a Welsh version of Geoffrey of Monmouth's History. It was printed as the basic text of AL G.C. II.xxix (vol.i, pp. 746-55), with the additional material from MS. *W*.

W: B.L. Cotton Cleopatra A.XIV (ff. 78v-82v), of about the same date. It is the "Cott. 6" of LW, and our text (from f.79r on) is printed at WML 91-8.

V: B.L. Harleian 4353 (f.37r-v, ending in a gap in the manuscript), of about the same date; in the same hand as the Book of Taliesin. It is the "H.3" of LW, and our text is printed at WML 89-90.

Mk: Bodorgan MS., the property of Sir George Meyrick, (pp. 78-83) of about the same date. It is the "M" of LW, and is printed here: v. *infra.*

X: B.L. Cotton Cleopatra B.V (ff.201r-205r), the "Cott. 5" of LW. This is a larger-paged manuscript in a more Gothic hand, perhaps intended for a library rather than for a practitioner's daily use; attributed by Gwenogvryn Evans to *circa* 1350 (*Rep.* ii.954), it is certainly later than the manuscripts "senior" to it.

Z: N.L.W. Peniarth 259[B] (ff.24v-26v), *Ponf.* in the *Deddfgrawn,* a paper manuscript of the mid-sixteenth century, but probably imitating in lay-out and in the forms of initial letters its earlier archetype.

MS. *Y* (N.L.W. 20143) is not included, since (though sometimes classed as a Cyfnerth manuscript) it follows the Blegywryd pattern in the chapters concerned with the Law of Women.

Because of the complicated relation of the manuscripts, it has not been found possible to present the material so as to give a clear idea of that relation, and the numbering scheme sometimes obscures its complexity by suggesting too much uniformity in the two chapters of the tractate. Since there is in the other manuscripts a substantial block of material not found in MS. *U*, it has been found convenient to treat this as a separate

---

[3] With the exception of *Mk* for the Bodorgan manuscript (not used for AL), the sigla are those used in AL.
[4] For this compilation by the seventeenth-century scholar, William Maurice of Cefn-y-braich, Llansilin, in two volumes now deposited in the National Library of Wales as Wynnstay 37, 38, see D. Jenkins, "Deddfgrawn William Maurice", (1941) 2 NLWJ 33-6.

chapter, numbered 73a. And as the lists given below will show, this particular tractate illustrates very well the way in which sentences, paragraphs, and whole chapters or tractates "float"—so that they are found in different contexts in different manuscripts.[5] In the list which follows, setting out the contents of the tractate as found in each manuscript, the references in square brackets are to material intruded into the tractate but having nothing to do with the Law of Women; where such material does not occur in MS. *U* (so that it has a simple numerical reference which gives an idea of its distance from §73 in that manuscript), it has been numbered as part of three blocks, α, β, and γ.[6]

> *U:* 73/1-30.
>
> *W:* 73/1, 2, 2a, 3-5, 6, 7, 7a, 8, 9, 9a, 10-13, 13abc, 14, 15, 15abc, 23, 23a, 24, 24a, 25-27, 33/2, [α/1, 2], 47/8;
> 73a/1-17; 73/19-21; 73a/18; 44/5; [β/1-11, 38/11].
>
> *V:* 73/1, 2, 2a, 3-7, 7a, 8, 9, 9a, 10-13, 13a ending in a lacuna in the MS.
>
> *Mk:* 73/1, 2, 2a, 3-7, 7a, 8, 9, 10-13, 13abc, 14, 15, 15abc, 23a, 24a, 25, 23;
> 73a/2-18; 38/10c, 44/5, [β/1-3, 5, 4, γ/1-3, β/7-11, 38/11].
>
> *X:* 73/1, 2, 2a, 3-5, 5a, 6, 7, 7a, 8, 9, 9a, 10-13, 13abc, 14, 15, 15abcd, 23, 23a, 24, 24a, 25-27, 33/2, [α/1, 2; β/1, 2, 8-10], 73/28-30, 47/8;
> 73a/1-17, [β/11, 38/11], 73a/17b.
>
> *Z:* 73/1, 2, 2a, 3-5, 5a, 6, 7, 7a, 8, 9, 9a, 10-13, 13abc, 14, 15, 15abc, 23, 23a, 24, 24a, 25-27, 33/2, [α/1, 2; β/1-5, 7-10], 73/28-30, 47/8;
> 73a/1-17.

A glance at these lists will suggest that to give a detailed account of all the differences between the manuscripts would be more confusing than helpful; it must suffice to draw attention to some salient points. The floating of a sentence within a tractate is highlighted by the position of §73/23 after §73/25 in the text printed below; it is even better illustrated by §73/19-21, which in MS. *W* follow §73a/17. The same sentences float outside the tractate in MS. *X*, where they appear in the company of other floating sentences, twenty pages after the end of the tractate on the Law of Women.

The two chapters, §73 and §73a, are close together in all the

---

[5] For the concept of floating sections see J. E. Powell, "Floating Sections in the Laws of Howel", (1937) 9 BBCS 27-34.

[6] §γ intrudes into the Law of Women only in that in MS. *Mk* it intrudes into the block which in MSS. *W* and *Mk* follows §73a (and is recorded at that point in those two manuscripts only to point the contrast with MSS. *X* and *Z*, in which it intrudes as a block into the body of the tractate). In MS. *W*, §γ occurs at a different point, away from the Law of Women. §γ/2 is almost the same as §β/7.

manuscripts which contain them, but only in MS. *Mk* do they directly follow each other. It is true that in MS. *X* §73a/1 immediately follows §73/30; but §73/28-30 are not an integral part of §73. They form a floating fragment, which in MS. *U* follows directly on §73/27, whereas in MSS. *W* and *Mk* it appears much earlier, in a different context, while in MS. *X* it has attached itself (with §47/8) to §73a/1, and is separated from the main body of §73 by seven sentences which have nothing to do with the Law of Women; two of these sentences also separate §73 from §73a in MS. *W*. The tractate as a whole is perhaps floating: in MS. *U* it follows a substantial tractate (§72) on Corn and Impounding; in MSS. *V* and *Mk* it follows tractates on the various forms of Contract; in MS. *W* it is separated from these latter by a short tractate on litigation for land; and in MS. *X* it is separated from §72 by a block of material from the second half of the Laws of Court.

The primary source of the text here printed is the Bodorgan MS., *Mk*, which was chosen because it has never before been published.[7] The manuscript was written in the early fourteenth century, probably in South Wales, in a hand not unlike (but not identical with) that of the Book of Taliesin.[8] In the Laws of the Country (but not in the Laws of Court) its contents and language closely resemble those of MS. *V*: this can be seen in the first sentences (which are all that remains in MS. *V*) of the present tractate. The tractate as found in MS. *Mk* is first printed; it is followed by the text of all material relating to Women which in any manuscript is found in association with the tractate. §73/28-30 are taken from another part of MS. *Mk*, and other material from MSS. *U*, *W*, and *X*. Variant readings from other manuscripts than that providing the main text have been confined to those which may be significant for substance or wording. The material has been edited in the usual way: italics (if not otherwise explained in footnotes) indicate the extension of abbreviations, words or letters in square brackets are editorial additions, some of which have been made by way of assurance to the reader that an unusual form is that of the manuscript rather than a misprint. Figures in square brackets give references to the pages of the manuscript. The manuscripts' punctuation has perhaps suffered cavalier treatment: this reflects their own frequently arbitrary practice, for it is quite evident that the scribes of the Welsh law manuscripts were by no means always fully awake to the meaning of what they were writing.

---

[7] Some variant readings and additional material from *Mk* were printed in LW.
[8] I thank Mr. Daniel Huws of the National Library of Wales for this information.

Cyfn §73

[Mk 78]

Seith punt y6 gobyr merch brenhi*n*, ac y'r vam y telir. [2]A'r g6r a tal y chowyll, kanys tir a tal idi. [2a]Pedeir punt ar hugeint y6 y heg6edi. [3]Or a merch breyr gan 6r yn llathrut heb rod kenedyl, pan atter sef uyd y heg6edi, whech eidon kyhyt eu kyrn ac eu hyscyfarn. [4]Y verch taya6c y telir tri eidon gogyfoet a rei hynny. [5]Or kymer g6r wreic o rod kenedyl, ac os gat kyn pen y seith mlyned, talet idi teir punt yn y heg6edi os merch breyr uyd, [6]a phunt a hanher yn y chowyll, [7]a hwheugeint yn y hamobyr. [7a]Os merch taya6c uyd, punt a hanher yn y heg6edi, a wheugeint yn y chowyll, a phedeir ar hugeint yn y hamobyr. [8]Os g6edy y seith mlyned y gat, bit ran deu hanher y rydunt, onyt breint a dyry ragor y'r g6r. [9]Deuparth y plant a da6 y'r g6r, nyt amgen yr hynaf a'r ieuhaf, a'r trayan y'r vam. [9a]Os agheu a'e g6ahan, bit ran deu hanher y rydunt o pop peth. [79] [10]Sarhaet g6reic 6rya6c herwyd breint y g6r y telir. [11]Pan lather g6r g6reigya6c, y sarhaet a telir yn gyntaf, ac odyna y alanas, kanys trayan sarhaet y g6r a telir y'r wreic. [12]G6reic g6r ryd a dicha6n rodi y chrys a'e mantell a'e phenlliein a'e hescityeu a'e bla6t a'e cha6s a'e* hemenyn a'e llaeth heb ganhat y g6r, ac a eill benffygya6 holl dootrefyn y ty. [13]Ny dicha6n g6reic taya6c rodi heb ganhat y g6r onyt y phenguch, ac ny eill benffygya6 onyt y gogyr a'e ridyll, a hynny hyt y cly6her y gal6 a'e throet 6rth y throtheu. [13a]Or a mor6yn wyra yn llathrut heb rod kenedyl, y that a dicha6n y hatt6yn o'e hanuod rac y g6r, ac ny

---

[73/5-7] *MSS. Mk, V, seem to have gone astray by incorporating* §73/5a *(as found in MS. W)* *in* §73/5, *no doubt with a view to conciseness, and running on to* §73/7. *MS. W has* *the reading:*
 [5]Or kymer g6r wreic o rod kenedyl, a'e hada6 kyn pen y seith mlyned, talet y heguedi idi. [5a]Os merch breyr uyd, teir punt uyd y heguedi. [6]Punt a hanher yn y chowyll. [7]Wheugeint yn y gobyr.
 This reading, followed by MSS. X and Z, seems preferable to that of our main text, *since it avoids any suggestion that* amobr *was payable to the deserted wife.*
[73/7] hamobyr: gobyr *UWVXZ*
[73/7a] hamobyr: gobyr *WVZ*
[73/11] y'r wreic: + ac ny cheiff dim *UX* o'r *U* o'e *X* alanas *UX*
[73/12] **MS.** hae.
 g6r ryd: g6r breinha6l *U*
 rody . . . ganhat y g6r: benffygya6 y chrys a'e mantell a'e phenlliein *UX* a'e hesgidiev *X* heb ganhyat y g6r *U* a roddi *UX* y b6yt a'e dia6t *U* y blawd a'e chaws a'e hemenyn a'e llaeth heb ganyad y gwr *X*
 bla6t: + a'i hyd *Z*
 ac a eill . . . ty: − *X*
[73/13] rodi . . . benffygya6 onyt y: roddi dim na'e uenffygya6 heb ganhyat y g6r, namyn y fengu6ch a'e *U* venthygiaw dim heb genad i gwr namyn i phegiwch a'i *Z*
 6rth y throtheu: ar i thomen *Z*
[73/13a] rod: canhat *WXZ*

Cyfn §73

The gobr of a king's daughter is £7, and it is paid to the mother. ²And the husband pays her cowyll, for he pays land to her. ²ᵃ Her agweddi is £24. ³ If a breyr's daughter elopes with a man without gift of kindred, when she is left her agweddi will be six bullocks whose horns are as long as their ears. ⁴ To a taeog's daughter are paid three bullocks of the same age as those. ⁵ If a man takes a wife by gift of kindred and if he leaves her before the end of seven years, let him pay her £3 for her agweddi if she is a breyr's daughter, ⁶ and £1½ for her cowyll, ⁷ and 120d. for her amobr. ⁷ᵃ If she is a taeog's daughter, £1½ for her agweddi, 120d. for her cowyll, and 24d. for her amobr. ⁸ If he leaves her after seven years, let there be sharing in two halves between them unless status gives the husband more. ⁹ Two-thirds of the children go to the husband, to wit the eldest and the youngest, and a third to the mother. ⁹ᵃ If it is death which separates them, let there be sharing of everything in two halves between them. ¹⁰ The sarhaed of a married woman is paid according to her husband's status. ¹¹ When a married man is killed, his sarhaed is paid first, and then his galanas, for a third of her husband's sarhaed is paid to the wife. ¹² The wife of a free man can give her shift and her mantle and her headkerchief and her shoes and her flour and cheese and butter and milk without her husband's leave, and can lend all the utensils of the house. ¹³ A taeog's wife cannot give away anything without her husband's leave but her headdress, and she cannot lend anything but her sieve and her riddle, and that as far as she can be heard calling with her foot on the threshold. ¹³ᵃ If a virgin maid elopes without gift of kindred, her father can re-take her from her husband against her will, and does not pay her amobr to the

thal y hamobyr y'r argl6yd. [13b]Or a g6reic hagen yn llathrut, ny eill neb y hatt6yn rac y g6r o'e hanuod. [13c]O'r lle y bo y hatlam y telir y hamobyr. [14]Y neb a dycco treis ar wreic, talet y hamobyr y'r argl6yd a'e dir6y, a'e dilysta6t a'e heg6edi a'e sarhaet a tal idi hitheu. [15]Or g6atta g6r treissa6 g6reic, ac os kadarnha y wreic yn y herbyn, kymeret hi y gala y g6r yn y lla6 asseu, a'r creir yn y lla6 deheu, a thyget ry* [80] d6yn treis ohona6 ef erni hi a'r gala honno, ac uelly ny chyll hi dim o'e ia6n. [15a]Y neb a wato treis, rodet l6 deg wyr a deu vgeint heb gaeth a heb alltut. [15b]O tri acha6s ny chyll g6reic y heg6edi kyt ada6ho y g6r: o clafyri, ac eisseu kyt, a dryc anadyl. [15c]Tri pheth ny chyll g6reic kyt gatter am y cham: y chowyll, a'e hargyfreu, a'e h6ynebwerth—nyt amgen wheugeint uyd y h6ynebwerth. [73/23 follows 73/25 below]. [23a]Teir g6eith y keiff g6reic y h6ynebwerth pan gyttyo ynteu a g6reic arall, ac os diodef dros hynny ny cheiff dim. [24a]Tri ll6 a dyry g6reic y 6r: pan enlliper gyntaf, ll6 seith wraged; ar yr eil enllip, ll6 pedeir g6raged ar dec; ar y trydyd enllip, ll6 deg wraged a deu vgeint; ac os diodef dros hynny, ny cheiff dim. [25]Na rodet neb wreic y 6r heb gymryt mach ar y gobyr y'r argl6yd, ag onys kymer, talet e hunan. [23]Ony wna mor6yn a vynho o'e chowyll kyn y chyfot y bore y 6rth y g6r, kyt uyd y rydunt.

Cyfn §73a

[2]Or yscar g6r a g6reic kyn pen y seith mlyned, val hyn y rennir y dootrefyn y rydunt: [3]Y g6r bieu a vo o'r dillat g6ely y ryda6 a'r lla6r, a'r [81] wreic bieu y teispan. [4]A'r g6r bieu yr yt oll; y wreic bieu y bla6t para6t. [5]Y g6r bieu y bryccan a'r nithlen a'r gobennyd tyle, a'r c6lltyr a'r u6ell gynnut, a'r lla6 u6ell a'r crymaneu oll eithyr vn cryman. [6]Y wreic

[73/13a] y hamobyr: gobyr Z
[73/14] hamobyr: gobyr UWXZ
a'e dir6y . . . hitheu: a'e hegwedi a'e dilysta6t U
hitheu: + ac or byd mor6yn talet y chowyll UWXZ
[73/15] *MS. yr.
gala: 6 followed by a gap Z
[73/15a] alltud: + a thri o'r gwyr yn ddiowredawc o dri pheth kyfreithion ac am drais nid oes
wyr dio[w]redawc o dyry l o wyr heb gayth heb alldud Z
[73/15c] nyt amgen . . . h6ynebwerth: pan gyttyo y g6r a gureic arall WXZ
[73/23a] h6ynebwerth: + y gan y g6r WXZ
[73/24a] pedeir . . . ddeg: xiij Z
ar y trydyd . . . dim: Ar dryded enllib llw .l. o wragedd am gusan ai gouysyau ai
hy[m]rain yw y tri llw. A'r gwr a ryd yr 6n llw y'w wraic briod. Y wraic am i gobyr llw
saith wragedd 6n vraint a hi Z
[73/25] ag [sic] . . . hunan: − UWXZ
[73/23] kyn . . . y g6r: kyn kychwynu y g6r y bore U

lord. [13b]If, however, a woman elopes, no-one can re-take her from her husband against her will. [13c]Her amobr is paid from the place where her residence is. [14]He who rapes a woman, let him pay her amobr to the lord and her dirwy; and her dilystod and agweddi and sarhaed he pays to her. [15]If a man denies raping a woman and the woman confirms it against him, let her take the man's penis in her left hand the relic in her right hand, and let her swear that she was raped by him with that penis, and so she will lose none of her right. [15a]He who denies rape, let him give the oath of fifty men without a slave and without an alien. [15b]For three causes a woman does not lose her agweddi though she leaves her husband: for leprosy, and want of connexion, and bad breath. [15c]Three things which a wife does not lose though she be left for her fault: her cowyll, and her argyfrau, and her wynebwerth—to wit, her wynebwerth is 120d. [73/23 *follows* 73/25 *below*]. [23a]Three times a woman has her wynebwerth [from her husband] when he has connexion with another woman, and if she suffers it beyond that she gets nothing. [24a]A woman gives three oaths to a husband: when she is accused first, the oath of seven women; on the second occasion the oath of fourteen women; on the third accusation the oath of fifty women; and if he suffers it beyond that he gets nothing. [25]Let no-one give a woman to a man without taking a mach for her gobr to the lord, and if he does not take it, let him pay himself. [23]If a maiden does not do as she wishes with her cowyll before she rises in the morning from her husband, it will be joint between them.

Cyfn §73a

[2]If a husband and wife separate before the end of seven years, this is how the utensils are shared between them: [3]The husband owns such of the bedclothes as are between him and the ground, and the wife owns the coverlet. [4]And the husband owns all the corn; the wife owns the prepared flour. [5]The husband owns the brycan and the winnowing-sheet and the bed-pillow and the coulter and the fuel-axe, and the hand-axe and all the sickles except one sickle. [6]The wife owns the broad axe and the

---

This chapter (73a) speaks of sharing *before* the end of seven years. This seems to be the result of a slip in the archetype of the manuscripts which contain the chapter; that the slip was not corrected is evidence that the material was not of living importance when the manuscripts were written.

bieu y u6ell lydan a'r s6ch a'r pal, a'r vn cryman, a'r perued taradyr; a'r g6r bieu yr heyrn oll eithyr hynny. [7]A'r wreic bieu karr yr ychen a'r g6edeu a'r llaethlestri oll onyt vn payol ac vn dyscyl y'r g6r. [8]Y wreic bieu yr emenyn oll onyt vn llestreit y'r g6r, ac o'r breuaneu heuyt y keiff y g6r vn. [9]Y wreic bieu y kic oll a vo ar y lla6r yn heli a heb halen arnunt, a'r ka6s a vo yn heli a heb halen; a'r g6r bieu y kic drychafedic a'r ka6s drychafedic oll. [10]Y wreic a dyly bot yn y thy yn arhos y ran o'r da hyt ym pen y na6uetdyd. [11]G6reic a dywetto y bot yn veicha6c pan vo mar6 y g6r, hi a dyly bot yn y thy hyny 6ypper a uo beicha6c; ac ony byd, talet* tri buhyn caml6r6 y'r brenhin, ac ada6et y ty y'r etiued. [12]Or byd d6y wraged yn kerdet y neb lle ac na bo vn dyn y gyt ac 6ynt, a dyuot deu 6r yn eu herbyn ac eu hymrein, ny diwygir udunt. [13]Or byd vn dyn hagen y [82] gyt ac 6ynt, yr y vychanet (onyt mab kefyn vyd), ny chollant dim o'e ia6n. [14]G6reic a el yn llathrut gan 6r a'e hatal o'r g6r hi ganta6 hyt ym pen y seithuet dyd heb wneuth[ur] ia6n idi, ny dyly ef wneuthur ia6n idi hyt ym pen vn dyd a bl6ydyn; yna hagen y dyly hi c6byl ia6n y ganta6. [15]G6reic a el yn llathrut gan 6r yn y haeduetr6yd, a'e d6yn o'r g6r hi y* l6yn neu y perth neu y ty, a'e hymrein, a'e goll6g o'r g6r trachefyn, a ch6yna6 oheni hitheu 6rth y chenedyl ac yn y dadleu: sef a dyly hi yn y diweirdeb, kymryt tar6 tri gayaf ac eilla6 y losc6rn a'e ira6 a g6er, ac odyna grynya6 y losc6rn tr6y dorgl6yt, ac odyna mynet y wreic y my6n y ty a dodet y throet 6rth y trotheu, a chymeret losc6rn y tar6 yn y d6y la6, a doet g6r o pop parth y'r tar6 ac erthi yn lla6 pop vn ohonunt y gymhell y tar6; ac or dicha6n hi y attal, kymeret yn y diweirdeb, ac onys dicha6n, kymeret a lynho o'r g6er 6rth y d6y la6. [16]G6reic a ymrotho e hunan yn ll6yn ac ym perth y 6r, a'e hada6 o'r g6r a gorderchu arall, a'e dyuot hitheu yg c6yn at y chenedyl ac y'r dadleu: os g6adu a wna y g6r, rodet y l6 y gloch [83] heb taua6t. [17]Os diu6yn a 6yn ynteu, talet idi geinha6c kyflet a'e thin. [18]Teir g6eith y drycheif ar sarhaet g6r pan ymreher y wreic.

[38/10c]G6reic 6rya6c a odiwether yg godineb, y heg6edi a gyll.

[73a/6] s6ch: − Z
    heyrn: dodrefyn Z
[73a/7] llaethlestri . . . dyscyl: llaethlestri oll, a'r dysglev oll, namwyn vn a baeol X
    payol ac: payol, a'r dysgleu oll eithyr WZ
    y'r g6r: bieu y g6r W
[73a/11] *MS. ta/talet
    brenhin: arglwyd X
    adawet y ty: + a'r tir WX
[73a/13] (onyt . . . vyd): − Z
[73a/15] *MS. y/y
    [kymeret yn y] diweirdeb: h6ynebwerth WX a'e diweirdeb W

ploughshare and the spade and the one sickle and the medium auger; and the husband owns all the irons except that. [7] The wife owns the ox-car and the yokes and all the milk vessels except one pail and one dish for the husband. [8] The wife owns all the butter but one vesselful for the husband, and of the querns of butter too the husband gets one. [9] The wife owns all the meat which is on the floor in brine and without salt on it, and the cheese which is in brine or without salt, and the husband owns all the raised meat and raised cheese. [10] The wife is entitled to be in her house waiting for her share of the property until the end of the ninth day. [11] A wife who says that she is pregnant when her husband dies, she is entitled to be in her house until it is known whether she is pregnant; and if she is not, let her pay three kine camlwrw to the king, and let her leave the house to the heir. [12] If two women are walking to any place and there is no person with them, and two men come upon them and copulate with them, no compensation is made to them. [13] If, however, there is one person with them, however small (unless it is a carried child), they lose none of their right. [14] A woman who elopes with a man and is kept with him till the end of the seventh day without doing right to her, he is not bound to do right to her until the end of a year and a day; then, however, she is entitled to full right from him. [15] A woman who elopes with a man in her maturity and is taken by the man to bush or to brake or to house and copulated with and released by the man again, and who complains to her kindred and in the sessions: this is what she is entitled to for her chastity—let a three-year-old bull be taken and its tail shaved and greased with tallow and then thrust through a door-hurdle; and then let the woman go into the house and set her foot against the threshold and take the tail in her two hands; and let a man come on each side of the bull with a goad in the hand of each to spur the bull; and if she can hold it, let her take it for her chastity; and if she cannot, let her take what sticks to her two hands of the tallow. [16] A woman who gives herself up in bush and in brake to a man and is left by the man, who takes another as mistress: if she comes to complain to her kindred and in the sessions, if the man denies let him give his oath to a bell without a tongue. [17] If he wishes to make compensation let him pay her a penny as broad as her buttocks. [18] Three times a man's sarhaed is augmented when his wife is copulated with.

38/10c A married woman who is taken in adultery loses her agweddi.

[44/5]Kyfreith magu ul6ydyn, buch a mantell a pheis a phenlliein a d6y escit, a charreit o'r yt goreu* a tyfho ar tir y g6r, a phadell troeda6c.

Additional material placed elsewhere in Mk

[Mk 55.15] [73/28]O rodir Kymraes y alltut, y phlant a geiff ran o tir eithyr yr eissydyn arbenhic. [29]H6nn6 ny chaffant hyt y tryded ach. [30]Ac o h6nn6 y da6 g6arthec dyfach, kanys or g6na h6nn6 gyflauan, kenedyl y vam a'e tal oll.

Additional material from other manuscripts

U (Peniarth 37): §73.

[U 83.5] [16]Gwreic a treisser, ony 6ybyd p6y a'e treisso ny thal amobyr. [17]Canys ketwis y bren*hin* hi rac treis y byd colledic ynteu o'e amobyr. [18]Ac od amheuir y wreic am hynny, rodet y ll6 na 6yr p6y a'e treiss6ys a'e ry treissa6 mal kynt. [19]Od ymda gwreic e hunan, a dyuot g6r idi a'e threissa6, os diwat a wna yr g6r roddet l6 deng wyr a deugeint, a thri oho-nunt yn diofreda6c, o uarchogaeth a lliein, a gwreic. [20]Ony myn diwat, talet y'r wreic y gwada6l, a'e dilysta6t, a dir6y a gwialen aryant y'r bren*hin* yn y wed y dylyo. [21]Ony eill y g6r y thalu [84] dyker y d6y geill. [22]Os d6y wraged y bydant, rodet y neill geill y hon a'r llall y'r llall or byd gantunt ell d6y.

[24]O rodir mor6yn aeduet y 6r, ac o dyweit y g6r nat oed uor6yn, ty*n*get y uor6yn ar y phymhet nat oed wreic, hi a'e that, a'e mam a'e bra6t, a'e chwaer.

[26]O d6c g6r wreic y neb ty, kymeret 6r y ty uach ar y gobyr, ac onys kymer, talet e hun. [27]Gobyr alltudes, pedeir ar ugeint.

W (Cotton Cleopatra A.XIV):

[W 80v.4, following 73/27] [33/2]Y penkerd bieu gobreu merchet y beird a u6ynt ydana6.

[44/5] The legal measure of a year's rearing is a cow and a mantle and a shift and a headkerchief and two shoes and a carload of the best corn that grows on the man's land and a pan with feet.

[73/28] If a Welshwoman is given to an alien, her children will get a share of land, except the special croft. [29] That they will not get until the third generation. [30] And from that come gwartheg dyfach, for if he [sc. one of the children] does an injury, his mother's kin pays it all.

[73/16] A woman who is raped, unless she knows who raped her she does not pay amobr. [17] Since the king did not keep her from rape he will lose his amobr. [18] And if the woman is doubted over that, let her give her oath that she does not know who raped her, and that she was raped, as before. [19] If a woman travels alone, and a man comes to her and rapes her, if the man denies let him give the oath of fifty men, three of them being under vows against horsemanship and linen and woman. [20] If he does not wish to deny, let him pay the woman her gwaddol and her dilystod, and a dirwy and a silver rod to the king in the manner which is right. [21] If the man cannot pay let his two testicles be taken. [22] If there were two women, let him give one testicle to one and the other to the other if he lies with both.

[24] If a mature maiden is given to a man, and if the man says that she was not a maiden, let the maiden swear as one of five that she was not a woman—herself and her father and mother and brother and sister.

[26] If a man takes a woman to any house, let the man of the house take a mach for her gobr, and if he does not take it, let him pay himself. [27] The gobr of an alien woman, 24d.

[33/2] The pencerdd owns the gobrau of the daughters of the bards who are under him.

[W 80v.7, following two sentences not concerned with women] [47/8] Pedeir ar hugeint y6 sarhaet guenida6l caeth nyt el yn ra6 nac ymreuan. [73a/1] Or kytya g6r gureiga6c a gureic arall talet wheugeint y'r wreic gyfreitha6l yn y h6ynebwerth.

X (Cotton Cleopatra B.V):

[X 202r.19, following 73/15c] [73/15d] Pan gyttyo gwr a gwreic arall, talhed idi y hwynep[202v]werth.

[X 205r.11, following 28/11] [73a/17b] Argyfurew gwreic yw y gwathawl.

[47/8] guenida6l: gwenygawl *X* gweinidawc *Z*
caeth: cyflogaeth *Z*

47/8 The sarhaed of a servient slave who does not go to spade or to quern is 24d. 73a/1 If a married man has connexion with another woman, let him pay 120d. to the lawful wife by way of wynebwerth.

73/15d When a man has connexion with another woman, let him pay her wynebwerth to her.

73a/17b Her gwaddol is a woman's argyfrau.

II. THE TEXT OF LATIN REDACTION A

taken from *The Latin Texts of the Welsh Laws*
edited by Hywel David Emanuel, Cardiff, 1967

THE text printed is that of MS. Peniarth 28 in the National Library of Wales, long believed to be the oldest surviving manuscript of Welsh law and to date from the late twelfth century. It has now been shown to be about a half a century later,[9] so that it is probably later than the oldest Welsh manuscripts and perhaps later than the incomplete manuscript of Latin Redaction C, B.L. Harleian 1796—but as the latter lacks our tractate, the text here printed is the oldest surviving Latin version of the Law of Women.

Since all the extant medieval Latin manuscripts were used by the late Dr. Emanuel, his text is printed here, with minor differences in presentation, and one alteration (the restoration of the manuscript reading *gurthung* in §52/55). For convenience of exact reference the three divisions of the text (indicated by rubrics) have been numbered as chapters, and the sentences in each chapter numbered in sequence. Letters or words in square brackets in text or translation indicate additions necessary for the sense; the footnote in square brackets is that of the translator and the present editors. References in square brackets of the form [LTWL 142] are to the pages of Emanuel's edition, those of the form [p.35, c.1] to the pages and columns of the manuscript.

[9] D. Huws, "Leges Howelda at Canterbury", (1976) 19 NLWJ 342-3.

[Peniarth MS. 28, p.34, c.2]

Lat A §51: De lege puellarum et feminarum

[LTWL 141.31] Si quis ducat uxorem datam ei a gente sua, et infra septennium eam dimittat, reddat ei suum *egwedy*. [2]Si vero post septennium dimittatur, de omni substancia debet habere dimidium, nisi vir per aliam libertatem possit plus habere. [3]De prole duas partes debet vir procurare, scilicet, maiorem et minorem; mater vero terciam. [4]Si insimul fuerint usque [p. 35, c. 1] ad alterius obitum sine herede, in duo dividatur tota substancia, scilicet, dimidium viro et dimidium uxori.

[LTWL 142] [5]Iniuria femine maritate secundum *breynt* viri sui redditur. [6]Si maritus eius occidatur, primo redditur *sayrhaed*, deinde precium eius; sed de *sayrhaed* eius coniux debet habere partem ut frater.

[7]Si quis acceperit uxorem et dederit ei dotem, et postea inpregnaverit, et antequam pariet dimissa sit, reputabitur illud tempus ei pro nutricacione a quo dimissa est. [8]Ipsa vero nutriet infantem, velit nolit, per annum et dimidium. [9]Ipse vero dabit ei pro nutricatione ovem fetam cum vellere et agno; deinde patellam ferream* vel iiii[or] denarios; deinde monocriam** frumenti ad faciendum ei pulmentum vel *rynnyon*; deinde tria palustra de lignis; deinde duas ulnas de albo panno ad cooperiendum eum, vel iiii[or] denarios; deinde nutrici eius duas ulnas de panno radiato, vel xii denarios; deinde vaccam fetam cum vitulo; deinde tria palustra, scilicet, unum de frumento, alium de ordeo, tercium de avena. [10]Hec omnia matri debentur reddere si illa voluerit.

[11]Si qua pregnans abortivum fecerit a quarto die usque ad [p. 35, c. 2] mensem integrum, ille cuius culpa hoc factum fuerit quartam partem precii eius secundum nobilitatem reddet; et propter hoc vocatur *gwayth kyndelwaut*, quia nondum sit formatum. [12]Si in secundo vel in tercio vel in quarto mense fecerit, terciam partem precii eius secundum nobilitatem reddet. [13]Si quis fecerit in quinto mense vel post animatum onus fuerit, dimidium precii eius reddet.

[14]Si quis cum muliere tribus diebus et tribus noctibus aperte et coram omnibus dormierit, et ita vadit in lectum antequam cooperiatur ignis, et non surrexerit ab ea mane donec discooperiatur ignis, tria animalia eiusdem longitudinis aures* et cornua debet mulier habere a viro illo [de]

51/9 *MS. patella ferrea.
**MS. monocria.
51/14 *MS. auris.

LATIN REDACTION A
translated by Ian F. Fletcher
Lat A §51: Concerning the Law of Girls and Women

If anyone take a wife given to him by her kindred, and send her away within seven years, let him render her *egweddi*. [2]But if she be sent away after seven years, she is entitled to have one half of the entire substance, unless her husband can have more through some other privilege. [3]Of the children, the husband should take two shares, that is, the eldest and the youngest; whilst the mother takes the third. [4]If they have been together without issue until the death of one of them, let all their substance be divided into two, that is, half for the husband and half for the wife.

[5]The *iniuria* of a married woman is rendered according to the *braint* of her husband. [6]If her husband is killed, first *sarhaed* is paid, then his price; but the wife should have a share of his *sarhaed* like a brother.

[7]If anyone has taken a wife and given her *dos*, and afterwards has made her pregnant, and she is sent away before she gives birth, that time from which she was sent away will be assigned as due to her for the rearing. [8]It is she who shall rear the child, whether she is willing or not, for a year and a half. [9]The father shall give her, to provide for the rearing, a fat sheep with its fleece and its lamb; and an iron pan or four pence; and a measure of corn for making pottage or *rhynion* for the child; and three loads of wood; and two ells of white cloth for swaddling him, or four pence; and two ells of striped cloth for his nurse, or twelve pence; and a choice cow with her calf; and three loads, that is, one of wheat, a second of barley, a third of oats. [10]All these are to be given to the mother if she should want them.

[11]If any woman, being pregnant, miscarry between the fourth day and the full month, let that person whose fault this act was, render a fourth part of its [sc. the child's] price according to its social elevation; and accordingly this shall be called *gwaed cyn delwawd*, because it is not yet formed. [12]If it happens in the second or third or fourth month, let him render a third of its price according to its social elevation. [13]If anyone does it in the fifth month or after the foetus has become quick, let him render half of its price.

[14]If anyone sleeps with a woman openly and in the sight of all for three days and three nights, and in this way goes to bed before the fire is covered over, and does not arise from her in the morning until the fire is uncovered, the woman is entitled to have from that man, by judgement, three beast of the same length of ears and horns, if she is sent away from

iudicio, si ab eo dimissa est. ¹⁵Et totidem habebit si qua in rapinam ierit. ¹⁶Et talis lex est earum que datoribus carent, sed proprio consilio taliter agunt.

Lat A §52: De separacione viri et mulieris

Si mulier habuerit datorem vel datores, sub dote sint usque ad vii^tem annos. ²Et si tres habuerint de septimo anno noctes*, omnis substantie eius medietatem mulier de iudicio habebit.

³Si quis uxorem suam sine lege dimiserit, et aliam superduxerit, [p. 36, c. 1] iuditio domum venire debet et femina repudiata, [et] in domo esse propria usque ad nonum diem. ⁴Et in illa die si dimissa sit, omnia que illius sunt de domo prius exeant, et post* ultimum numerum ipsa de domo exeat.

⁵Vir habebit omnes sues, mulier oves. ⁶Vir habebit omnes equos [LTWL 143] et equas, boves et vaccas, iuvencos et iuvencas; mulier capras. ⁷Postea suppellex sic dividatur. ⁸Omnia vasa lactis, preter unum *bayol*, mulieris sunt; et omnes disci*, preter unum vernum, id est, *kycdyschil*, viri sunt. ⁹Palustrum vero et iugum unum mulieris sunt. ¹⁰Omnia dolia et omnia vasa potus viri sunt. ¹¹De vestimentis* lecti vir habebit omnes vestes que subtus sunt, mulier que supra. ¹²Postquam aliam* duxerit uxorem, vir debet mittere vestimenta lecti mulieri** quam repudiavit.

¹³Vir habebit caldarium, et *brecchan*, et pluvinar, et *nythlen*, et cultrum, et securim lignorum, et terebrum, et retentaculum, et falces omnes preter unam falcem, et cratem. ¹⁴Mulier habebit patellam et tripodem, dolabrum et cribrum, vomerem et unam falcem, linum et lini semen, et *trychwt*, preter aurum et argentum. ¹⁵Que [p. 36, c. 2] duo si fuerint*, id est, *thelesseu*, in duo equalia dividantur. ¹⁶Tela si fuerit, in duo equalia dividatur*, tam linea quam lanea.

¹⁷Vir habebit horreum et annonam, et quicquid super terram et in terra continetur, et gallinas et omnes aucas et unum cattum; et si plures fuerint, omnes mulieris sunt, preter unum, ut supra dictum est. ¹⁸Mulier habebit carnem salsatam et iacentem super terram et caseum recentem

---

52/2 *MS. noctis.
52/4 *MS. postea.
52/8 *MS. discos.
52/11 *MS. vestimento.
52/12 *MS. alia.
    **MS. mulier.
52/15 *MS. fuerit.
52/16 *MS. dividant.

him. [15]And any woman shall have the same if she elopes. [16]Such too is the law of those women who lack givers, and act in this way of their own accord.

Lat A §52: Concerning the separation of husband and wife

If a woman has a giver, or givers, let her be subject to *dos* for seven years. [2]And if they have three nights from the seventh year the woman shall have by judgement one half of all his substance.

[3]If anyone send away his wife without lawful cause, and take another in her place, by judgement the woman who has been put out is entitled to come to her home, and be in her own home until the ninth day. [4]And if on that day she is sent away, first let all the things which are hers go out from the house, and after the last of the number, let her herself go out from the house.

[5]The husband shall have all the pigs, the wife the sheep. [6]The husband shall have all the horses and mares, the oxen and cows, bullocks and heifers; the wife shall have the goats. [7]Next the household equipment shall be divided as follows. [8]All the vessels for milk, except one *baeol*, are the wife's; and all the dishes, except one meat dish, that is *cigddysgl*, are the husband's. [9]One car and yoke are the wife's. [10]All the jars and all the drinking vessels are the husband's. [11]Of the bedding, the husband shall have all the bedclothes which are beneath, the wife those which are above. [12]After he has taken another wife, the husband is obliged to send the bedding to the wife whom he has repudiated.

[13]The husband shall have the cauldron, and *brycan*, and the pillow, and *nithlen*, and the coulter, and the wood-axe, and the gimlet, and the fire-dog, and all the sickles except one, and the gridiron. [14]The wife shall have the pan and the tripod, the broad-axe and the sieve, the ploughshare and the one sickle, the flax and the linseed, and the *trythgwd* except gold and silver. [15]If there has been anything of these two, that is, *tlysau*, they shall be divided into two equal shares. [16]If there are products of the loom, they shall be divided into two equal parts, both as to linen things and as to woollen things.

[17]The husband shall have the barn and the grain and whatever there is above ground and in the ground, and the hens and all the geese and one cat; and if there are several [cats] all are the wife's except the one, as stated above. [18]The wife shall have the meat which is salted and lying on the ground, and the cheese that is fresh on the ground; but after the

super terram; sed postquam elevantur carnes et casei, nichil de illis mulier de iure habebit. ¹⁹Vas butyri, si non sit plenum, mulier habebit, et pernam* similiter, si non fuerit integra, et caseum, si non fuerit integer**, et tantum de farina quantum ipsa poterit inter manus suas ferre de cella in domum cum genuum*** fortitudine. ²⁰Unusquisque habeat vestimenta sua congrua, preter pallia, que dividi debent.

²¹Et postquam sic egerint, si vir aliam duxerit uxorem, sit ipsa libera a viro suo, id est, *dilyss*, quia de iure nullus vir debet habere duas uxores.

²²Si quis dimiserit uxorem suam et postea eum facti penituerit, et illa a primo libera alteri viro data sit, si potest prior vir eam attingere habentem unum pedem in lecto cum alio viro et [p. 37, c. 1] alterum pedem ultra lectum, prior vir de iure debet eam habere.

²³Si quis duxerit puellam in *llatruth*, et dicat puella: 'Quantum mihi dabis?', et ille dixerit:* 'Tantum', firmans illud fide sua vel super reliquias, et postea negaverit, accipiat puella reliquias, et iuret quod tantum promiserat ei. ²⁴Et sic nullo modo potest contradici, quia testimonium eius testimonium est.

²⁵Si quis duxerit uxorem quam putaverit esse virginem, et [LTWL 144] invenerit eam corruptam, et secundo eam cognoverit, et cum ea usque mane dormierit, nil de iure puelle potest ei* auferre. ²⁶Si vero, postquam noverit, surrexerit ad nupciales viros et eis testificaverit, nil ei de iure debet reddere. ²⁷Si in crastina temptet eam, et contradicit femina, tunc consideretur eius etas. ²⁸Si matura sit in pilis et uberibus, et si venerint muliebria eius, septem de proximis ei* cognatis cum utroque parente eam purgent; eodem modo si matura sit. ²⁹Si pro certo habeatur corrupta, seccetur camisia eius ante et retro, et bubulus unius anni uncta* cauda tradatur. ³⁰Si in manu eius permanserit, sit ei pro dote.

³¹Uxor optimatis potest dare camisiam suam [p. 37, c. 2] et clamidem et peplum et subtalares, farinam, lac, et butyrum, et caseum, sine licentia mariti sui; omnemque suppellectilem domus sue potest commodare.

52/19 *MS. perna.
**MS. integram.
***MS. genu.
52/23 *MS. dixit.
52/25 *MS. eum.
52/28 *MS. eis.
52/29 *MS. iuncta.

meats and cheeses are hung up, the wife shall have none of them by right. [19]The vessel of butter, if it be not full, the wife shall have, and the ham likewise unless it be unbroached, and the cheese unless it be unbroached, and so much of the flour as she herself can manage to bring in her own hands from the granary into the house with the strength of her knees. [20]Each one of them shall have his personal clothing, except the cloaks, which should be divided.

[21]And after they have carried this out, if the husband have taken another wife, let the first woman be free from her husband, that is, *dilys*, because in law no man is entitled to have two wives.

[22]If anyone has sent away his wife and afterwards repent of the deed, and the wife, being freed from her first husband, has been given to another, if the first husband can catch hold of her whilst she has one foot in the bed with her second husband, and the other foot outside the bed, the first husband is entitled to have her by law.

[23]If anyone takes a girl in *llathrudd*, and the girl says: "How much will you give me?" and he says "So much", swearing this by his faith or upon relics, and afterwards he deny it, let the girl take up the relics, and swear that he promised her so much. [24]And in this way it is impossible for there to be denial, because her testimony is [conclusive] testimony.

[25]If anyone has taken a wife whom he thought to be a virgin, and has found her to be deflowered, and subsequently he has intercourse with her and sleeps with her until morning, he can take nothing away from that which is the girl's by right. [26]But if, after he has found it out, he goes up before the wedding guests and attests it to them, he is not bound to render anything to her of her legal right. [27]If upon the next day he makes trial of her, and the woman denies it, then let her age be considered. [28]If she is mature as regards her pubic hair and her breasts, and if menstruation has occurred, let seven of her near relatives (including both her parents) clear her by compurgation; this is the procedure to be followed if the woman be mature. [29]If she be held to be deflowered for certain, let her shift be cut both in front and behind, and a yearling steer be handed to her by its greased tail. [30]If it remain in her hand, let her have it for her *dos*.

[31]The wife of an *optimas* can make a gift of her shift and cloak and veil and footwear, flour, milk and butter, and cheese, without the permission of her husband; and she can lend out all the equipment of her house.

³²Uxor villani nichil potest dare sine licencia villani nisi mitram suam, nec commodare nisi cribrum, quo possit audiri stans in limine domus* sue dum propter illud clamet.

³³Quamvis puella eat in *llatrut* cum viro sine licentia parentum suorum, illi tamen cum suo domino eam possunt* retrahere, licet invitam, sed cum suo iure; tunc etiam non cogetur pater eius mercedem reddere. ³⁴Si femina eat in *llathrut* que ante virum cognoverit, hec potest cum suo viro invitis parentibus remanere; sed ubicumque eius sit mansio, ibi merces eius querenda est.

³⁵Si quis violenter puellam cognoverit, reddat domino mercedem et *dyruy*, puelle* vero suam iniuriam et *egwedy* et *e dylesruyt* det. ³⁶Si autem vir violenciam negat, et mulier hoc affirmare velit, capiat eius membrum pudibundum in leva manu, reliquias vero in dextra, et iuret quod cum membro illo* vim ei intulerit; sicque nichil perdet.

³⁷Si quis vim intulerit puelle vel femine que sola ambulat, et negaverit, [p. 38, c. 1] det iuramentum quinquaginta virorum, quorum tres erunt continentes et abstinentes a carne et equitatione. ³⁸Si vero confessus fuerit, puelle vel femine reddet ius suum et quietam clamabit. ³⁹Regi vero reddet virgam argenteam altam usque ad os eius, ita grossam sicut [digitum] medicum eius; et cyphum aureum super virgam in quo possit sustineri plenus potus regi, ita spissum sicut* unguis aratoris pollicis qui per septennium aratrum tenuerit.

⁴⁰Si due femine sole ambulaverint et inde passe fuerint, nil de iure consequentur. ⁴¹Si vero socium habuerint secum ambulantem, licet parvum puerum, dummodo non feratur in dorso, ius suum plenarie habebunt.

⁴²Si mulier lectum viri sui sine causa reliquerit, antequam a viro [LTWL 145] suo iterum in lecto recipiatur, iii^{es} vaccas *camlury* reddat ei, eo quod dominus eius est.

⁴³Si mulier viro verbum irrogaverit verecundum, id est, *geyr kewylyt* iii^{es} vaccas *camlury* ei reddat, quia dominus eius est.

⁴⁴Si sine causa a viro suo mulier vapulaverit, secundum dignitatem suam ei [in]iuriam vir suus reddat. ⁴⁵Quisquis coniugem alicuius verberaverit, vir eius habebit dimidium *sayrhaed*.

³²The wife of a villein can make a gift of nothing but her own headband without the villein's permission, nor lend out anything except the sieve, where she can be heard calling for it while standing on the threshold of her house.

³³Although a girl may go in *llathrudd* with a man without the permission of her parents, yet can they, together with her lord, reclaim her, even if she be unwilling, but with her legal right; in that case also her father will not be compelled to render her *merces*. ³⁴If a woman go in *llathrudd* who has previously had intercourse with a man, this woman can remain with her man against the wishes of her parents; but wherever her dwelling place may be, there is her *merces* claimable.

³⁵If anyone has had intercourse with a girl by force, let him render her *merces* and *dirwy* to her lord, and to the girl let him give her *iniuria* and *egweddi* and her *dilysrwydd*. ³⁶But if the man denies that it was forceful, and the woman wishes to affirm this, let her take his shame-bringing member in her left hand, and relics in her right, and let her swear that with that member he forcefully entered her; and in this way she loses nothing.

³⁷If a man rapes a girl or woman who is walking alone, and he deny it, let him give the oath of fifty men, of whom three shall be continent and abstainers from meat and from horse riding. ³⁸If on the other hand he makes confession of it, let him render the girl or woman that which is her right and he shall claim his peace. ³⁹Furthermore let him render to the king a silver rod as high as is his [sc. the king's] mouth, and as thick as is his middle finger; and a gold cup in addition to the rod, in which it is possible to contain a full draught for the king, as thick as is the thumb nail of a ploughman who has been at the plough for seven years.

⁴⁰If two women have been walking alone and then have suffered, they shall obtain nothing by right. ⁴¹But if they had a [male] companion walking with them, even a small boy, provided that he is not carried on their back, they shall have their right in full measure.

⁴²If a woman leave her husband's bed without lawful cause, before she is again taken to bed by him let her render him three cows *camlwry*, because he is her lord. ⁴³If a woman utter a shameful word to her husband, that is, *gair cywilydd*, let her render him three cows, because he is her lord. ⁴⁴If a woman be beaten by her husband without cause, let her husband render her *iniuria* corresponding to her social dignity. ⁴⁵Whosoever beats the wife of another man, her husband shall have one half *sarhaed*.

⁴⁶Si qua [p. 38, c. 2] mulier habuerit rem turpe[m] cum alio viro osculo, id est, *cussan*, quartam partem *sayrhaed* ei reddet, nisi in ludo qui dicitur *llawan*, et in convivio, et quando aliquis de longe venerit. ⁴⁷Similiter et de *gouissiau*. ⁴⁸Qui autem coitum fecerit, totum restituet *sayrhaed*.

⁴⁹Si femina habens maritum de alio infametur, si tamen incertum sit, septem mulierum manu se expurget. ⁵⁰Si iterum eodem modo infametur, iuramento xxᵗⁱiiiiᵒʳ mulierum manu se expurget*. ⁵¹Si tercia vice 'cum quadam certitudine hoc affirmetur, iuramento quinquaginta mulierum manu se expurget. ⁵²Hec infamia tribus modis oritur: scilicet, si quis viderit de luco venientem, virum autem ex alia parte lusci eiusdem eadem hora egredientem; vel si visi fuerint sub uno pallio; vel si vir visus fuerit inter femora eius. ⁵³Adulter si negaverit adulterium, det iuramentum quinquaginta virorum.

⁵⁴Tribus de causis potest femina habere suum *egwedy*, licet ipsa virum relinquat: scilicet, si sit leprosus vir; et si habeat fetidum anhelatum; et si cum ea concumbere non possit.

⁵⁵Si mulier opposuerit alicui viro quod vis ei illata* sit ab eo, et ille negaverit, et si contradictio [p. 39, c. 1] fuerit inter eos, mulier debet habere ab eo *lw gweylit*; et si mulier fecerit iuramentum contra, id est, *gwrthung*, debent ire in novam domum sub nigro panno, et coram omnibus debet vir probare si possit an non**.

⁵⁶Tria sunt que non possunt mulieri auferre, licet ob suam dimitatur culpam: scilicet, *cowyllh*; et *argeuereu*, id est, animalia que secum a parentibus adduxit; et animalia que redduntur pro *uynebwerth* si maritus eius aliam cognoverit.

⁵⁷Si filia alicuius, vel neptis, vel alia que in custodia illius fuerit, cum aliquo in rapinam ierit, pater reddet domino ius suum, sive awnculus eius sit, quia eam non custodivit. ⁵⁸Si femina eat, ipsa sola reddat ius suum, vel vir eius, vel qui eam rapuit.

⁵⁹Cum *cowyllh* reddatur cuidam puelle, si de illo non facit voluntatem suam antequam a viro suo mane surgat, commune erit inter eos.

52/50 *MS. expurgent.
52/55 *MS. allata.
[**The text is confused and probably corrupt. The beginning of the sentence seems to refer to a charge of rape, the end to disproof of an allegation of impotence under §52/54: cf Ior §54/1-3. The phrase "vis ei illata (*or* allata) sit ab eo" perhaps results from miscopying of the archetype or mistranslation of some expression in the original Welsh.]

[46] If ever a woman engage in disgraceful conduct with another man by kissing, that is, *cusan*, he shall render a fourth part of *sarhaed* to him [sc. her husband] unless it occurred in the game which is called *llawan*, or at feasting, or when someone has come from afar. [47] Likewise in the case of *gofysio*. [48] But the man who has intercourse shall make restitution of the full *sarhaed*.

[49] If a woman who has a husband is defamed with reference to another man, if the matter be yet uncertain, let her clear herself by the hand of seven women. [50] If she be defamed again in the same manner, let her clear herself with an oath by the hand of 24 women. [51] If this be asserted a third time with some degree of certainty, let her clear herself with an oath by the hand of fifty women. [52] This infamy arises in three ways: that is, if someone has seen her coming from a grove, and a man going out from another part of the same grove at the same time; or if they have been seen beneath the same coverlet; or if the man has been seen between her thighs. [53] If the adulterer deny the adultery, let him give the oath of fifty men.

[54] A woman can have her *egweddi* upon three grounds, even if she leaves her husband: these are, if the husband be leprous; or if he have stinking breath; or if he cannot have intercourse with her.

[55] If a woman brings an allegation against any man that force was used against her by him, and he denies it, and if their evidence is contradictory, the woman should have from him *llw gweilydd*; and if the woman makes an oath to the contrary, that is, *gwrthtwng*, they should go into a new house beneath a black bedcover, and in the presence of all, the man should prove if he can or not.

[56] There are three things which they cannot take away from a woman, even if she is sent away for her own fault: these are, *cowyll*; and *argyfrau*, that is, the animals which she brought with her from her parents; and the animals which are rendered for *wynebwerth* if her husband has intercourse with another woman.

[57] If anyone's daughter, or niece, or other female who was in his care, elopes with someone, her father, or uncle as the case may be, shall render the lord that which is his right, because he has not guarded her. [58] If a woman elopes, let her alone render [sc. to the lord] that which is his right, or her husband, or the man who took her. [59] When *cowyll* is rendered to any girl, if she does not exercise her will over it before she rises from her husband in the morning, it shall be held in common between them.

[LTWL 146] [60]Femina legaliter maritata* ter habebit *uynebwert* si maritus eius aliam cognoverit: primo, dimidium libre; secundo, libram; tercio, cum omni dote sua et iure suo libera discedat. [61]Verum si ipsa hoc ulterius paciatur, numquam habebit *uynebwerth.*

[62]Si puella aliqua [p. 39, c. 2] detur viro, et vir* dicat eam invenisse corruptam, ipsa debet affirmare se esse incorruptam iuramento quinque hominum, id est, patris et matris, fratris et sororis, et suo proprio.

[63]Si quis ducat uxorem in *llatruth*, et eam ad domum ducat cuiusdam optimatis, ille accipiat a viro fideiussorem de mercede eius domino suo danda*, aut ipse reddat, sed antequam insimul dormiant. [64]Nemo debet dare feminam antequam accipiat fideiussorem de mercede eius domino suo danda*.

[65]Triplex est pudor puelle: primus, cum pater suus ea presente dixerit se illam viro dedisse; secundo, cum viri lectum intraverit; tercio, cum a lecto surgens inter homines venerit. [66]Et ideo pro primo datur *amwabyr*, pro secundo *cowyllh*, pro tercio *egwedy* si relicta fuerit.

Lat A §53: De *amwabereu*

[1]Merces filie *penkenedyl* est libra. [2]Merces filie *mayr*: libra* et dimidia. [3]Merces filie *kymmellaur*: libra. [4]Merces filie optimatis qui habet hereditatem, id est, *swyd*: dimidium libre; sine *swyd*: lx^a denarii. [5]Merces filie villani: xx^{ti}iiii^{or} denarii. [6]Merces filie cuiusdam advene sive extranee: xx^{ti}iiii^{or}, si in terra regis [p. 40, c. 1] a viro ducatur. [7]Merces filie cuiusquam illorum qui sunt *suydogyon pennadur* curie libra est. [8]Merces filie cuiuslibet aliorum curialium: dimidium libre. [9]Merces filie fabri curie: dimidium libre. [10]Merces filie *bonhedic kanhuynaul*: xx^{ti}iiii^{or} denarii.

$^{52/60}$ *MS. maritate.
$^{52/62}$ *MS. ubi.
$^{52/63}$ *MS. dandam.
$^{52/64}$ *MS. dandam.
$^{53/2}$ *MS. libram.

[60] A woman legally married shall have *wynebwerth* three times if her husband has intercourse with another woman: for the first time, half of a pound; for the second time, a pound; for the third time, let her depart free together with her entire *dos* and that which is hers by right. [61] But if she suffer this thing further, she shall have no more *wynebwerth*.

[62] If any girl be given to a man, and the man says that he found her defiled, she herself should affirm that she is undefiled, with the oath of five persons, that is, of her father and mother, her brother and sister, and her own oath.

[63] If anyone take a wife in *llathrudd*, and bring her to the house of some *optimas*, let the latter take from the man a guarantor for her *merces* to be paid to her lord, or let the man himself render it, but [let this be] before they sleep together. [64] No one should give a woman before he receives a guarantor for her *merces* to be paid to her lord.

[65] The shame of a maiden is threefold: first, when her father declares in her presence that he has given her to a man; secondly, when she enters her husband's bed; thirdly, when upon rising from the bed she comes among people. [66] And therefore, for the first *amwabyr* is given, for the second *cowyll*, for the third *egweddi* if she is left.

Lat A §53: Concerning *amwabrau*

The *merces* of the daughter of the *pencenedl* is a pound. [2] The *merces* of the daughter of the *maer*: a pound and a half. [3] The *merces* of the daughter of the *cymellawr*: a pound. [4] The *merces* of the daughter of a noble who has an *hereditas*, that is, *swydd*: half a pound; without *swydd*: sixty pence. [5] The *merces* of the daughter of a villein: twenty four pence. [6] The *merces* of the daughter of any stranger or foreigner: twenty four pence if she be married within the king's dominions. [7] The *merces* of the daughter of any of those who are *swyddogion penadur* of the court is a pound. [8] The *merces* of the daughter of anyone of the other courtiers: half a pound. [9] The *merces* of the daughter of the court smith: half a pound. [10] The *merces* of the daughter of a *bonheddig canhwynawl*: twenty four pence.

III. THE "IORWERTH" TEXT
edited and translated by T. M. Charles-Edwards

THE text presented here is that of Peniarth MS. 35 (Aneurin Owen's *G*). In its present form, this manuscript is made up of two unrelated parts in different hands; the part with which we are concerned is in the same hand as MS. *U* of the Cyfnerth tradition, and is therefore of the early fourteenth century.[10] Its text of the tractate on the Law of Women agrees closely with the Iorwerth tradition as represented by the comprehensive manuscripts, and it has been chosen as the basis of the present text for two reasons.

First, it is not yet possible to reconstruct the archetype of all the manuscripts. The willingness of scribes to introduce small changes of wording makes such a reconstruction extremely difficult. Secondly, MS. *G* has been neglected by previous editors. It was the only available early manuscript whose variants were not quoted in AL. Dr. Aled Wiliam did not make any use of it in the text of *Llyfr Iorwerth*, but his stemma rightly shows it as independent of any other manuscript.[11]

The publication of this manuscript's version of the tractate makes available the variants of all early manuscripts. Some sentences of the tractate are, however, missing from MS. *G*, and these have been supplied from Peniarth MS. 32 (the *D* of AL), a manuscript of the Red Book of Hergest school, written in the early fifteenth century in an orthography not too dissimilar from that of MS. *G*. The following sentences (italicised in the text) derive from MS. *D*: §44/7-8, §44/10-§45/1, §52/2. The reference system is that of Wiliam's *Llyfr Iorwerth* with the addition of numbers for the sentences of that edition: thus §44/10 is the tenth sentence of §44 there. As the punctuation of the present text often diverges from that of Wiliam's edition, some sentences appear here without a number, while others have more than one number. The sentence numbered 5/4 in §44 is a detached portion of §44/5: it is the part which follows the seventh punctuation mark in Wiliam's edition.

---

[10] *Supra*, p. 133.
[11] Ior p.xxix.

Ior §44
Kyureitheu g6raged

[G 90r.1]

²O deruyd y wreic bot rodyeit idi, ydan y hangwedi y dyly bot hyt ym pen y seith mlyned; ac o cheiff teir nos o'r seith[u]et bl6ydyn ac yskar onadunt, rannent yn deu hanher pob peth a uo ar y helo oc a uo udunt. ³Y wreic bieu raṅnu a'r g6r dewissa6. Y moch y'r g6r, a'r deueit y'r wreic. Ony byd ont y neill, eu rannu yn deu hanher. Ac os deueit a ge[i]uyr a uyd, y deueit y'r g6r, a'r geiuyr y'r wreic. Ony byd ont y neill, eu rannu yn deu hanner. ⁴O'r meibon y d6y raṅ y'r tat, yr hynaf a'r ieuhaf, a'r peruedhaf y'r uam. ⁵Y dotdrefyn ual hyn y rennir: llestri y llaeth oll, eithyr un bayol ac un dysgyl, y'r gwreic yd a, a'r deu hynny y'r g6r. ⁶Y wreic a dyly karr a ieueu. ⁵/⁴Y g6r a dyly holl lestri y llyn. ⁷ *Y g6r a dyly y ridyll a'r wreic y gogyr man.* ⁸ *Y g6r a dyly y maen uchaf o'r vreuan, a'r wreic yr issaf.* ⁹Y dillat gwely a uo arnadunt y wreic bieiuyd. Y dillat a uo adanunt, y g6r bieu yny wreicaho. Ac g6edy g6reicao, ellyṅget y dillat y'r wreic. Ac os g6reic arall a g6sc ar y dillat, talet y h6ynebwerth iddi. ¹⁰ *Y g6r bieu y galla6r a'r bryccan a gobennyd y tra6sdyle a'r k6lltyr a'r v6yall gynnut a'r taradyr a'r pergyg a'r crymaneu oll dyeith[yr] vn cryman, a h6nn6 y'r wreic.* ¹¹ *Y wreic bieu y badell a'r trybed a'r u6yell lydan a'r g6dyf a'r s6ch a'r llin achlan a'r llinat a'r g6lan a'r trithg6t dyeithyr eur neu aryant, a h6nn6, o byd, y rannu. Ac y sef y6 y trithg6t y lla6gyteu ac a vo yndunt odieithyr eur ac aryant.* ¹² *Or byd g6eeu, eu rannu. Y pelleneu y'r meibyon or bydant; ac ony bydant, eu rannu.* ¹³ *Y g6r a dyly a vo uch daear ac is daear o yt.* ¹⁴ *Y g6r a dyly yr ieir oll ac vn cath, a'r rei ereill oll y'r wreic.* ¹⁵ *Y b6yt ual hynn y rennir: y wreic bieu y kic yn heli, a'r g6r bieu g6edy croccer;* ¹⁶*y wreic bieu y kic b6lch a'r ka6s b6lch;* ¹⁷*y wreic bieu kymeint [o ula6t] ac a allo y r6ng nerth y d6y vreich a'e deu lin y d6yn o'r gell hyt y ty.* ¹⁸*Pob un onadunt bieu y dillat dyeithyr y mentyll; a'r mentyll, eu rannu.* ¹⁹*Os y g6r a vyd*

Ior §44
The Laws of Women

²If it happens that a woman has givers, she is entitled to be under her *egweddi* until the end of seven years. And if she gets three nights from the seventh year and they part, let them divide into two halves everything that is theirs which is in their possession. ³It is for the woman to divide and the man to choose. The pigs go to the man and the sheep to the woman. If they have only one kind, they are to be divided into two halves. And if there be sheep and goats, the sheep go to the man and the goats to the woman. If they have only one kind, they are to be divided. ⁴Of the children two parts go to the father, the eldest and the youngest, and the middle to the mother. ⁵The household goods are divided as follows: all the milk vessels, except for one pail and one dish, go to the woman, and those two go to the man. ⁶The woman is entitled to a car and yokes. ⁵/⁴The man is entitled to all the drinking vessels. ⁷The man is entitled to the riddle and the woman to the fine sieve. ⁸The man is entitled to the upper stone of the quern and the woman to the lower. ⁹The bed-clothes which are over them shall belong to the woman. The clothes which are under them belong to the man until he marry. And when he marries, let him release the clothes to the woman. And if another woman sleeps upon the clothes, let him pay her face-value to her. ¹⁰To the man belong the cauldron and the blanket and the pillows of the bed and the coulter and the wood-axe and the auger and the *pergyng* and all the sickles except one sickle, and the latter goes to the woman. ¹¹To the woman belong the pan and the tripod and the broad axe and the billhook and the ploughshare and all the flax and the linseed and the wool and the *trithgwd* except for gold or silver, and the latter, if there is any, is divided. By the *trithgwd* is meant the handbags and what is in them except for gold and silver. ¹²If there are webs they are divided. The balls [of wool] go to the sons, if there are any; and if there are none, they are divided. ¹³The man is entitled to the corn which is above ground and below ground. ¹⁴The man is entitled to all the hens and one cat, and all the others go to the woman. ¹⁵The food is divided as follows: to the woman belongs the meat which is in salt, and after it is hung up it belongs to the man; ¹⁶to the woman belongs the cut meat and the partly-used cheese; ¹⁷to the woman belongs as much flour as she can carry by the strength of her arms and her knees from the larder to the house. ¹⁸To each of them belong their clothes except for the cloaks; and the cloaks are to be divided. ¹⁹If the man is privileged, let him reveal his privilege before the divi-

breinha6l, dangosset y vreint kynn rannu. A g6edy kaffo ef y vreint, ranher mal y dywedassam ni uchot.

Ior §45

Eu dylyedyon talent yn deu hanner. [90v] ²Os ky*n*n y seithuet ul6ydyn yd ysgarant, talher idi y hegwedi a'e hargyfryeu, a'e chowyll os yn uor6yn y rodir—yr hyn a uo ar garn o'r petheu hynny*. ³Os kynn y seithuet ul6ydyn yd edeu hi y g6r, c6byl o hynny a gyll, eithyr y chowyll a'e h6ynebwerth. ⁴Os y g6r a uyd clauur, neu anadyl drewedic, neu na allo ymrein, os o achos un o'r [try] pheth hynny yd edeu hi euo, hi a dyly caffel c6byl o'r eidi. ⁵Os o uar6 [y gwahanant], hi a dyly pob peth yn deu hanher, eithyr yr yt. Ny dyly g6reic caffel rann o'r yt, onyt g6reic p6ys. ⁶Ac os o uy6 a ma*r*6 y gwahanant, rannet y claf, a'e perigla6r y gyt ac ef, a dewisset yr iach*. ⁷Ny dyly y claf kymynnu* namyn** y dayret y'r egl6ys, ac y'r argl6yd, a'e dyledyon. A chet ys kymynno, y mab a eill torri y ky*m*myn h6nn6. A h6nn6 a elwir y mab anwar. ⁸P6y bynhac a torho kymyn k*yureitha*6l, dayret a dyledyon*, ysgy*m*mun uyd uegys publican neu pagan. ⁹Os o uywyt y gwahanant, trigyet hi [91r] a'r eidi yn y ty hyt [ym pen] y na6 nos a'r na6 nieu* y vybot ae k*yureitha*6l y bu y gwahan. Ac os ia6n uu y gwahan, aet hi a'r eidi o'r ty ym pe*n*n y na6uet dyd, y da o'r blaen, ac ar ol y keinha6c diwethaf aet e hun.

Ior §46

Sarhaet g6reic 6rya6c vrth ureint y g6r yd a; nyt amgen trayan sarhaet y g6r. Ky*n*n y rodi y 6r, hanher sarhaet y bra6t. ²Y galanas, na hi a uo gwed6 na hi a uo g6rya6c, hanher galanas bra6t. ³Or mynn g6r wreic arall g6edy yd ysgarho a'r gyntaf, ryd uyd y gyntaf. ⁴O d*e*ruyd y 6r ysgar a'e wreic, a mynnu o honno vr arall, a bot yn ediuar gan y g6r kyntaf ry ysgar a'e wreic, a'e godiwes ohona6 a'r neill troet yn y gwely, a'r llall eithyr y gwely, y g6r kyntaf a dyly caffel y wreic.

⁵O d*e*ruyd y wreic vrya6c g6neuthur kyulauan dybryt, ae rodi cussan y 6r arall, ae gadel y gouyssya6, ae gadel y hymrein, sarhaet y g6r y6 hynny. ⁶Os y hymrein, y sarhaet honno a dyrcheuir ar uod y hanher yn

⁴⁵/² *This punctuation seems to give the right sense while doing as little violence as possible to the punctuation of the manuscript.*
⁴⁵/⁶ *MS. ia6ch with punctum delens under 6.*
⁴⁵/⁷ *The scribe seems to have written kyminnu or kymunni (without dotting the i) and then turned the letter after the m into a y.*
**namyn added in the margin.*
⁴⁵/⁸ *The second y of dyledyon is written on an o.*
⁴⁵/⁹ *MS. niei with the second downstroke of the u expunged or obscured.*

sion. And when he has received whatever his privilege entitle him to, let the division proceed as we have said above.

Ior §45

Let them each pay a half of their debts. [2]If they part before the seventh year, let her be paid her *egweddi* and her *argyfrau*, and her *cowyll* if she is given as a virgin—that part of these things which is on the hoof. [3]If she leaves her husband before the seventh year, she loses all that, except her *cowyll* and her face-value. [4]If the man is leprous or his breath stinks or he cannot copulate—if she leaves him because of one of these three things—she is entitled to have all that which is hers. [5]If they part through death she is entitled to an equal share of everything, except for the corn. A woman is not entitled to a share of corn unless she be a "woman of weight". [6]And if they part through life and death [one living, the other dying], let the sick divide in the presence of his parish priest, and let the healthy choose. [7]The sick person is not entitled to bequeath anything except tribute to the church and to the lord, and his debts. And though he bequeath it, his son can break that bequest. And he is called the cold son. [8]Whoever breaks a legal bequest, tribute and debts, he shall be excommunicate like a publican or a pagan. [9]If they part while alive, let her remain with what is hers in the house until the nine nights and the nine days [are up] to know whether the parting was legal. And if the parting was proper, let her go with what is hers from the house at the end of the ninth day, the goods in front, and after the last penny let her go herself.

Ior §46

The *sarhaed* of a married woman is according to the status of her husband, namely a third of the husband's *sarhaed*. Before she is given to a man, it is half the *sarhaed* of her brother. [2]Her *galanas*, whether she be single or whether she be married, is half the *galanas* of her brother. [3]If a man would take another wife after he has parted from the first, the first shall be free. [4]If it happens that a man parts from his wife, and she wants another man, and the first man repent of having parted from his wife and overtake her with one foot in the bed and the other out of the bed, the first man is entitled to have the woman.

[5]If it happens that a wife commit an unseemly offence, either giving a kiss to another man, or allowing herself to be fingered, or allowing intercourse with her, that is *sarhaed* to her husband. [6]If there has been inter-

u6y, canys o kenedyl elynyaeth yd hen[y]6. [91v] [7]Os y gouyssya6 a deruyd, talet ida6 sarhaet, a honno heb ardyrchauel. [8]Os cussan uyd, taler ida6 deuparth sarhaet, canyt gweithret c6byl. [9]Os gwadu y gaffel r6ng y deu uord6yt a wna y g6r, ll6 de*ng* wyr a deugeint, a de*ng* wraged a deugeint y gan y wreic*. [10]Os gwadu y gouyssya6 a wna, rodet l6 pedwar gwyr ar dec, a ll6 pedeir g6raged ar dec ar wreic. [11]Os gwadu rodi cussan a wna, rodet y g6r ll6 seith wyr, a'r wreic l6 seith wraged, a hynny og eu kyfnesseiueit y am eu mameu a'e tadeu a'e brodyr a'e chwioryd.

Ior §47

P6ybynhac a dycco mor6yn lathrut a chyn bot achos ida6 a hi gouyn ida6, "Beth a rody di y mi?", a meintoli ohona6 ef pa ueint a rodei idi, a hynny ar y gret, ket keissyo ef y wadu g6edy hynny, os gyrr hi arna6 ef, credad6y y6 hi, canys yna* y mae geir y geir ar y gwerynda6t, can duc ef hihi y'r lle nyt oed neitha6rwyr. [2]O rodir mor6yn y 6r, a'e* chaffel hi o'r g6r yn [92r] llygredic, a'e diodef hi y uelly hyt trannoeth, ny dyly ef d6yn dim tranoeth o'e dylyet hi. [3]Os ef a wna ynteu [kyuodi] ar y neitha6r g6edy as caffo yn llygredic, ac na chysgo y gyt a hi hyt trannoeth, ny dyly dim tranoeth y ganta6 ef. [4]O de*r*uyd dyuot bronneu a chedor arnei, a'e blodeua6, yna y dyweit y k*y*ureith na 6yr neb beth y6 ae mor6yn ae g6reic, achos ry dyuot ar6ydon mab arnei. Vrth hynny y gat y k*y*ureith y diheura6 hi o l6 seith nyn, y am y that a'e mam a'e brodyr a'e chwioryd. [5]Os hitheu ny mynn y diheura6, lladher y chrys yn gyuu6ch a'e gwerdyr, a roder dinawet bl6yd yn y lla6 g6edy ira6 y losg6rn. Ac o geill y gynhal, kymeret yn lle y ran o'r argyfreu. Ac ony eill y kynhal, bit heb dim.

Ior §48

P6y bynhac a rodo g6reic y 6r, ef bieu talu* y hamobyr, neu ynteu a gymero meicheu y genti hi ar y talu. Ac os hitheu ehun a ymryd, talet y hamobyr*, canys hi ehun a uu rodyat [92v] arnei. [2]O d6c g6r wreic

---

46/9 *a deng . . . wreic *in the margin.*
47/1 *yna *inserted above the line.*
47/2 *e *inserted above the line.*
48/1 *talu *in the margin.*
  **ha*m*/mobyr *across a hole in the parchment.*

course with her, that *sarhaed* is increased by a half, for it derives from enmity between kindreds. [7]If she has been fingered, let him pay to him the *sarhaed*, and that without augment. [8]If there be a kiss, let two thirds of the *sarhaed* be paid to him, since it is not a complete act. [9]If the man denies being found between her two thighs, an oath of fifty men [is required], and fifty women from the wife. [10]If he deny fingering her, let him give an oath of fourteen men, and an oath of fourteen women for the wife. [11]If he deny giving a kiss, let the man give an oath of seven men, and the wife an oath of seven women, and they are to be from their nearest relatives including their mothers and fathers and brothers and sisters.

Ior §47

Whoever should abduct a virgin and before he has intercourse with her she asks him, "What will you give me?", and he specifies how much he would give her, and that upon his faith, though he try to deny it afterwards, if she charges him, she is to be believed, for in that case her word is a [conclusive] word, since he took her to a place where there were no wedding guests. [2]If a girl is given to a man, and the man finds her to have been deflowered and put up with her in that condition until the next day, he is not entitled to subtract anything the next day from her due. [3]If he gets out of bed during the wedding celebrations after he has found her to have been deflowered, and does not sleep with her until the next day, she is not entitled to anything the next day from him. [4]If it happens that her breasts and pubic hair have grown and she has menstruated, then the law says that it does not know what she is, whether girl or woman, because the signs of child[bearing] have appeared. Therefore the law allows her to be vindicated by the oath of seven persons, including her father and her mother and her brothers and her sisters. [5]If she does not wish to be vindicated, let her shift be cut off as high as her genitals and let a year-old steer with its tail greased be put into her hand. And if she can hold it, let her take it in place of her share of the *argyfrau*. And if she cannot hold it, let her have nothing.

Ior §48

Whoever gives a woman to a man, it is for him to pay *amobr* for her, or he shall take sureties from her for its payment. And if she gives herself, let her pay her *amobr*, for she herself has been her own giver. [2]If a man

lathlut, a'e dyuot y ty mab uchel6r y gysgu genti, ac na chymero y g6rda mach ar y hamobyr, talet ehun yr amobyr.

²O deruid y 6r d6yn g6reic lathrut, bit hyt ym pen y seith mlyned ar tri eidyon kyhyt eu kyrn ac eu hysgyfarn. A chan colles ehun y breint, bit hitheu ehun ar y breint h6nn6. ⁴O byd argyureu idi bit h6nn6 yn ditreul hyt ym pen y seith mlyned. ⁵Os hitheu a ganhata y treula6, ny diwygir dim idi o treul deint ac ystlys. ⁶O pen y seith mlyned allan rannu deu hanner uegys a g6reic a rodyeit arnei, ⁷cany phara g6reic nac o lathrut nac o rod ar ureint y hegwedi namyn hyt ym penn y seith mlyned, ac nat agwedya6l hitheu o penn y seith mlyned allan. Vrth hynny rannent deu hanner.

⁸P6ybynhac a gysco teir nos gan wreic o'r pan anhudher y tan hyt pan datanhudher tranoeth, a mynnu ohona6 y wadu*, talet idi eidyon a talo ugeint ac arall [93r] a talho dec ar ugeint ac arall a talho tri ugeint. Ac os d6c ar ty ac anll6yth a'e bot y gyt ac ef hyt ym penn y seith mlyned, rannu a hi uegys a g6reic a rodyeit arnei.

⁹Teir hegwedi kyureitha6l yssyd: egwedi merch brenhin, nyt amgen, pedeir punt ar ugeint; a'e chowyll vyth punt; egwedi merch g6rda, teir punt, a'e chowyll punt; hegwedi merch mab eillt, punt; y chowyll pedwar ugeint.

Ior §49

O deruyd y vr ueichogi g6reic o l6yn a pherth, ef a dyly gossymdeitha6 y mab, canys y* kyureith a dyweit na dyly hi gaffel treul o achos y g6r cany chauas y u6ynant, ac 6rth hynny y dyly ynteu meithrin y mab. ²O deruyd y 6r ysgar a'e wreic a hi yn ueicha6c pan ysgarer a hi, gatter idi o'r pan ysgarher a hi yny angho yg kyueir hanher bl6ydyn o ueithrin y mab. Ac gwedy ganher y mab hitheu bieu y ueithrin ef eilweith ul6ydyn—mynho na uynho ³ys dir idi y ueithrin yr da y gan y g6r. Sef y6 messur [93v] y da: bu6ch ulith, a pheis a talo pedeir keinya6c kyureith, a phadell a talo .i. kyureith* a charreit o'r yt goreu a tyuo ar tref y dat, a hynny idi yr y ueithrin ul6ydyn. Hitheu ehun g6edy hynny bieu y ueithrin ef hanner

---

⁴⁸/⁸ *Other MSS. have gadu, which the sense seems to require.
⁴⁹/¹ *MS. y mab, with a line through mab and dots under it.
⁴⁹/³ *The scribe seems to have used the abbreviation for kyureith by mistake, instead of that for keinya6c.

abducts a woman and comes to the house of a *mab uchelwr* to sleep with her, and the householder does not take a surety for her *amobr*, let him pay the *amobr* himself.

[3] If it happens that a man abducts a woman, let her be until the end of seven years upon [i.e. with a contingent entitlement to] three bullocks whose horns are as long as their ears. And since she herself has lost her status, let her remain with that status. [4] If she has an *argyfrau* let it remain unconsumed until the end of the seven years. [5] If she herself allows it to be consumed, no compensation is made to her by reason of wear by teeth and body. [6] From the end of the seven years onwards there is a division into two halves as with a woman with givers for her, [7] for no wife, whether by abduction or by gift, remains of the status of her *egweddi* save until the end of the seven years, and she is not entitled to *egweddi* from the end of the seven years onwards. Therefore let them take equal shares.

[8] Whoever sleeps with a woman for three nights from the time when the fire is covered up until it is uncovered the next day, and wishes to repudiate her, let him pay her a bullock worth twenty pence and another worth thirty and another worth sixty. And if he takes her to house and holding, and she is with him until the end of the seven years, he shares with her as with a woman who had givers.

[9] There are three legal *egweddïau*: the *egweddi* of a king's daughter, namely twenty-four pounds, and her *cowyll* is eight pounds; the *egweddi* of a *gwrda*'s daughter, three pounds, and her *cowyll* a pound; the *egweddi* of a villein's daughter, a pound; her *cowyll*, four score pence.

Ior §49

If it happens that a man impregnates a woman of bush and brake, he is obliged to maintain the child, for the law says that she ought not to incur expense because of the man since she has not received benefit from him, and therefore he is obliged to rear the child. [2] If it happens that a man parts with his wife and she is pregnant when he parts from her, the period from the parting until she gives birth is to be allowed her as six months' rearing of the child. And after the child is born it is for her to rear him for a further year—whether she be willing or not, [3] she must rear him in exchange for goods from the man. This is the measure of the goods: a milch cow and a tunic worth four legal pence and a dish worth one legal penny and a car-load of the best corn that may grow on the holding of his father, and that goes to her for rearing him for a year. After that she

bl6ydyn. Ac o hynny allan ny ellir kymell erni y ueithrin namyn y ra*nn* ehun, onys mynn ehun. ⁴Ac o hynny hyt ym pedeir blyned ar dec y deu parth ar y tat o'r meithrin, a'r trayan ar y uam. Ac ym pe*nn* y pedeir blyned ar dec y mae ia6n y'r tat d6yn y uab ar y argl6yd. Ac y mae ia6n y'r mab g6rhau ida6 ef. ⁵Ac o hynny allan bit 6rth ossymdeith y argl6yd.

Ior §50

O de*r*uyd y wreic dywedut ar 6r d6yn treis arnei, a gwadu o'r g6r, rodet ll6 de*ng* wyr a deugeint heb alltudyon heb wyr not. ²O de*r*uyd idi hitheu gyrru yn k*yureith*a6l arna6 ef, ky*mm*eret kala y g6r yn y lla6 asseu a'e lla6 deheu ar y kreireu, a thy*n*get hi y'r kreireu hynny y ry ymrein hi a'r gala honno y treis arnei, a ry [94r] wneuth*ur* meuel a sarhaet ohona6 ef idi hi, ac o'e chenedyl ac o'e hargl6yd. ³Rei o'r ygneit ny adant wat yn erbyn hynny. Y k*yureith* eissoes a dyweit ual y dywedassam ni uchot. ⁴O de*r*uyd y 6r adef d6yn treis ar wreic, talet deudeng mu y'r brenhi*n* a'e hamobyr y hargl6yd; ac os morwyn uyd, y chowyll a'e hegwedi yn y ueint u6yhaf y dylyo, a'e h6ynebwerth, a'e dilyssr6yd; ac os g6reic vrya6c uyd y sarhaet, gan y hardyrchauel ar uod y hanher, o'e g6r.

⁵O de*r*uyd y 6r d6yn mor6yn lathrut, y hargl6yd a'e chenedyl a eill y d6yn y ganta6, kyn bo dr6c ganta6 ef*. Ac o bu gynt gan vr, ny ellir y d6yn y gan y g6r a'e duc g6edy hynny hi lathrut, onyt ehun a'e myn.

Ior §51

Tri phriuei g6reic: y chowyll, a'e gouyn, a'e sarhaet. Sef achos y gelwir yn tri phriuei g6reic vrth eu bot yn [tri] phria6t g6reic, ac na ellir* eu d6yn o neb achos y genti. ²Sef y6 [y] chowyll, yr hyn a gaffei am y g6erynda6t. ³Sef y6 y sarhaet pob maedu [94v] a wnel y g6r arnei. Eithyr am tri pheth, sarhaet y6 idi. Sef y6 y tri pheth hynny y dyly y maedu: am rodi peth ny dylyho y rodi, ac am y chaffel gan 6r, ac am una6 meuel ar y uaraf. Ac os am y chaffel gan vr y maed, ny dyly o diu6yn namyn hynny, kany dylyir diu6yn a dial* am un gyflauan. ⁴Sef y6 y gouyn: o cheiff y g6r

---

⁵⁰/⁵ *Wiliam emends the ganthau of his MS. (B) to genthy, but the archetype clearly had ganthau. However, Cyfn §73/13a, Lat A §52/33, Bleg 63.3-6, and Col §63 all refer to the girl's willingness, not the man's.
⁵¹/¹ *MS. eillir.
⁵¹/³ *a dial written above the line and very faint.

herself is to rear him for six months. And from then on she cannot be compelled to rear him except for her own share, unless she herself wishes it. [4] And from then until fourteen years two thirds of the rearing fall upon the father, and a third upon the mother. And at the end of the fourteen years it is proper for the father to take his son before his lord. And it is proper for the son to do homage to him. [5] And from then on let him be maintained by his lord.

Ior §50

If it happens that a woman says that a man has raped her, and the man denies it, let him give the oath of fifty men without foreigners without designated men. [2] If it happens that she legally charges him, let her take the man's penis in her left hand and put her right hand upon the relics, and let her swear to those relics that he penetrated her with that penis by rape upon her, and that he caused shame and insult to her, and to her kindred and to her lord. [3] Some judges do not allow a denial against that. The law, however, says as we have said above. [4] If it happens that a man admits raping a woman, let him pay twelve cows to the king and her *amobr* to her lord; and if she be a virgin, her *cowyll* and her *egweddi* according to the greatest amount to which she may be entitled, and her face-value and her *dilysrwydd*; and if she be a wife then his *sarhaed*, augmented to the extent of a half, goes to her husband.

[5] If it happens that a man abducts a virgin, her lord and her kindred can remove her from him, though he object. And if she has been with a man previously, she cannot be removed from the man who afterwards abducted her, unless she herself wishes it.

Ior §51

The three privities of a woman: her *cowyll* and her *gowyn* and her *sarhaed*. This is the reason why they are called the three privities of a woman, because they are the three appropriated things of a woman, and they cannot be taken from her for any reason. [2] Her *cowyll* is what she received for her virginity. [3] Her *sarhaed* is every beating which her husband gives her. Except for three things it is *sarhaed* to her. Those three things for which it is right to beat her are: for giving something which she is not entitled to give, for being found with a man, and for wishing shame upon his beard. And if he beats her for being found with a man, he is not entitled to any compensation save that, for there is no right to compensation and revenge for any offence. [4] The *gowyn* is, if she find her

gan wreic arall, talet y g6r idi y treigyl kyntaf chweugeint, a'r eil treigyl
punt. Os keiff y tryded [weith], ysgar a eill heb golli dim o'r eidi. ⁵A'r da
a gaffo am y tri pheth hynny a dyly uot yn wahanedic y vrth y g6r.

⁶G6reic y brenhin a eill rodi heb ganyat trayan a del o dofot y gan y
brenhi*n*. ⁷G6reic mab uchel6r a eill rodi y mantell a'e chrys a'e phenlliein
a'e hesgidyeu a'e b6yt a'e dia6t a chra6n y chell, a benffygya6 y holl
dodrefyn. ⁸G6reic taya6c ny eill rodi dim namyn y phengu6ch, na
benffygya6 namyn y gogyr a hynny hyt y clywer y llef y ar y tom o'e d6yn
adref.

⁹Tri gor[95r]ssaf g6reic: pan kysger genti, ny dyly kychwyn odyno hyt
ym pe*n*n y na6uet dyd; a phan ysgarho a'e g6r, ny dyly kychwyn hyt y
na6uet dyd, ac [y]na ar ol y k*einya6c* diwethaf; a phan uo mar6 y g6r, ny
dyly kychwyn hyt y na6uet dyd, ac yna ar ol y k*einya6c* diwethaf.

¹⁰O tri mod y dylyir amobyr: o rod ac estyn kyny chysger genti; yr eil
y6 o kywelyogaeth honneit kynny bo rod; y trydyd o ueichogi.

¹¹Amobyr merch maer kyghella6r, punt. Amobyr merch maer,
chweugeint. Amobyr merch penkenedyl, chweugei*n*t a phunt. Amobyr
merch uchel6r, chweugeint. Amobyr merch mab eillt, pedwar ugeint.
Amobyr merch alltut, pedeir ar ugeint. Amobyr merch pob
pe*n*ns6yda6c, herwyd rei punt, herwyd ereill chweugeint*. Amobyr
merch pob un o'r s6ydogyon ereill, herwyd rei chweugei*n*t, herwyd ereill
tri ugeint. Amobr merch kaeth, deudec k*einya6c*.

Ior §52

O beichogir gwenidya6c [95v] o kaeth, y neb a'e beichoco a dyly rodi
g6reic arall y wassanaethu yn y lle yny angho [a meithryn y mab g6edy
angho] yn dilesteir y'r neb a wassanaetha hi, ac o byd mar6 yn eghi talu y
gwerth y hargl6yd. ²*Ebedi6 ystauella6c o wreic: vn ar bymthec.* ³O
de*r*uyd mar6 alltut o wreic yn mynet tr6y wlat, talet y'r neb bieiffo y tir
un ar pymthec yn y uar6 tywarchen. ⁴O de*r*uyd i vr ysgar a'e wreic a

husband with another woman, let her husband pay her six score pence the first time, and a pound the second time. If she find him a third time she can part with him without losing anything of what is hers. ⁵And it is right that the goods which she gets for those three things be separate from her husband.

⁶The wife of the king can give without permission a third of the casual acquisitions which come from the king. ⁷The wife of an *uchelwr* can give her cloak and her shift and her headkerchief and her shoes and her food and her drink and the store of her larder, and can lend all her household goods. ⁸The wife of a villein cannot give anything except her headgear, nor lend anything except her sieve, and that [only] as far as her voice may be heard from the dunghill calling for it to be brought home.

⁹Three stoppings of a woman: when she is slept with, she is not obliged to move from there until the end of the ninth day; and when she parts from her husband, she is not obliged to move until the ninth day, and then after the last penny; and when the husband dies she is not obliged to move until the ninth day, and then after the last penny.

¹⁰In three ways *amobr* becomes due: by gift and handing over though she be not slept with; the second is by open cohabitation though there be no gift; the third by pregnancy.

¹¹The *amobr* of a *maer cynghellor*'s daughter, a pound. The *amobr* of a *maer's* daughter, six score pence. The *amobr* of the daughter of the head of a kindred, a pound and six score pence. The *amobr* of an *uchelwr*'s daughter, six score pence. The *amobr* of a villein's daughter, four score. The *amobr* of a foreigner's daughter, twenty-four. The *amobr* of the daughter of any chief official, according to some a pound, according to others six score. The *amobr* of the daughter of any one of the other officials, according to some six score, according to others three score. The *amobr* of a slave's daughter, twelve pence.

Ior §52

If a slave woman is made pregnant, the man who impregnated her is obliged to provide another woman to serve in her place until she give birth, and to rear the child after she has given birth without any expense falling upon the man whom she serves; and if she dies in childbirth to pay her value to her lord. ²The *ebediw* of a woman having a chamber: sixteen pence. ³If it happens that a foreign woman dies while travelling through a district, let the owner of the land be paid sixteen pence for the "death-sod". ⁴If it happens that a man parts with his wife and wants another,

mynnu arall, dilis eu kany dyly un g6r bot d6y gwraged ida6. [5]Pob g6reic
a dyly uynet y fford y mynno kany byd karrdychwel ac ny dylyir idi dim
namyn y hamobyr, canyt oes y wreic ebedi6 namyn y hamobyr. [6]Ny
chegein g6reic yn uach nac yn tyst ar 6r. [7]O de*r*uyd gwelet g6reic yn
dyuot o'r neill parth y'r ll6yn a'r g6r o'r parth arall, neu yn dyuot o
wacty, neu y dan un uantell, os g6adu a wnant, ll6 de*n*g wraged a
deugeint ar y wreic, a'r gymeint o wyr ar y g6r.

Ior §53

O de*r*uyd rodi Kymraes y alltut, vrth ureint yr alltut [96r] yd a y sarhaet
yny uo mar6 yr alltut, ac g6edy bo mar6 yr alltut yny uynho vr arall;
canyt ymchoel y breint hi dracheuyn ar y chenedyl. [2]O de*r*uyd rodi
Kymraes y alltut a bot plant meibon udunt, y plant a dyly tref tat o
uam6ys eithyr na dylyant ra*n*n o'r tydyn breina6l hyt y trydydyn, eithyr
mab alltut o pe*n*naeth: h6nn6 a keiff rann o c6byl. [3]Meibon y ry6 wraged
hynny y telir gwarthec dyuach onadunt. Sef achos y gelwir yn warthec
dyuach, canyt kenedyl y tat a'e tal namyn kenedyl y uam.

[4]Ny dyly g6reic prynu na gwerthu ony* byd pria6t heb ganyat y g6r.
O* byd pria6t hi a dyly prynu a gwerthu.

[5]Teir g6raged a dyly eu meibon uam6ys herwyd k*y*ureith: mab
Kymraes a roder y alltut*, a mab g6reic a 6ystler y wlat a*n*ghyfieith, o
cheiff beichogi a'e g6ystla6 o'e chenedyl a'e [96v] hargl6yd, a gwreic a
dycco alltut treis [arnei].

[6]O de*r*uyd rodi mor6yn y 6r ac na ouynher y chowyll kyn y chyuodi
y ar y gwely tranoeth, ny dyly ef atteb idi o hynny allan. [7]O de*r*uyd y
uor6yn na defnydyo y chowyll ky*n*n y chyuodi y ar y gwely tranoeth, ny
dyly y chowyll o hynny allan namyn yn gyffredin y rydunt.

[8]Ny dyly merch o da y that namyn hanner a gaffo y bra6t. Ac ny dyly
talu o alanas namyn hanner a talo bra6t idi, a hynny dros y phlant. Ac

---

53/4 *Both words have been doctored. After the O of the first, two letters have been rubbed out, but a half-crossed-out r seems to be legible in photograph. The second word
has been wholly rubbed out, but the photograph suggests that at some stage Ony was
squeezed into the space of two letters.
53/5 *a mab . . . alltut repeated by dittography.*

she [the first] is immune [from any claim by him] since no man is entitled to have two wives. [5] Every woman is entitled to go wherever she may wish since there will be no car-return and nothing is due from her except her *amobr*, for a woman has no *ebediw* save her *amobr*. [6] No woman is competent as a surety or a witness upon a man. [7] If it happens that a woman is seen coming from one side of a bush and the man from the other side, or coming from an empty house, or under one cloak, if they deny it, an oath of thirty women [is required] for the woman, and the same number of men for the man.

Ior §53

If it happens that a Welshwoman is given to a foreigner, her *sarhaed* follows the status of the foreigner until the foreigner dies, and after the foreigner has died until she takes another husband; for her status does not return again to her kindred. [2] If it happens that a Welshwoman is given to a foreigner and they have male children, the children are entitled to a patrimony in virtue of succession through the mother, except that they are not entitled to a share of the privileged toft until the third generation, except for the son of a foreign chief: the latter gets a share of everything. [3] It is the sons of such women for whom "cattle of dark ancestry" are paid. This is the reason why they are called cattle of dark ancestry, because it is not the kindred of the father which pays them but the kindred of the mother.

[4] A wife is not entitled to buy or sell, unless she be *priod*, without the permission of her husband. If she be *priod*, she is entitled to buy and sell.

[5] Three women whose sons are entitled to inheritance through the mother, according to law: the son of a Welshwoman who is given to a foreigner, and the son of a woman given as a hostage to a country with another language, if she becomes pregnant and has been given as a hostage by her kindred and her lord, and a woman who is raped by a foreigner.

[6] If it happens that a virgin is given to a man and her *cowyll* is not requested before she rises from the bed the next day, he is not obliged to answer her henceforth. [7] If it happens that a virgin does not use her *cowyll* before rising from the bed the next day, she is not entitled to her *cowyll* from then on, but it remains in common between them.

[8] Of her father's goods a daughter is entitled to only half what her brother gets. And of *galanas* she is obliged to pay only half what a brother of hers pays, and that is on behalf of her children. And if she has

ony [byd] plant idi, a thy*n*gu ohoni na bo byth, ny dyly talu dim. Ac o byd plant idi ac eu mynet yn oet k*yureith*a6l, talent ehun drostunt o hyn allan. [9]Ny dyly un wreic talu k*einya6c* paladyr na hen uo na ieuanc.

Ior §54

O de*r*uyd y wreic, [o] achos mynnu yscar, dywedut na allo y g6r y hymrein, k*yureith* a eirch y proui. [2]Sef ual y prouir: ta*n*nu llenlliein we*n*n newyd olchi adanadunt; a mynet y g6r ar warthaf honno y uot genti; a phan del y ewyllis y ell6ng ar y llenlliein. [3]Ac o geill hynny ual y gwelher [97r] ar y llenlliein, dogyn y6 ida6*, ac g6edy hynny ny eill hi yscar ac euo o'r achos honno. Ac ony eill ynteu hynny, hi a eill yscar ac ef a mynet a'r eidi yn c6byl.

[4]O dyweit mor6yn ar 6r d6yn treis arnei, a'r g6r yn g6adu, a dywedut o'r uorwyn ony duc ef treis arnei hi y bot yn uor6yn etwa, y k*yureith* a dyweit bot yn ia6n proui ae mor6yn ae nat mor6yn, canys y bot yn uor6yn y6 y hardel6. [5]Sef a dyly y proui yr edling. Ac os keiff yn uor6yn ryd uyd y g6r y dywesp6yt arna6 y threissa6, a hitheu heb golli y breint. [6]O dygir treis ar wreic vrya6c, ny dylyir talu amobyr canys hi ehun a'e tal6ys pan vrha6ys.

[7]O de*r*uyd y wreic d6yn map yn k*yureith*a6l y 6r, ket as gwatto y g6r, y k*yureith* a dyweit gwedy as dycco hi un weith y 6r na dyly hi y d6yn ef y arall byth, cany byd karrdychwel y 6rth y neb y ducp6yt yn kyntaf ida6.

[8]O de*r*uyd rodi g6reic y 6r ac enwi da ida6 genti, a chaffel c6byl o'r da hyt yn oet un [97v] k*einya6c*, ac na chaffer honno, y k*yureith* a dyweit y geill y g6r yscar a hi, ac na chaffo dim o'r eidi, a honno a elwir yr un k*einya6c* a d6c cant. [9]Nyt reit mach ar dilysr6yd da a del yn canhysgaed gan wreic.

Ior §55

Y wreic a dyly trayan sarhaet y g6r, nac o lad y sarhaer nac o peth arall. [2]Ny dyly reith o wraged y gyt a g6reic, nac am ledrat nac am alanas nac am uach namyn reith o wyr.

[54/3] **MS*. idia6 *with punctum delens under the second* i.

no children, and she swears that she will never have any, she is not obliged to pay anything. And if she has children and they have reached legal age, let them pay themselves on their own behalf from then on. [9]No woman is obliged to pay a spear penny, whether she be old or young.

Ior §54

If it happens that a woman, because she wants a parting, says that her husband cannot copulate with her, the law requires it to be proved. [2]This is how it is proved: a white sheet newly washed is stretched under them, and the man goes onto it to have intercourse with her; and when his desire comes let him ejaculate it upon the sheet. [3]And if he can do that so that it is seen upon the sheet, it is sufficient for him, and after that she cannot part with him for that reason. And if he cannot do that, she can part with him and take all that is hers.

[4]If a virgin should say that a man has raped her, and the man deny it, and the virgin say that if he has not raped her she is still a virgin, the law says that it is right to test whether she be a virgin or not a virgin, for it is her plea that she is a virgin. [5]The person who should test it is the *edling*. And if he finds her to be a virgin, the man said to have raped her shall be free, and she will not lose her status. [6]If a married woman is raped, there is no obligation to pay *amobr*, for she herself paid it when she married.

[7]If it happens that a woman legally fathers a child upon a man, though the man deny it, the law says that after she has fathered it once upon a man she is not entitled ever to father it upon another, for there shall not be a car-return from the man upon whom it was first fathered.

[8]If it happens that a woman is given to a man and goods to accompany her are specified to him, and all the goods are received up to the last penny, and that one is not received, the law says that the man can part with her, and that he gets nothing of what is hers, and that is called the one penny which brings a hundred. [9]There is no need for a surety on the immunity from claim of goods which come as a dowry with a wife.

Ior §55

The wife is entitled to a third of the *sarhaed* of her husband, whether he suffered *sarhaed* by being killed or by something else. [2]There is no entitlement to a group of oath-helpers composed of women with a woman, either for theft or for *galanas* or for surety, but only a group of oath-helpers composed of men.

[3]*Kyureith* a dyweit na dyly g6reic cowyll g6edy blodeuho onys diheura y chyfnesseifeit hi y am y that a'e mam a'e brodyr a'e chwioryd, a hynny yny uo seith nyn. [4]Sef y dyly blodeua6 o'e phedeir bl6yd ar dec allan; o hynny hyt y deugein ml6yd y dyly ymd6yn. Sef y6 hynny pedeir bl6yd ar dec a deugeint; a hyt hynny y byd yn y ieue*n*gtit, ac gwedy hynny pe[i]dya6 ac ymd6yn.

[5]O de*r*uyd rodi mor6yn y 6r a heb gysgu genti caffel cam ohoni, vrth ureint y g6r y diwygir idi, ac nyt [98r] vrth ureint y bra6t, [6]a honno a elwir mor6ynwreic. Ac o dygir treis arnei, ef a dylyir talu cowyll idi. [7]O de*r*uyd enllibya6 g6r ar wreic, y treigyl kyntaf ll6 seith wraged, yr eil treigyl ll6 pedeir g6raged ar dec, y trydyd treigyl ll6 pedeir g6raged ar ugeint, ac o hynny allan, ll6 de*n*g wraged a deugei*n*t pob treigyl. [8]O de*r*uyd y wreic llad g6r* hi a dyly caffel k*einya6c* paladyr , a h6nn6 y6 y dyn a'e keiff ac nys tal.

[9]Pob argl6ydes a dyly amobyr g6raged y chyuoeth. [10]G6reic maer bisweil a dyly amobreu g6raged* y uaertref.

[11]Nyt oes ureint y putein ket dyccer treis arnei; ny dyly caffel ia6n. [12]O serheir hitheu, talher y sarhaet vrth ureint y bra6t, a'e galanas o lledir.

[13]Pob kyflauan* a wnel g6reic, talet y chenedyl drosti ual dros vr, ony byd g6rya6c. O byd g6rya6c hitheu, talent hi a'e g6r y dir6y a'e chaml6r6. [98v]

[14]Tri a*n*ghyuarch g6r y6, nyt amgen a'e uarch a'e arueu, a'r hyn a del ida6 o dayret y tir, a'r trydyd yr hyn a del ida6 yn y 6ynebwarth y gan y wreic am y owg*. Ny dyly ynteu rannu yr un o'r tri pheth hynny a'e wreic.

[15]Tri aghyuarch g6reic y thri phrifei; a hynny ny dyly hitheu y rannu a'r g6r.

[55/4] *This figure of fiftyfour is only arithmetical confusion created by adding fourteen to forty: cf. Ior 99/6 for an accurate version.*
[55/8] *MS.* kelein *crossed through, with* g6r *added at the end of the previous line.*
[55/10] *MS.* g6reged.
[55/13] *MS.* aghyflauan.
[55/14] *MS.* am yo hegw. *MS. D has* ohebu, *which implies the same kind of contumelious conduct as the suggested* owg *(which is related to* gowyn: *see Glossary, S.V.).*

[3] The law says that a woman is not entitled to a *cowyll* after she has menstruated unless she be vindicated by her close relatives, including her father and her mother and her brothers and her sisters, and that up to the number of seven persons. [4] The period during which she should menstruate is from fourteen years onwards; then until she is forty she should bear children, that is to fifty-four*, and till then she is in her youth, and after that she ceases to bear children. [5] If it happens that a virgin is given to a man, and before being slept with suffers injury, compensation is paid to her according to the status of her husband, and not according to the status of her brother, [6] and she is called a virgin-wife. And if she be raped there is an obligation to pay her a *cowyll*. [7] If it happens that a wife is accused [of adultery with] a man, the first time an oath of seven women, the second time an oath of fourteen women, the third time an oath of twenty-four women, and from then on an oath of fifty women each time. [8] If it happens that a woman a kills a man she is entitled to receive a spear penny, and that is the person who receives it and does not pay it.

[9] Every lady is entitled to the *amobr* of the women of her lordship. [10] The dung-*maer*'s wife is entitled to the *amobrau* of the women of the *maerdref*. [11] A whore has no status even though she be raped; she is not entitled to receive compensation. [12] If she suffers *sarhaed*, let her *sarhaed* be paid according to the status of her brother, and her *galanas* if she be slain.

[13] Every offence which a woman may commit, let her kindred pay for her as for a man, unless she be married. If she be married, let her and her husband pay her *dirwy* and her *camlwrw*.

[14] The three things for which a man may not be asked are, namely, his horse and arms, and that which comes to him in the way of land-rent, and the third, that which comes to him as his face-value from his wife when she has reviled him. He is not obliged to share any of those three things with his wife.

[15] The three things for which a woman may not be asked are her three privities; and she is not obliged to share these with the husband.

RELATIONSHIP OF THE TRACTATES IN LATIN REDACTIONS A AND B TO THOSE IN LLYFR IORWERTH AND LLYFR CYFNERTH

ONE of the reasons for reprinting the tractate on the law of women from Latin Redaction A is that it supplies a clue to the history of other texts. It has two headings:

the first (to §51) reads *De lege puellarum et feminarum*,
the second (to §52) reads *De separacione viri et mulieris*.

The table set out below shows that the appearance of two headings is due to a compiler's use of a text belonging to the Cyfnerth family and another of the Iorwerth family. The table also suggests that the Latin Redaction B is independent of Redaction A since it includes matter deriving from Cyfnerth and Iorwerth manuscripts which is lacking from Redaction A (note Red. B 14, 15, 85, 102-105, 73/2).

The material taken from a Cyfnerth source consists, in the main, of two sequences: Lat. A §51/1-6 (+ Lat. B 14, 15) = Cyfn. 73/5, 8-11 (+ 3, 4), and Lat. A §52/54-66 = Cyfn. 73/15ab, 23-25. On the whole the Latin material seems closest to *W* among the surviving Cyfn. manuscripts; but perhaps the most striking point to emerge from a comparison is that it lacks the information on the values of *gobr, agweddi* and *cowyll* found in the earlier part of Cyfn. Instead it appears, to judge by Redaction A §53, to have had a separate list *De amwaberau*. It may well be that an early version of the Cyfnerth tractate similarly lacked information on the values of *gobr, agweddi* and *cowyll*, and that the surviving Cyfnerth manuscripts show contamination (of varying degree) from separate lists like Lat. A §53. This early Cyfnerth version would then be the source used by the compiler of the common exemplar of Redactions A and B. Although in other respects this early version of Cyfn. is close to *W*, the latter has taken the process of inserting values of *gobrau* etc., as far, or further, than the other Cyfn. manuscripts. The textual history suggested by this comparison is exhibited in the following stemma:

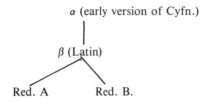

α (early version of Cyfn.)

β (Latin)

Red. A   Red. B.

It should, perhaps, be emphasised that this stemma may only be true of the tractate on the law of women.

The material deriving from a version of the Ior. tractate occurs in one main sequence: Red. A 52/1-30 (+ Red. B 102-105). The principal source is a version of Ior. 44 and 47. So far as the evidence goes this source may be a manuscript of the *Iorwerth* text rather than a version itself related to the *Iorwerth* text. Lat. A §52/6 is different from Ior. §44/3/4, but since this sentence does not occur in Lat. B it may be an innovation peculiar to Lat. A. The position of Red. A §52/9 confirms that MS. *B* of Ior. has innovated as against the other MSS. Lat. A §52/27 supplies a connection lacking in Ior., but this may be a relatively late attempt to make the transition clearer. Now that the MS. of Redaction A, Peniarth 28, is dated to the mid-thirteenth century (*supra*, p. 147), there is no need to suppose a source other than *Llyfr Iorwerth* itself, for the material common to the Latin Redactions and the early manuscripts of *Llyfr Iorwerth*.

Much of the material taken from Cyfnerth and Iorwerth sources concerns the consequences of *ysgar, separacio*, when the partners are both living and when their union was by gift of the woman to the man. It seems as though the compiler of β in the stemma had it in mind to provide himself with a tractate which would contain both sources and provide a conspectus of Welsh legal doctrine on this topic. On the other hand there is a significant amount of material which seems to come neither from Ior. nor from Cyfn. Not all of this material is triadic.

A complete stemma would, therefore, be as follows:

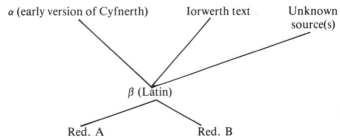

α (early version of Cyfnerth)   Iorwerth text   Unknown source(s)

β (Latin)

Red. A   Red. B

The other Latin redactions that contain a complete copy of the tractate, Redactions D and E, also derive from β the bulk of their material. I shall not discuss the question whether they do so directly or *via* Redactions A and B. It is, however, worth noting that, for this tractate at least, the WV recension of Cyfn. resembles Bleg. not because it has been influenced by Bleg., but, primarily, because an early version of Cyfn. influenced a remote ancestor of Bleg.

The numbering of Lat. A, Cyfn. and Ior. in the table is as in texts printed in the present volume, except that where necessary a third number indicates a particular clause within a sentence. Thus Ior. §52/1/1 refers to the first clause of the first sentence, or period, in §52 of *Llyfr Iorwerth*. The numbering of Lat. B is by sentence of its tractate on the law of women printed at LTWL 220-26. The presence of material in addition to that in a compared version is indicated by (+), of less material by (−). The contrasted sentences or clauses do not exhaust the number which could be so contrasted. The main purpose was to show the break between the Ior. sequence ending with Lat. A §52/30 and the second Cyfn. sequence starting with Lat. A §52/31.

TABLE

Lat A	Lat B	Ior	Cyfn
139. 21-22	1 ⎫ 2 ⎭	52/1/1	
139. 22-25	3	52/1/2	
140. 31-32	4		
140. 32-33	5		
139. 19-21	6		
§51/1 = 141.31	7		§73/5
2	8		8
3	9		9
4	10		9a
5	11		10
6	12-13 (+)		11
	14		3
	15		4
7			
8			
9			
10			
11			

Lat A	Lat B	Ior	Cyfn
12			
13			
14 ⎫	50	contrast 48/8	
15 ⎬			
16			
§52/1		42/2	
2		42/2	
3	76	45/9/1	
4		45/9/2	
5	84	44/3/2	
	85	44/3/1	
6		contrast 44/3/4	
7	86	44/5/1	
8/1	89	44/5/2	
8/2	90	44/5/3	
9	91	44/6	
10	92	44/5/4	
11	87	44/9/1-2	
12	88	44/9/3	
13	93	44/10	
14	94 ⎫	44/11	
15 ⎫	94-95 ⎬		
16 ⎬		44/12/1	
17	96-97	44/13-14	
18	98-99	44/15	
19	100	44/16-17	
20	101	44/18	
	102	44/3/5	
	103	44/3/4	
	104	44/19	
	105	45/1	
	106 ⎫		
	107 ⎬ triad	contrast 53/5	WML. 126.14-22
	108 ⎬		
	109 ⎭		
21	77	⎰ 52/4 ⎱ contrast 46/3	
22	78	46/4	
23 ⎫		47/1	
24 ⎬			
25	65	47/2	
26	66	47/3	
27	67		

Lat A	Lat B	Ior	Cyfn
28	68	47/4 (+)	
29 30 }	69	{ 47/5/1 47/5/2	
31	16	contrast 51/7	§73/12 (WV)
32	17	contrast 51/8	13 (W)
33	18-19	contrast 50/5	13a
34	20-21		13b
35	22	contrast 50/4	14 (W) (+)
36	23	contrast 50/2	15
37	71		19
38	72 }		20
39	73/1 }		
	73/2		21
40	74		§73a/12
41	75		13
42	49		
43	47 (+)		
44	48		
45			
46	51 }		
47	52 }	contrast 46/5-8	
48	53 }		
§52/49	29 }	contrast	} §73/24a
50	30 }	55/7	
51	31 }		
52	79	contrast 52/7 (Dw.Col.243)	WML. 127.7-11
53			
54 (triad)	24	contrast 45/4	15b
55 (corrupt)	62-63		
	64		
56 (triad)	25	contrast 51/1	15c
57 58 }	70 (corrupt)		
59	26 (+)		23
60 61 }	27 (−)		} 23a (−)
62	28		24
63	33		
64	32		25
65 66 } (triad)	54 55 }		} WML. 135.3-10

Lat A	Lat B	Ior	Cyfn
§53/1	34		
2 } 3 }	contrast 35		
4			
5	38		
6	39		
	40		
	41		
7	36		
8	37		
9	42		
10			

GLOSSARY

THIS glossary aims at being useful rather than exhaustive or even consistent. Its first purpose is to elucidate the words which have been left in their Welsh form in the translated texts, but it includes other words also. Some of these are English words which have been used in the translations to render Welsh technical terms, and are included here in order to alert the reader to the technicality of the Welsh terms. Some are terms which are common currency in Law or Legal History but may be unfamiliar to non-lawyers. But most space is taken up by the Welsh technical terms, for which the Glossary may add something to the discussion in the studies, or may suggest a reconciliation of divergent views expressed by different contributors. At some points our notes summarise the results of study which it is hoped to publish more fully elsewhere.

The order of the English alphabet has been followed, even for Welsh digraphs: it is thought that this will help non-Welsh readers more than it irritates Welsh ones.

affaith, pp. 61-5. In most examples in the lawbooks, the meaning is clearly *accessory,* and the word has been accepted as derived from Latin *affectus* (rather than *affectio*), though the recorded meanings in classical and later Latin do not suggest *accessory,* and some examples in Welsh literary texts seem to require another meaning, see Col pp. 88-9. This supports the view expressed at pp. 61-5 that an *affaith* was originally a cause rather than an accessory.

agweddi, egweddi. The word appears in forms representing *agweddi, egweddi,* and *engweddi,* but the medieval examples representing *engweddi* all seem to be in the hand of the same scribe, who was probably misinterpreting his exemplar. It has two senses: (*a*) a part of the property to which a wife was entitled on separation from her husband in certain circumstances; (b) in the *Naw Cynyweddi,* the second class of marital union.

This is one of several words connected with marital union and containing the element *-weddi*: see *cynyweddi, dyweddi.* Two roots **wedh* were inherited in Celtic: (a) one meaning "to lead" (cf. Irish *fedid*); (b) one meaning "to bind", found in Welsh *gwedd,* "yoke" (and thence "team" of oxen or horses). The analogy of Latin *coniugium* suggests that the root in our words might be the second, but Pedersen (VKG ii. 301, 517) and Benveniste (i. 240) derive *dyweddi* from the first root and connect it with the use of the same root in other Indo-European languages as a term for leading a bride in marriage, semantically comparable with the use of *ducere* in Latin. The prefixes in *agweddi* and *egweddi* present more of a problem: the form with *a-* occurs most frequently in northern, and that with *e-* most frequently in southern, texts, and several prefixes may be involved, such as *e <*eks,* "out of" or *a <*ate,* "to, at". The prefixes present other problems, and analogy may have influenced the final forms; *a-* and *e-* are interchangeable in other Welsh words, see GPC for such forms as *aderyn/ederyn.* If we accept *e <*eks* as the prefix, we could postulate a meaning "leading out", which would be a possible interpretation of a term both for an unconfirmed (and possibly impermanent) union, and for the share of the common pool taken by the wife on the break-up of such a union.

In sense (*a*) *agweddi* means the specific sum from the common pool of matrimonial property to which the wife was entitled on a justified separation from the husband before the union had lasted seven years. The measure of this sum depends on the natal status of the wife, which is determined by her father's status, whereas after the union has lasted seven years her natal status is irrelevant, since she takes a half of the pool; this provides one more illustration of the ambivalent position of the woman between two kins. Some texts seem to indicate that the name *agweddi* was originally given only to the entitlement of a wife given by her kindred, but at a later stage the smaller entitlements of women not so given were certainly sometimes called *agweddi*: see pp. 79-80 and n.49.

(*b*) In the *Naw Cynyweddi*, agweddi means a class of union inferior to *priodas*. If the entitlement was called *agweddi* only when the wife had been given by her kindred, the union called *agweddi* was probably one created by gift but not yet matured into *priodas* by the lapse of seven years.

agweddïol (of a woman) *entitled to agweddi* (q.v.): her union with a man is recognised as established, but is not fully matured. Since some jurists did not use the name *agweddi* for the entitlement of women not given in marriage by their kindred, they may not have treated these women as *agweddïol*: see p. 80.

aillt, *villein.* Though the texts show traces of a distinction in meaning between *aillt, bilain,* and *taeog,* the three words were virtually synonymous in the thirteenth century, and all were used pejoratively in the fourteenth: Col §14*n*; originally, however, *aillt* meant *client*, whether free or unfree: cf. Irish *céile*. The expression *mab aillt*, which is occasionally found, means *male aillt* rather than *aillt's son*; it may owe something to the Irish cognate *mac ailte*, meaning a son brought up in fosterage: *Bürgschaft* 11, §36.

alien, Cyfn §73/28, translating *alltud* (q.v.), elsewhere translated *foreigner*.

alltud, translated *alien, foreigner*. The word is exactly cognate with Anglo-Saxon *æltheodig,* and means "[one] from another country". The Welsh law texts show no sign of the development towards the meaning *exile from one's own country* (or, roughly, *pilgrim*) discussed by T. M. Charles-Edwards in 11 *Celtica* 43-59; for the lawbooks the word has the original legal meaning of the Latin *peregrinus,* i.e. one who is in our country without being of it. For Welsh law, the *alltud* came from outside Wales: though T. P. Ellis cites no authority for the statement "No free Welshman could be an 'alltud' in Wales" (WTL i. 455), the rule seems to be implied by the provision that a freeman (*canhwynol,* see *bonheddig canhwynol*) from one of the three divisions of Wales (Deheubarth, Gwynedd, and Powys) was not entitled to *mamwys* in another: Col §606, Ior §86/11.

The rule is also implied in the decision by Prince Edward of Caernarvon in 1305 that Welshmen moving from one *patria* in Wales to another should not be regarded as *adventicii* or required to put themselves in *advocaria*: Rec. Caern. 212. *Advocaria* corresponds to the client-patron relationship between the alien and some "lord" which Welsh law required: the alien must attach himself to the king, to a *breyr*, or to a villein, and his status depended on that of his lord. The bond between alien and lord could be freely dissolved, but if the alien left his lord voluntarily, he must leave half his goods to the lord, whose claim extended to the *argyfrau* of the alien's wife: DwCol §355. If the alien and his descendants stayed with the same lord and his descendants for four generations, the right to break the relationship was lost: *priodolder* had then been established, DwCol §§478, 479. The lord was *priodor* of the alien; if the king was his lord, the alien was *priodor* of the land given him, and had the status of a Welshman: DwCol §476.

amobr, the fee payable to a woman's lord in respect of a sexual relationship. Originally perhaps payable for loss of virginity (actual or presumed), it was certainly sometimes claimed in respect of a second union, and though originally paid to a patron-lord (of whatever political status) it became a part of the income of the territorial lord, see pp. 88-90. In the Latin texts the Welsh word, when it appears, has the form *amwabyr* (pl. *amwabereu*), but the translation *merces* is more often found; the Latinised *amobragium*, which is usual in record sources, does not seem to occur in the lawbooks.

The word, a derivative of *gobr* (q.v.), has the air of having been coined for use in a restricted sense in place of *gobr*, which was also used in a wider sense for other payments; the form *amwabyr* suggests that the coining was early. The derivative *amobrydd* (for the lord's collector of *amobr*) appears in fifteenth-century precedents: AL XII.xi.

amod (1) the ordinary word in the law texts for contract in general; for the etymology cf. Irish *ben imtha*, see Binchy, CLP 115; (2) the name of a form of contract (often distinguished as *amod ddeddfol*) in which the existence of a contract was proved by the oath of a party and its terms by the statement of *amodwyr*: see Col §§133-5n.

It was an old principle of Welsh law, expressed in proverbial form (*Amod a dyr ddeddf, Trech amod no gwir*) that rules implied by law could be excluded by the contract of the parties; this principle was applied to *cowyll* (see p. 76) and probably to the sharing of property on separation (see p. 84) cf. p.41 n.8.

amodwyr, p. 95, the witnesses who proved the terms of a contract made in the form of *amod ddeddfol:* see *amod*.

arfoll, p. 33, q.v. It could be argued that in the expression *llw ac arfoll* the two words are not synonymous but complementary, with *llw* meaning *oath* and *arfoll* meaning *agreement*. In the Law of Women a quite different meaning is possible, since the verb *arfollaf* is attested with the meaning *conceive:* LlA 159. *Llw ac arfoll* could then mean "oath and conception", and imply that an oath amounting to a promise of marriage, followed by a pregnancy, made an effective union; this would be a parallel to the rule of English common law that a promise to marry in the future was fulfilled by subsequent sexual intercourse, without any further ceremony or formality whatever. As the result of this rule it was very rarely that the plaintiff in an action for breach of promise of marriage alleged that she had suffered loss by sacrificing her virginity in reliance on the promise, since proof of the sacrifice would disprove the breach. This interpretation of *llw ac arfoll* would explain how the much more probably correct reading *ar liw ac ar olau* might have been changed in the β version of the *Naw Cynyweddi*.

arglwydd, the ordinary Welsh word for *lord,* in both secular and religious contexts. In the lawbooks it appears in three senses: (1) for the patron of a client, whether free, villein, or alien; (2) sometimes alternating with *brenin (king),* for the territorial ruler: see "Kings, Lords, and Princes", (1976) 26 BBCS 451-61; (3) by mistranslation of Latin *dominus,* for *owner.* When it is said that a woman's husband is her lord (p. 52), the original sense was perhaps (1), but the provision for paying *camlwrw* to him implies sense (2). For the feminine *arglwyddes,* see *lady.*

argyfrau: the goods (Lat A §52/56 *animalia*) brought by the wife to a union. In the translation of the Statute of Wales (1284) in MS. Peniarth 41, *argyfrau* translates *dos* in the English technical sense of *dower* (not *dowry* as in GPC), but *dowry* is the appropriate translation for the word as used in the lawbooks. The *argyfrau* was not to be consumed during the seven-year *agweddi* period; after that it fell into the common pool of matrimonial property, but it was treated as part of the common pool during the seven years in one case: if the husband of an *agweddïol* wife was an alien who left his lord, he was bound to leave half his goods for the lord, and his wife's *argyfrau* was treated as part of his property: DwCol §355.

barn y diddim, p.99, "the judgement of the [one] without anything". The *diddim* is one of the *Tri Chadarn Byd* (three mighty ones of the world), "because where there is nothing, nothing can be compelled (*or* extorted)", WML 139.18-19, cf. DwCol §135: this triad also occurs in the earliest set of gnomic triads found in Welsh in the White Book of Rhydderch.

beichiogi: this may be either an abstract noun or a verb-noun from *beichiog (pregnant,* literally *burdened),* and is found in the lawbooks in two senses: (*a*) making or becoming pregnant, see pp. 25, 32; (*b*) the state of pregnancy or the unborn child, as in the triad *Tri gwerth cyfraith beichiogi gwraig:* cf. *gwaed cyn delwawd.*

bilain, *villein;* cf. *aillt, taeog,* which seem to be synonymous in thirteenth-century law, and see *breyr.* Since initial *v-* in Welsh is always a mutation of *b-* or *m-,* the borrowed *villein* was re-formed in Welsh as *bilain* and *milain.* The latter form has survived in modern Welsh (together with another form, *mileinig*), having the pejorative transferred meaning of *fierce, savage,* or the like. The use of the English word *villein* must not be taken as implying any particular view of the implications of the status: the whole question of dependent status in medieval Wales awaits scientific examination.

bonheddig canhwynol, p. 42, the ordinary freeman, who had not ascended to the status of *breyr* by the death of all his male ancestors; if a non-*breyr* held office in the court, his status as *bonheddig canhwynol* was masked by the official status, but no doubt continued. The noun *bonheddig* is the adjective from *bonhedd* (modern Welsh *bonedd*), the abstract noun meaning *lineage* or *origin,* from *bôn,* which is *stock* in the literal sense. The *bonheddig* is thus the man of known stock, as the *generosus* or *gentleman* is the man of known *gens.*

Canhwynol (GPC s.v. *cynhwynol,* but the form in all the published law texts seems to be with *can-*) is usually understood as meaning natural-born, but the use of the word shows too little variety for confidence: the definition of a *bonheddig canhwynol* as a Welshman by mother and father (*Cymro fam tad,* WML 44.9-10, Bleg 58.17-18) excludes those sons of Welsh freewomen by aliens who were entitled to patrimony by *mamwys* (in right of the mother), though they presumably had *bonheddig* status and certainly had their status by birth. In the rule of Col §606, Ior §86/11, that a *canhwynol* from one of the three divisions of Wales was not entitled to *mamwys* in another, the implication seems to be that the *canhwynol* was entitled to an inheritance in his homeland, but since a man would retain his status as *bonheddig canhwynol* even if all his land was given up in payment of *galanas* (Col §607, Ior §87/2, 3), the right to land cannot be essential to the status.

braint, Cyfn §73/8, 10, Ior §46/1, translated *status;* Ior §44/19, translated *privilege; *briganti,* "freedom, privilege", see T. M. Charles-Edwards, "Native Political Organization . . .", *Antiquitates Indogermanicae* (ed. M. Mayrhofer et al., Innsbruck, 1974) 42. In modern Welsh meaning *privilege,* it is in the lawbooks the ordinary word for the status of persons, land, and offences. *Galanas, sarhaed, agweddi, amobr, cowyll,* and *ebediw* are all payments governed by an individual's status.

breyr, a freeman of the highest natural status, attained by succeeding to his patrimony as the result of the death of his last direct male ancestor; though his name is derived from **brogo-rix*, the *breyr* might be a very small freeholder: cf. *uchelwr* and see p. 70 n.3. According to Bleg 5.12 the three kinds of men were king, *breyr*, and villein, with their members, thus treating the *alltud* (alien, foreigner) and the slave (*caeth*) as non-human. The lawbooks, however, show the *alltud* as fully human, since both *galanas* and *sarhaed* are payable for offences against him; the slave was human for the law of *sarhaed,* but for that of homicide he was treated as a chattel whose value was paid to the owner if it was destroyed: see pp. 42-3. The subsumption of the "members" under the three heads makes it clear that the *breyr* was not of a different class from the ordinary freeman (*bonheddig*), though his status within the class (as measured by *galanas* and *sarhaed*) was higher: cf. *mab uchelwr.*

brwydr gyfaddef, p. 99, literally *admitted battle.* The expression does not seem to occur in the lawbooks, but *ymlad kyfadef* ("admitted fighting", WML 123.17, 20) may have the same force. Several of the cases in the court records speak of *brwydr gyfaddef* because each of the parties complains of the other ("Brothergavetheu quia uterque queritur de alio in placito transgressionis", S.C. 2/216/2, m.4; Dyffryn Clwyd, 1319); this suggests that the parties were deemed to have admitted the fighting by their cross-summonses. This may be compared with rulings in the lawbooks that the defendant was to be treated as *lleidr cyfaddef* ("admitted thief"): Ior §115/1 (defendant vouches to warranty, and vouchee fails to warrant); WML 123. 21-4 (compurgators fail to support defendant's denial); DwCol §448 (defendant taken in possession of goods fails to make one of the admissible pleas).

brycan, Cyfn §73a/5, Lat A §52/13; at Ior §44/10 translated *blanket*, but the rules for sharing the bedclothes (Cyfn §73a/3, Lat A §52/11, Ior §44/9) suggest a more specialised meaning. The word is a borrowing from Old Irish *breccan,* "speckled cloth", which became in eighteenth-century Scotland the name of "a length of flannel of various colours, which is their cloak by day, their bedcloth by night, and their shroud in the grave" (*Arch. Brit.* 233); hence Aneurin Owen's *plaid* as translation of Ior §140/2, though he has *bed-coverlet* at Ior §44/10. As the *brycan* was one of the three indispensables of a *gwrda* (Ior §42/3), a dual-purpose article seems probable enough.

bush and brake, Ior §49/1, Cyfn §73a/15, 16, translating *llwyn a pherth;* see *gwraig llwyn a pherth.*

caeth (Latin *captus*), the ordinary word for *slave;* see *breyr, servient slave.* If a female slave was made pregnant, the man responsible must provide her owner with a substitute in the same way as the man who incapacitated a working animal.

camlwrw, the minor financial penalty of three kine or 180*d.,* cf. *dirwy.* The word has the air of having been deliberately coined from the elements *cam (wrong)* and *llwrw (track);* cf. English *misdemeanour* as contrasted with the older word *felony* for the more serious offences. *Camlwrw* has replaced an earlier *camgwl,* found in LL 120, in which the second element *cŵl* (cf. Ir. *col*) also means *wrong.* In Lat A §52/42 *camlury* probably represents an alternative form comparable with *lludy* for *lludw.*

car, Cyfn §73a/7, Ior §44/6, translates Welsh *carr,* which should probably be understood as meaning a sledge (in modern Welsh distinguished, when necessary, as *car llusg,* "dragged car") rather than a wheeled vehicle.

caradas, p. 16, **caraddas,** p. 30 n.16, the third of the marital unions listed in the *Naw Cynyweddi:* the early manuscript spellings are consistent with either transcription, but *caradas* is supported by the *cynghanedd* in the line *Gŵyr ei awdl o garadas* (Madog Benfras, DGG 119) as well as the Irish *carthach.* In the Cotton Cleopatra text of *Brut y Brenhinedd* (ed. J. J. Parry; Cambridge, Mass., 1937) 10-11, Assaracus (born of a Trojan woman to a Greek father), a son *o garadas,* is contrasted with a son *or gwely priawd:* the Latin has *ex concubina.*

car-return, Ior §§52/5, 54/7, translates Welsh *carddychwel,* which can be understood as a noun, but in some passages must be an adjective referring to the person concerned. The discussion at p. 21 supports the evidence of the medieval spelling with *karr-* that the first element is *car,* not *câr.*

casual acquisitions, Ior §51/6, translating *dofod.* What these casual acquisitions were, in which the queen was entitled to share, appears from a comparison of Col §654 and Ior §91/1 with Bleg 48.8-12 and

WML 28.8-13. According to Col and Ior the *maer* and *cynghellor* take a half of the *dofod*, except for the value of land, theft, and a corpse; Ior speaks of taking a half of everything "against the king" except these three. Bleg and WML give the two officers a third part instead of a half, and specify the sources: the *gobrau* of villeins' daughters, the *camlwrw* and *ebediw* of villeins, the corn of a fugitive villein, and the corn and food left by a dead villein. There is an overlap between these and the list of the king's eight "packhorses" (*wyth pynfarch brenin*: Ior §43/1, WML 65.1-4, Bleg 47.1-6)—the sea, a waste, a needy stranger, a thief, a childless man suddenly dead, *ebediw, dirwy,* and *camlwrw:* the common factor in all these is that they are items of income which cannot be relied on (as *gwestfa* and *dawnbwyd* can). They can be compared with the incidents (as contrasted with the services) of English feudal tenure. Thus *ebediw* (like *relief*) is certain to be payable sooner or later, but it is uncertain when it will be paid, and other sources (like *wardship* or *marriage*) may not materialise at all. *Dofod* is used for anything casually found when walking, and for the casual earnings of bards "whether by *erchi* (request to a patron) or by *cyfarws neithior*", DwCol §78.

cattle of dark ancestry, Ior §53/3, translating *gwartheg dyfach,* q.v.

cenedl, p. 105, in modern Welsh *nation,* in medieval Welsh *kindred.* For inheritance of land a man's *cenedl* were the persons related to him by descent through males from a common ancestor: the rules of *mamwys* alone infringed the agnatic principle here. But in measuring relationship for blood-feud and compurgation both female and male links were taken into account. See p. 55, where the special importance of the narrowest group of kin is shown: cf. *derbfine* (q.v.).

cenedl elyniaeth, p. 53: *kin-enmity,* rather than "the nature of enmity" as in AL.

chastity, Cyfn §73a/15, translating *diweirdeb,* q.v.

chief official, Ior §51/11, translating *penns6yda6c;* see *swyddogion penadur.*

cigddysgl, Lat A §52/8. The Welsh word seems to mean just what its elements indicate, i.e. *meat-dish;* its inclusion is evidence of translation, and of difficulty in finding a Latin equivalent: *vernum* seems to be known only in medieval Latin, and from British sources.

coemptio, p. 122, is usually understood as *buying;* Alan Watson, *Rome of the Twelve Tables* (Princeton, 1975) 94, shows that "the original meaning of *emere* was 'to take'", so that *coemptio* might mean *"mutual taking"*.

confarreatio, p. 39, literally apparently a joint taking of a cake, "was a religious ceremony, necessary for and probably confined to the members of certain priesthoods" (Nicholas).

cowyll, the "morning-gift" made to a virgin bride by her husband. The basic meaning of the word is a veil or head-covering, cf. Latin *cucullus,* English *cowl*, and the triad *Tri chowyllawg llys*, which were, according to Bleg 118.20 a vat of mead, a friar, and a song before being shown to the king, and according to DwCol §257 a justice, a priest, and a bard. We seem to have here a hint of the symbolism of a change of headdress as a mark of marriage.

croft, special, Cyfn §73/28, translating *eissydyn arbenhic;* cf. *toft, privileged. Eisyddyn* is being treated by GPC as a variant of *syddyn,* which according to JD was for Dyfed what *tyddyn* was for Gwynedd, namely *tenementum*, i.e. a holding. Both words occur in Bleg (*eissydyn* 74.26, 81.8; *tydyn* 74.22), and (so far as we know) only *tyddyn* in the Latin texts; this may be an indication that the passages concerned were derived from material in Welsh from Gwynedd.

cusan, Lat A §52/46, the ordinary Welsh word for a kiss (a borrowing from Anglo-Saxon *cuss* or *cyssan,* GPC) seems otiose as a gloss on *osculo*. The kiss was the least serious of the three grades of *cyflafan ddybryd:* see *cyflafan* and p. 53; it was also a sign of kinship, given when a child was affiliated: see p. 92.

cyfeddach, p. 53, basically "taking mead together", is used in the lawbooks for the feasting at court.

cyflafan, Cyfn §73/30, translated *injury; cyflafan ddybryd,* Ior §46/5, translated *unseemly offence.* No single translation is satisfactory in all law contexts, and explanations have tended to narrow the sense too much, perhaps under the influence of the primary sense of *battle, fight, struggle*: GPC s.v., sense (*a*). Thus in GPC the Welsh explanations show that the definition of sense (*b*), *injury, wound; blow, bite,* is to be understood as referring to bodily hurt, while sense (*c*), *crime, felony,* *heinous deed, outrage* (like Jones Pierce at MWS 21 etc.) lays exclusive stress on the criminal aspect of the wrongdoing. Cyfn §73/30 is concerned with the civil aspect of the wrong, for the question is who is to pay with the alien's son for the damage done by him. *Damage* would often be the best translation, as for instance in the opening manifesto of Llyfr y Damweiniau, Pob kyflauan a wnel dyn o'y anuod, dywyget o'y uot, "Every damage which a man does involuntarily, let him compensate for voluntarily" (DwCol §1). In *cyflafan ddybryd* the stress is on the wrongful act rather than on its effects, and *outrage* would not be inappropriate: see p. 53. The adjective *dybryd* (in which *dy-* negates *pryd,* "form": cf. Isaiah liii.2, *ni bydd pryd fel y dymunem ef,* "no beauty that we should desire him" RSV) has developed from the presumed original *deformed* to its modern meaning of *gross, excessive, serious;* see GPC s.v.

cyfneseifiaid, p. 9, "next of kin": the English rendering must not be understood in its technical legal sense; if either parent was alive, the brothers and sisters would not be next of kin in English law.

cymellawr (MS. *kymmellaur*), the form in Lat A §53/3 of the word whose usual forms imply *cynghellor* (not *canghellor* from Latin *cancellarius*). The *cynghellor* was a royal official charged with administrative and minor judicial duties in a limited district: see (1976) 27 BBCS 115-18, and cf. *maer.*

cynghellor, see *cymellawr, maer.*

cynhysgaeth, Ior §54/9, translated *dowry.* In the lawbooks the word is perhaps used in the more general sense of *provision,* rather than with the technical sense which it shows in the later court records referred to at pp. 99-100 and nn.15, 17; see pp. 28, 82 n.66.

cynnwys, p. 107 and n.43. After 1284 *cynnwys* (variously spelt in the records as the result of dialect differences) appears as the name of a device used by the Welsh to circumvent the prohibition in the Statute of Wales of inheritance by sons regarded by the Church as illegitimate. Presumably the illegitimate claimant brought a collusive action against his legitimate brothers, alleging that he was on the verge of ceasing to be a proprietor (see *priodor Wallicus*) and so raising the obscurely named *diasbad uch annwfn;* "and then law orders that he be heard and given *cynnwys* of as much as one of the men who were occupying the land against him, according to number" (i.e. *per capita*): Col §580 and n.

cynyweddi, Cyfn §73/30 (variant reading), *marital union*. For the structure of the word cf. *agweddi* and *dyweddi*: with the initial element **kon-, together or joint, cynyweddi* is appropriate for the whole concept of marital union as a mutual leading together; cf. p. 27.

cywyres, p. 21. The word is found only in the law texts, see the forms (with aspirate mutation) *chyhwres* (Lat D 374.25) and *chywyres* (Bleg.116.27); it is evidently *cy-* + *gŵr* + *-es*, the woman who shares a man with the prior wife: see the Cyfnerth form of the triad *Tri hwrdd ni ddiwygir* ("three thrusts which are not compensated") from which the examples are taken: where Bleg/Lat D speak of the *cywyres,* WML 133.11-15 speaks of the jealousy of a married woman against another woman on account of her husband (*guneuthur eidiged o wreic 6rya6c 6rth wreic arall am y g6r*).

daered, p. 85; at Ior §45/7 translated *tribute*. The word occurs in the law texts in two contexts: (*a*) that of a money payment to the king, supplementary to the renders in kind, the *gwestfa* and *dawnbwyd* (or their commutation, the *twnc*); (*b*) that of the dying man's disposal of his goods, as in the passage in question here and in the rules for the disposal of the goods of a thief who is hanged (Col §393, DwCol §503). The Iorwerth text here printed supports the view of Donald Howells (8/9 SC 57) that both church and lord took *daered* from the goods; this provides confirmation for his argument "that in the first instance the *daered* was the whole fief, and the *daered* payment the total dues paid in return . . . However, by the time of the lawbooks, or at least the later ones, the word *daered* had been almost completely superseded by the newer *twnc*, and retained only to denote some supplementary charge" (ibid. 56-7). The tribute to the lord, which is taken from the dead man's goods, will then be the return of the fief (in cattle, not land) given by his lord; as this seems to be equivalent to *ebediw* (q.v.), the reading of MS. *D* in Ior §45/7, which gives *daered* to the church and *ebediw* to the lord, may be seen as a justified modernisation of the text.

damdwng, p. 99, literally "swearing about" the goods concerned, in two contexts: (*a*) when claiming property found in another's possession, the claimant (by a procedure resembling the *vindicatio* of Roman law) swears that the property is his; (*b*) in other cases *damdwng* means swearing to the value of an item: e.g. where compensation is claimed for an article which has no standard legal value.

Damweiniau, p. 6, literally *accidents, happenings,* an expression for case-law material, derived from the title *Llyfr y Damweiniau,* applied at least from the fourteenth century to a collection of rules stated as applicable to particular cases, which may be hypothetical and must certainly not be regarded as authoritative precedents laid down in court.

defod, p. 118, n.15. In modern Welsh the word means *rite* or *ceremony,* which agrees with the use of OBreton *domot* to gloss *ritum*; in the law texts it means rather *custom:* thus the *swyddogion arfer o ddefod* ("officers usual by custom") in the court are contrasted with those provided by the law: Ior §30/1. There is nothing to show under what conditions a *defod* would be *cyfiawn* so as to override law; it would be rash to assume anything corresponding to the modern English law's requirements of certainty, reasonableness, and immemorial continuity.

degwm rhoddi, pp. 105, 112, "tithe of giving".

derbfine, p. 55, the four-generation family group basic to the Irish system of land-holding (Binchy, CLP 102) and payment of compensation for homicide (Thurneysen, *Ir. Recht,* Díre section 15). The meaning of Welsh *gwely* is similar, but it is not yet possible to say with authority that it is identical, and there is no connection between the Welsh and Irish words. The element *derb* is found in the Welsh words for first and second cousins, *cefnderw* and *cyfyrderw*. Charles-Edwards has shown that these terms reflect relationships which were originally within the limits of the old Celtic inner kindred: 24 BBCS 107.

dial, Ir. *di-gal,* Corn. *dyal,* < **dē-gal,* "aversion of heat" (see *galanas*) is used for an act or transaction which in law ended a state of hostility, by revenge or compensation: see p. 68. In the tractate *Saith Esgopty Dyfed, dial* (Bleg 84.25) corresponds to *redditionis* at Lat D 391.18: see T. M. Charles-Edwards, 24 BBCS 254-5; but in the rule that a victim is not entitled to both *diwyn* and *dial* (e.g. Ior §51/3), *dial* (for vengeance) is contrasted with *diwyn* (q.v.) for compensation.

diddim, see *barn y diddim*.

dilys, Lat A §52/21, "free from her husband" (as in the Latin glossed), immune from claim by him: see *llys*.

dilysrwydd, Ior §54/9, there translated "immunity from claim"; in Lat A §52/35 the meaning is the same as that of *diweirdeb,* q.v.; see *llys*.

dirwy, in modern Welsh the ordinary word for a financial penalty of any amount, but in the lawbooks a fixed penalty (usually twelve kine or £3) for the more serious offences against state or society: cf. *camlwrw*. The similarity of the penalty for rape (*dirwy trais*) to the king's *sarhaed* confirms the principle expressed in DwCol §436, that it is because the offence has caused him loss that the king is entitled to a payment from the offender: see p. 49. For the Irish cognate *díre* see p. 68.

divorcium, pp. 110, 112. Now suggesting the total dissolution of a valid marriage, the word had at earlier periods the more general meaning of separation, with or without such a dissolution of the union as would entitle each spouse to take another partner.

diweirdeb, Cyfn §73a/15, translated *chastity,* the word's basic meaning at all periods. As the name of part of the compensation for rape, it alternates with *dilystod* and *dilysrwydd,* for which see *llys*.

diwyn, p. 41, *compensation,* verb-noun of the verb *diwygaf,* see p. 68. The Irish cognate of *diwygaf* has as its verb-noun the etymologically unconnected *di-gal,* cognate with *dial*. The development of the diphthong (originally *ŵy*) in this word and *gowyn* (q.v.) deserves further examination.

dofod, Ior §51/6, translated *casual acquisitions,* q.v.

dominus, p. 88 n.90, *lord,* but sometimes *owner*: see *arglwydd*.

dos, Lat A §51/7, §52/30, 60, left untranslated because the Latin word is ambiguous, see pp. 81, 127. In §51/7 the payment seems to be *cowyll,* in §52/30, 60, *agweddi* or *argyfrau*.

dower, the life-interest of a widow in part of her late husband's land, under English law.

dowry, see *agweddi, argyfrau, cowyll, dos.*

droit de seigneur, "lord's right", see p. 73 and n.17, and cf. *ius primae noctis.*

dung-maer, Ior §55/10; Welsh *maer biswail:* see *maer.*

dyweddi, p. 27, must be understood as *dy* + *weddi,* from **do-wed,* cf. *agweddi,* q.v. Pedersen (ii.517) compares the form with Breton *dimezin* (< **do-ambi-wed*), meaning both *betroth* and *marry,* and Cornish *domethys.* Though common in the literature, it is rare in the lawbooks; since AL V.ii.100 treats the *dyweddi* as incomplete until *amobr* is paid (*kannyt c6byl y dywedi yny daler y hamobyr*), it must mean more than the betrothal or engagement which the word suggests in modern Welsh.

ebediw, p. 89, a payment due on death; the word, previously explained as compounding the element *-bad-* (for *death*) is more likely to incorporate *eb-* (*horse,* cf. Latin *equus*), so that it originally meant the return to the patron of a horse provided for his client: Howells, 8/9 SC 49-51. In the classical law, *ebediw* has an increasingly feudal connection with land holding. See also *daered.*

edling, Ior §54/5, a borrowing from Anglo-Saxon *ætheling,* which developed in Welsh the narrower meaning of *heir-apparent.* It is hardly likely that the rule of Ior §54/4,5 was ever applied in practice; the provision seems intended rather to discourage the use of a plea which is open to the most obvious abuse.

egweddi, see *agweddi.*

eillt, see *aillt.*

eisyddyn, see *croft,* cf. *toft.*

enllib, p. 33, **cadarn enllib,** pp. 33, 52. In the technical Welsh language now being developed for English law, *enllib* is reserved for *libel;* in the lawbooks it is best understood as *scandal,* which becomes *cadarn* ("confirmed") when supported by evidence of one of the kinds specified in the triad cited at p. 52.

face-value, Ior §45/3, translating *wynebwerth,* q.v.

fidejussores, p. 109. The word normally means *sureties*; in the Latin texts of Welsh law *fideiussor* usually translates *mach,* q.v. If it had this sense in the record here cited, the *fidejussores* would be persons guaranteeing the validity of the union, but it is surprising to find a reference to twelve for a single transaction.

fire-dog, Lat A §52/13, translating *retentaculum,* in reliance on Bleg 65.16, which has *pentan hayarn* for the *retentaculum* of Lat D 344.29; but as its position in the list corresponds to that of *pergyng,* it may represent that instrument.

foreigner, Ior §53/1, 2, translating *alltud,* q.v.

frankmarriage, p. 127. The grant of land with a bride by way of *liberum maritagium* created in English law a tenure under which the land was inalienable for three generations; the tenure was in effect replaced by the estate tail during the thirteenth century: see PM ii.16 n.2.

gafael, p. 102. In the document there quoted, *gafael* is the name of Welsh tenure of land; this is a development not evidenced in the lawbooks. The basic meaning of the word is *hold* or *grip:* hence it comes to mean a holding of land. In the land-law texts *gafael* is a (probably purely theoretical or notional) measure of size, of sixteen or 64 Welsh acres according to different texts (see Col §649*n*); in the extents and surveys it is sometimes apparently a subdivision of *gwely,* but perhaps more properly to be regarded as the same thing seen as a holding, whereas *gwely* first meant the group of close relatives (corresponding more or less exactly to Irish *derbfine,* q.v.), who held the land.

gair cywilydd, Lat A §52/43, *a word of shame.*

galanas, cf. Irish *galnas, galannas,* "slaughter"; Cumbric *galnes/ galnys,* used in the *Leges inter Brettos et Scottos* (LHEB 10, 653 n.1; Loth, 47 RC 383-400) for part of the compensation for homicide; Breton *glanasoc,* glossing *uir sanguinosus,* DGVB 176. The word is used with three meanings: (*a*) in most examples it means *life-price* (the Anglo-Saxon *wergild*), and alternates with *gwerth* (q.v.) or in Latin *precium*; (*b*) it has the meaning *homicide,* alternating with *llofruddiaeth, lladd* *celain*, and *homicidium*; (*c*) it is occasionally used for feud or enmity. There is a historical connection between all three meanings of the word: its root *gal*, "heat, valour, steam", connects it with many other words, e.g. Welsh *gelyn*, "enemy", and *dial* (q.v.), Irish *galann*, "enemy", M. Corn. *gal*, "evil, wickedness", Breton *gal*, "force, power": see J. Lloyd-Jones, *Feilscribhinn Torna* (ed. S. Pender; Cork, 1947) 83-9, and Myles Dillon, 8 Celtica 196-200. A state of enmity between kins was at one period created by other actions, as well as by homicide (which in time became the only source of feud): see pp. 61-5. This enmity was probably originally settled by a payment agreed between the two kins; the payment later became a fixed sum which varied according to the status of the victim and was related to the *sarhaed*, q.v.

gelyniaeth: enmity; see *cenedl elyniaeth, galanas.*

gobr, Cyfn §73/1 etc., see *amobr, merces.* The basic meaning of the word is *payment* or *fee*, and it occurs in the lawbooks for the fees payable to court officials and for *reward* or even *bribe*, as well as in the special sense for which *amobr* is reserved. It is connected with the verb *gobrynaf*, which incorporates *prynaf* (I buy: see *tir prid*) and is cognate with Irish *fo-cren*, whose verb-noun *fochraic* glosses *stipendium, remuneratio*, and *praemium.*

gofysio, Ior §46/5, 7, 10, translated literally by *finger*, the second degree of *cyflafan ddybryd*. In the light of the Latin cited at p. 53, and of MS. *D*'s variant reading to Ior §46, *dodi byssed yndi* ("to put fingers into her"), the word must be understood as implying an indecent contact.

goŵyn, p. 20, *offence* or *offence-payment:* for the connections of the word see pp. 65-8.

gwaddol, Cyfn §73a/17b; see p. 17. In modern Welsh this is the ordinary word for a bride's *dowry* and for the *endowment* of (say) a charity. In the lawbooks it hardly has a technical sense: Cyfn §73a/17b supplies the technical term for the non-technical *gwaddol*; cf. Lat D 376.23, *argyfreu*, id est *guadawl*. In the light of the cognates MBret. *gudul* and OIr *fodáil*, meaning *share, distribution,* and of the instances of the related verb *goddolaf* in CA, the original meaning of *gwaddol* seems to be a sharing or distribution. This meaning may be present in the law texts at Ior §113/9, where liability for *cyhyryn canastr* attaches to the receiver of meat whether he receives it by gift or by buying or by *gwaddol*; and in the matrimonial context the original meaning may have been the bride's share of her father's goods, which might or might not be given to her on her marriage. In Bleg 64.31 *bit y gwr dan y gwadawl* is a mistranslation of Lat D 344.14, *sit vir sub dote*: the sense requires *agweddi*.

gwaed cyn delwawd, Lat A §51/11, literally "blood before shaping", "pro sanguine ante liniamenta menbrorum" (Lat D 342.9): the embryo for the first month of pregnancy. The treatment of the compensation for abortion shows perhaps the most extreme example of variation in arrangement and in substance to be found in the lawbooks. In Cyfn (WML 128.23-129.5) and Bleg (112.26-32) the material is one of the big collection of triads; in Lat D it appears at 336.12-15 as one of four triads in Welsh appended to the treatment of *galanas* and at 342.6-12 (in a paragraph not in Bleg), as also in Lat A, Lat B (223.3-5), and Lat E (471.32-34), as part of the tractate on the Law of Women; in Ior (§97/2) it begins the tractate on Children and Affiliation; and in Col (§332) it comes with other statements of the measure of *galanas* at the end of the *Galanas* tractate. Each placing is justifiable, and since the variations in placing do not correspond to those in substance, they suggest how ready the compilers of the lawbooks must have been to re-arrange their material.

In substance, Cyfn and Bleg agree with Lat A and Lat D in recognising the embryo (*gwaet kyn delwat/delwad* [*sic*]) as the first stage, and in the characteristics of the other two stages, but they do not fix the length of the stages, and they make the compensation for the embryo 48d., whereas the quarter-*galanas* (given by Lat A) would be 236¼d. even if the child had only the status of a villein's alien. Lat B, Lat D (in both versions), Lat E, and Col agree in giving a third of the *galanas* if the foetus is not quickened; if it is quickened (*animatum,* "o byt eneyt endau"), Lat B, Lat E, and Col give two-thirds, and Lat D 342 one half, of the *galanas*. All these texts imply that full *galanas* was payable only after the child was born, and this may well have been the original rule. In Ior and Lat D 336 the full *galanas* is payable for the last trimester of the pregnancy, and this is given as the opinion of some in Lat D 342; Ior explains that this is because the foetus is then complete in limbs and life ("kyulaun o aelodeu ac eneyt"). Ior's division of the period of pregnancy into three trimesters corresponds to a traditional medical practice, and its description of the foetus as white in the first trimester (with one-third *galanas*) and red in the second (with two-thirds *galanas*) may have a basis in the appearance of the foetus.

gwartheg dyfach, Cyfn §73/30, left untranslated; Ior §53/3, translated "cattle of dark ancestry". The expression was evidently obscure to the thirteenth-century compilers of texts, for they are uncertain whether the cattle are so called because *meichiau* are given or because they are not given: see the readings of the three manuscripts of Bleg 81.22. If the *meichiau* are not given, the adjective must be *di-fach*; if they are given, it is the suffixless adjective derived from *difeichiaf* or *dyfeichiaf*, either of which can mean *I give* (or perhaps *become*) a *mach*. The cattle in question are paid in compensation for a homicide committed by the son of a Welshwoman by an alien, and it has been persuasively argued that they are cattle without *mach* because they are part of a fief which never became the full property of the client: see D. Howells, 8/9 SC 60-61. Cattle without *mach* could equally be those brought by the wife from her kindred, for which no *mach* was given, see pp. 82-3 and Ior §54/9. The greatest difficulty in the way of this explanation is that many of the manuscript readings imply *dyfach*, which cannot mean "without *meichiau*" though it can mean "with *meichiau*".

Charles-Edwards's translation assumes that *dyfach* has no connection with *mach*, but is to be understood as *dyf-ach,* where *ach* is the common word for ancestry or degree of kin, and *dyf-* is the form of the adjective *du,* "black", reduced at an early period in pretonic position: **dubo-dyf-,* see LHEB 276. The point of the expression is elucidated by comparison with such Irish terms as *glasfine,* "grey kinsman", for the son of an Irishwoman and an alien from outside Ireland (a *cú glas*), *dubfine,* "black" or "dark kinsman", for a man who purports to be a relative but is outside the prescribed degrees of kinship. The cattle are then of "dark ancestry" because they are paid by the maternal kin of a foreigner's son. The name of Pwlldyfach, where Hywel ab Edwin ab Einion "defeated the Gentiles who were ravaging Dyfed" in 1042 (BTPTr 13) may incorporate the term.

gweddw, Ior §46/2, translated *single.* In most cases, *gweddw* means *widow,* like other cognates of that English word, but the context shows that here it must mean *single,* i.e. without a husband, rather than deprived of a husband; cf. *fedb.*

gwely, see *derbfine, gafael.*

gwerth, p. 41, *value,* sometimes used instead of *galanas* for the compensation payable for killing even a free man. The word is appropriate for the compensation for killing a slave, which is paid to his owner like the value of an animal.

gwg, p. 15, in modern Welsh meaning *frown* or *scowl,* is one of several words involving the same root and in the law texts has the more positive meaning of blow or insult, see pp. 67-8, and cf. the form *gowg* found in MS. *L* of Bleg.

gŵr priod, p. 17 and n.31; see *priodas.* In modern Welsh *gŵr priod* means a married man, i.e. we know that he has a wife, but not who she is; in the lawbooks *gŵr priod* seems to reveal something about the woman rather than the man, i.e. we know that she has a man proper to her, a man of her own.

gwraig, *female, sexually-experienced female, wife,* according to context, see p. 5. The second seems to be the primary meaning, see PKM 74, where Goewin, after Gilfaethwy's intercourse with her, tells Math to seek another virgin (*morwyn*) in her place, for "Gwreic wyf i"—"I am a woman." A man's *gwraig* is his wife, but the texts give little indication of where the line was drawn between the status of a wife (established in one of the less formal ways) and a casual relationship evidenced by intermittent cohabitation. A very casual relationship would make *amobr* payable, but it does not follow that either party could claim rights as a result: the woman might not be entitled to any share of property on a separation, nor the man to *sarhaed* from a third party for misconduct with the woman.

gwraig briod, see *gŵr priod, gwraig, priodas.* The lawbooks' use of *gwraig briod* does not seem to correspond to that of *gŵr priod:* see p. 17.

gwraig llwyn a pherth, pp. 26, 27, 32, *woman of bush and brake.* According to GPC 1698c, the expression means *harlot, strumpet, prostitute,* which follows LW 574; but the examples cited hardly justify this very definite interpretation. *Putain* (q.v.) is used in other contexts for *prostitute,* a concept which seems to have an element of publicity in contrast with the secrecy implied in "bush and brake".

gwraig wriog, p. 44, *woman having a man.*

gwreictra, "woman-feud", one of the *naw affaith galanas* according to the men of Powys, and a ground of *llys* (objection) against a witness: see p. 62 and cf. *llys.*

gwriog, *having a man, married,* without any implication as to the form of the union, or perhaps of its implication for status; see p. 44 n.19.

gwrthdwng, Lat A §52/55, *counter-swearing,* cf. Old Irish *fortoing,* see CG 534. The manuscript of Latin A has *gwrthung,* a possible form, but in the translation the usual form has been used.

gwyry always means *virgin* (with which it is cognate, cf. Breton *guerh-*); ct. *morwyn* and see p. 5.

healsfang, p. 56, Anglo-Saxon, literally "neck-taking"; the first instalment of wergild, reckoned as a tenth of the total payment, and made by an inner circle of the kin, sometimes defined as all those within the knee: see Liebermann ii.489, 490.

hereditas, Lat A §53/4, left untranslated because there explained as meaning *swydd,* q.v.

iniuria, Lat A §52/35, left untranslated because English has no convenient word for the Latin *iniuria,* which "in its widest sense . . . denotes simply unlawfulness or the absence of a right. As the name of a particular delict . . . it embraced any contumelious disregard of another's rights or personality" (Nicholas 215-6). It is used in Latin for *sarhaed.*

injury, Cyfn §73/30, translating *cyflafan,* q.v.

ius primae noctis, "right of the first night", see p. 73 and cf. *droit de seigneur.*

lady, Ior §55/9, translating *argl6ydes:* the only meaning which suggests itself is "female lord" ("the superior of a district in her own right", AL i.103 *n.*b), and the appearance of the rule only in Ior may mean that it is due to a realisation that political changes might lead to a woman's exercising the rights of a lord. An *arglwyddes* was exempt from the incapacity of women to act as *mach:* see Col §113n, but it is to be doubted whether the *arglwyddes* so exempted was a political superior: see SEIL 233. The rule can hardly mean that the *amobrau* of a lordship went direct to the lord's wife.

leyrwite, in medieval England payment to the lord in respect of a female villein's fornication: cf. *merchet.* The section in Lat D (346.1-11) corresponding to Lat A §53 is headed *De leyrewittis.*

llathlud, llathrudd. The form with -*l*- is usual in manuscripts from northern, that with -*r*- in those from southern, Wales. It has been usual (perhaps under the influence of compounds such as *llofrudd*) to understand the -*r*- form as *llathrudd,* but most manuscript forms (such as *llathrut* Cyfn §73/3) imply *llathrud*; the strongest evidence for *llathrudd* seems to be the *llathruth* of Lat A §52/23. The first element in both forms is possibly that found, with the sense of stealth, in *lladrad* (theft).

The *rapina* sometimes used in Latin for *llathlud* has to modern ears too strong a sense for the period of the texts: though *abduct* may represent accurately enough the force of "to take *llathlud*", *elope* is the best word for "to go *llathlud*". The use of the same term in both contexts has continental parallels: *raptus* was applied in Germanic law to a taking of a woman without her relatives' consent even when she was willing: Brunner ii.860-61.

llawan, Lat A §52/46. Glossed by Aneurin Owen in this passage *iocosus* (as though it were *llawen*), the word corresponds to the *rhaffan* of Col §22, which is derived from a Latin source: cf. Bleg 66.30 = Lat D 345.31, Lat B 223.22. *Rhaffan* is assumed to be a derivative of *rhaff,* a rope (see p. 53 n.51) and *llawan* may have a similar meaning and be derived from the element found in *cynllyfan* and *llywanen*; cf. Irish *loman, a* rope.

llw ac arfoll, see *arfoll.*

llw gweilydd, Lat A §52/55, not translated or explained in the Latin. Aneurin Owen glosses this example and the corresponding Lat B 223.42 *iuramentum voluntarium*; the examples in the Welsh texts, however, he translates "oath of an absolver", while in the Glossary he gives the translation *spare oath.* According to GPC the meaning *voluntary* for *gweilydd* is derived only from dictionaries, and the basic meaning (found in the modern use of *gweili* in several dialects for e.g. a horse without a cart or a load) seems to be *unaccompanied*. This meaning accords with that in *llw gweilydd*, which is always the unsupported oath of a suspect, taken at the instance of the suspector; if the oath is refused, no counter-oath (*gwrthdwng*, q.v.) is required from the suspector before further procedure can follow.

llwyn a pherth, see *gwraig llwyn a pherth.*

llys, objection, bar. *Llys* is the root of a series of technical terms (*llysu, dilys, dilysu, dilysrwydd* and *dilystod, annilys, annilysu*) which cannot be put into English effectively as a parallel series, though there is a similar series in Irish: cf. CG, Glossary s.v. *díles. Llys* is used especially for objection to a witness, compurgator, or *mach,* or the bar which is the ground of that objection: according to Col §§528-31 and Lat E 457.12-20 (which has *causa reprobacionis* for *llys*) there were three classes of *llys.* The verb *llysu* (found in Acts iv.11, corresponding to Vulgate *reprobatus est,* A.V., R.S.V., and N.E.B. *rejected*) is used for challenging a person by invoking a *llys.*

The adjective *dilys,* with the negating prefix *di-,* means "without bar" or "without defect", i.e. *authentic, unchallengeable,* or *valid.* It is clearly appropriate for those who have rebutted an attempted *llys* or have not been challenged, but is also used in other contexts: thus *dylyed dilys* (Bleg 79.5) means "unchallengeable entitlement" (to land). The woman who after parting from her husband is said to be *dilys* or free from him when he takes a second wife (Ior §52/4, Lat A §52/21) is free, not so much from him as from any challenge to her single status. Further derivatives are used in connection with the transfer of property, *dilysu* meaning to show that the transferor had good title or that the transfer was validly carried out, *annilysu* meaning to show that the title or the transfer was invalid.

The abstract noun *dilysrwydd* then means in all contexts the quality of being free from objection, and it occurs most often in the context of title to property: at Bleg 92.5, 94.3 the seller of livestock, who must guarantee their freedom from specified physical defects for specified periods, must guarantee their *dilysrwydd* for their lifetime: that is, he is always liable if a defect is shown in his title to the stock. It was usual to give a *mach* for the *dilysrwydd* of property transferred, but no *mach* was needed for money or weapons, or for a ring, a knife, or a belt: Ior §66/13,

DwCol §189; the latter text goes on to explain that this was because these things cannot be followed to show them as *annilys:* "urth na ellyr herlyn ev hannylleseu" (DwCol §190): they cannot be identified.

In the Law of Women, *dilysrwydd* and the variant *dilystod* name a payment made for rape of a virgin, in some texts called *diweirdeb*, i.e. chastity. Here the idea is evidently that an unmarried girl is *dilys* only if she is a virgin, and the payment is a compensation for the loss of this *dilysrwydd*. There is no indication of the measure of this compensation, and it is not quite clear why it is paid. The victim's economic loss is measured by her *cowyll*: if she afterwards takes a husband, she can claim no *cowyll* from him because she is not a virgin. *Dilysrwydd* may have begun as an explanation of the ground for paying *cowyll* to the raped virgin, if it is not to be regarded as a compensation for the girl's injured feelings, additional to the *sarhaed* which she would receive for any assault.

mab anwar, Ior §45/7, translated "cold son"; see p. 85 and n.77.

mab llwyn a pherth, pp. 32-3, "a son of bush and brake", cf. *gwraig llwyn a pherth*.

mab uchelwr, synonymous with *uchelwr*, cf. *aillt, mab aillt,* and see *breyr*.

mach, Cyfn §73/26 etc., in our Ior text translated *surety,* following the practice of most earlier translators, including those who in the medieval Latin texts used *fideiussor* for *mach*. The translation is correct if *surety* is understood in the widest sense, as in Binchy's paper, "Celtic Suretyship, a fossilized Indo-European Institution" (in *Indo-European and Indo-Europeans* (ed. G. Cardona et al., Philadelphia, 1970), reprinted at 7 *Irish Jurist* (new series) 360-72), but misleading if a surety is regarded as guaranteeing performance of the primary obligation and himself performing if the principal fails. The *mach* (though in some cases he might become personally liable) was in origin a privately-recruited enforcer of legal rights: he might be introduced in order to ensure effective conveyance of property (in which case he would be called on, if necessary, to prevent the transferor from re-taking possession of it), or the performance of a promise (so that he might be called on to compel the promisor to perform, as a result of which the giving of *meichiau* was probably the oldest formal contract in Welsh law). A special case of promise was the promise to abide by the decision of a tribunal: the normal procedure of the lawbooks required the giving of *mach ar y gyfraith*, even though submission to the jurisdiction of the tribunal was no longer voluntary.

maer, Lat A §53/2, a local official of the king, responsible with the *cynghellor* (see *cymellawr*) for administration of royal rights within a given area, perhaps the commote. The office of *maer* was honourable; the contemptuously-named dung *maer* (*maer biswail*, Ior §55/9) who organised labour on the royal demesne (*maerdref* or *tir bwrdd*), was, like the English reeve, of villein status, and was given no compensation if the servants of the festive court did him *sarhaed:* Bleg 27.21. The *maer cynghellor* of Ior §51/11 presumably combined the two offices: in 1315 and again in 1325 there are references in English records to the office of *meyryd kynkellorion* in the commote of Ardudwy: *Calendar of Close Rolls (1313-18)* 256; N. M. Fryde, *List of Welsh Entries in the Memoranda Rolls* (Cardiff, 1974), 67 (no 564).

maerdref, Ior §55/10, see *maer.*

merces, Lat A §52/63-§53/10, left untranslated, to show that this Latin word is used in the sense of *amobr.* Since *merces* has no specialised meaning in Latin, the translator may have thought of *gobr* as *fee* rather than as a special technical term.

merch, p. 117. The basic meaning is *daughter,* but the word can be used in modern Welsh for a female of any age.

merchet, in medieval England payment to a lord in respect of a female villein's marriage, cf. *leyrwite.* The correspondence of the spelling with a medieval spelling of *merched* (pl. of *merch,* q.v.) or *merchedd* (a conceivable abstract noun from *merch*) is fortuitous: the word's associations are rather with *market:* SOED, and cf. L. O. Pike in Y.B. 15 Ed. 3 (Rolls Series, 1891) xv ff.

morwynwraig, "virgin wife", see pp. 5, 6, 15 n.25, and *rhodd ac estyn.*

nawdd, pp. 49-50, *protection.* The Laws of Court in the Welsh lawbooks specify for each officer the period for which or the distance to which he can grant protection.

neithior, p. 72, *wedding-feast*. For the significance of the poets' function at wedding feasts in Celtic society generally, see Mac Cana, 9 *Celtica* 178-9; for later developments in Wales, see Ceri W. Lewis in *A Guide to Welsh Literature,* ii (ed. A. O. H. Jarman and G. R. Hughes; Swansea, 1979) 63.

neithiorwyr, *wedding guests*.

next of kin, p. 9, see *cyfneseifiaid*.

nithlen, Lat A §52/13, *winnowing-sheet*.

nobilis, p. 70 n.3, *breyr* or *uchelwr*, q.v.

noble, Lat A §53/4, translating *optimas*; here a *breyr* is meant.

optimas, Lat A §52/31, *breyr*; for the same word in Lat D, Bleg 62.9 has *gwr ryd,* "free man".

pencenedl, pp. 42, 92, "head of kindred", a *breyr* who had a position of some authority over other relatives besides those descended from him: see Col §658 and note. Like that of his Irish counterpart, the *ceannfine,* the *pencenedl's* position "with regard to his kinsmen must . . . have varied not only between area and area but between one individual clan and another" (Kenneth Nicholls, *Gaelic and Gaelicised Ireland* (Dublin, 1972) 64). The office of *pencenhedlaeth* over members of the lineage of Hwfa ap Cynddelw was claimed by Llywelyn ap Gruffudd ab Iorwerth in 1318-19: W. Rees (ed.), *Calendar of Ancient Petitions relating to Wales* (Cardiff, 1975) 84; this suggests that in Gwynedd the unit over which the *pencenedl* exercised authority would be one of the fifteen tribes which came to be known as *Pymtheg Llwyth Gwynedd.* The kindreds which had no *pencenedl,* whose case is envisaged in the lawbooks, might then be those not attached to any of the fifteen. In thirteenth-century Powys, the office had perhaps acquired a territorial basis, for Gruffudd ap Meurig, *pencenedl* of Cegidfa (Guilsfield) is found attesting a grant of Gruffudd ap Gwenwynwyn in 1271: J. G. Edwards (ed.), *Littere Wallie* (Cardiff, 1940) 132.

pencerdd, usually translated "chief of song", and understood as meaning the chief poet (cf. Lat B 222.37, "princeps poetarum, id est *penkerd*); but as the reference at HGK 21.13 to "Gellan telynyaur penkerd" ("harpist pencerdd") suggests, a pencerdd might be a musician or a poet; cf. DwCol §75. Moreover, since *cerdd* originally meant *craft*, the original force of the name may have been "chief of the craft"; in the lawbooks the *pencerdd*'s status, like that of the court smith, is certainly that of the head of his profession, and both men take their places at the royal court, not among the twenty-four "statutory" officers, but among what Ior §30/1 calls "the officers of usage and custom who will be in a court". It seems likely that the *pencerdd* and the court smith exercised their functions within a defined area and attended the king only when he came to that area: cf. the Irish *Ollam*, whose territory was the *tuath*. It may be significant that according to Bleg 25.13 it is *pennkerd y wlat* (*Penkert patrie* Lat D 330.27) who is entitled to the *gobrau* of the *cerddorion* who are under him, and as Mr. Eurys Rowlands has put it, the lawbooks show an attempt to reconcile the tradition which gave a poet a definite function under royal patronage, and that which gave him accepted authority independent of the political power: 7 *Llên Cymru* 218. The *pencerdd*'s function at a *neithior* reflects his pre-Christian status as a pagan priest: see P. Mac Cana, 9 *Celtica* 178-9; for Irish parallels, see Binchy, "Secular Institutions", in *Early Irish Society* (ed. M. Dillon; Dublin, 1954); D. Greene, "The Professional Poets", in *Seven Centuries of Irish Learning* (ed. B. Ó Cuív; Dublin, 1961); E. J. Gwynn, (1940) 13 Eriu 31.

pergyng, Ior §44/10. The spelling of MS. *D*, in which vowel *y* usually represents *y,* has been retained, though most later examples suggest the spelling *perging*; the scribe of *D* may have copied his exemplar exactly because the word was unfamiliar. Most recorded examples of the word come from poems of praise in which the sense is metaphorical; the literal sense seems to be more or less that suggested by Aneurin Owen in a note to VC III.xxii.5 (= Ior §140/6), "it may be the perch, or brandrith, for the boiler". The Breton *percig uel bach*, found as a gloss on *ligo* (DGVB 284), confirms this view. The definition in TR (following LW 74*b*), "a little cauldron" is not acceptable.

prid, see *tir prid.*

prifai, in one version of the *Naw Cynyweddi* a mistranslation of Latin *privigni* (*stepsons*), see p. 26; elsewhere one of the woman's "privy things", which were reserved to her on a separation: see pp. 65-8, 76 and n.30, 81.

priod, see *gŵr priod, gwraig briod, priodas*.

priodas: this is the ordinary word in modern Welsh for *marriage* both in the sense of the marital relation (German *Ehe*) and in that of the ceremony which creates the relation (modern English *wedding*, German *Hochzeit*). In the legal material the ceremony (if any) is *neithior*; *priodas* is rare and designates in the oldest material only a marital union of the highest status: see the discussion at pp. 27-30. The basis of the word *priodas* is *priod*, whose essential meaning is *proper, appropriate*; another derivative is *priodor*, usually translated (accurately enough) *proprietor*: see *priodor Wallicus*. The *gŵr priod* and *gwraig briod* (married man and married woman, as contrasted with bachelor, widow, etc., in modern Welsh) will then be the "proper husband" and "proper wife", or even the "proprietary husband" in the sense of the husband proper to a particular woman; the *gŵr priod* and *gwraig briod* perhaps acquire their rights in each other as the first *priodor* acquires his proprietorship in land—by prescription. It is clear from the law relating to *agweddi* (q.v.) that a marital union was not regarded as fully matured until it had continued for seven years, and it can be argued that *priodas* is the name for the fully matured union (and perhaps even for such a union only if it was begun by gift of kindred); see pp. 16-18, 28. On this assumption, the *gwraig briod* (who might be entitled to buy and sell: Ior §53/4) would be the wife whose union had matured fully; since she would now be entitled to a half share of the pool of matrimonial property, she would share in any loss caused by her buying and selling, as she would not do while she was *agweddïol*, during the first seven years. The *gŵr priod*, whom her *gwaddol* was to secure for a daughter, was perhaps a "man appropriated to her [exclusively]", and would have that character from the beginning of the *agweddi* period, though it was of course contemplated that the union would mature fully in due course. In Ior §87/5 (cited at p. 28), however, *gwraig briod* cannot have this technical meaning of Welsh law, but must mean the woman recognised by the Church as a wife and not a concubine; so too in Bleg 79.11, *priodas*, as the factor which gives a legitimate son priority over an illegitimate one, must mean a union so recognised. This does not imply that any religious ceremony or the presence of a priest was necessary.

priodor Wallicus, p. 104 n.30, "Welsh proprietor". Under Welsh law, continued occupation of land for four generations created *priodolder*. The word suggests a *proper* relation to the land, i.e. *property* or *proprietorship:* cf. *priodas.* From the fourth generation on, the occupier was *priodor,* and in legal theory *priodolder* was not lost by non-occupation for nine generations, see *cynnwys, tir prid.*

privity, Ior §§51/1, 2; 55/15, translating *prifai,* q.v. The lawyers among the contributors, embarrassed by the technical sense of *privity* in English law, have used *privy things* for *prifai.*

procreatrix, p. 107, *producer, bearer.*

pudor has in Latin the senses found in English *shame:* on the one hand the subjective feeling of the person concerned, and on the other hand the objective public ignominy to which the person may be exposed. The subjective sense is nicely exemplified in the euphemism *membrum pudibundum* of Lat A §52/36.

puella, p. 117, in Lat A translated *girl,* and corresponding to *morwyn* in the Welsh texts; the ordinary Latin word for an unmarried girl.

putain, p. 35, *harlot*; a borrowing from the French *putain* of the same meaning; see *gwraig llwyn a pherth.*

rhodd ac estyn, Ior §51/10, *gift and handing-over.* The double expression may be mere hendiadys, as Wiliam (Ior Index, s.v.) suggests; but as it seems to appear only in the Ior/Col text (though the triad of Ior §51/10 has been taken into Cyfn MS. *Mk* at p. 119.11-14), it may reflect a late refinement of the concept of giving a wife. In medieval Welsh *estyn* must be an abstract noun, for the verb-noun (which in modern Welsh is *estyn*) is *estynnu*; it is derived quite regularly from Latin *extendo,* and occurs in other contexts in the lawbooks, in all of which the reference seems to be to a handing over—of office (Ior §§15/6, 94/1, 6), of a horse given by the king (WML 21.8), of the privileges of a church (Ior §71/5), of land (Ior §§84/6, 87/7, DwCol §258). Hence in the Law of Women *rhodd* may refer to the intention and *estyn* to the act of giving; or *rhodd* may refer to the oral expression of the intention to give, as *estyn* surely implies a physical act, such as would amount to *traditio* (handing over) in Roman law. The virgin-wife (*morwynwraig,* q.v.) would have her special status in the period between *rhodd* and *estyn.* A similar separation between the gift and the transfer is found in Germanic law: see Lizzie Carlsson, *Jag giver dig min dotter,* i (Stockholm, 1965), especially c.III.

rhynion, Lat A §51/9. Left untranslated in the Latin, the word is usually rendered *groats* (defined by SOED as "hulled, or hulled and crushed grain" or "naked oats"); for *rhynion* JD has *farina crassa, crassamen,* and TR "large oat-meal, groats".

sarhaed, literally *insult,* has the primary meaning of the offence (which can be compared with the Roman law *iniuria* (q.v.), and the secondary meaning of the compensation payable to the victim, which varies according to his status. In the Law of Women a distinction is drawn between *sarhaed* and *wynebwerth* or *gowyn, q.v. Sarhaed* is the abstract noun from *sarhau,* and has been compared with Irish forms derived from *sár,* a noun meaning *outrage,* which gives a deponent verb *sáraigidir* and a verb-noun *sárugud,* both referring to the act of infringing honour. *Sárugud* is not used for the compensation for insult, for which the Irish words are based on *díre* and *enech:* see *dirwy, wynebwerth.* The modern Welsh form *sarhad* means only *insult,* and the medieval form *sarhaed* has been kept for the technical senses of medieval law; there is no justification for the spelling *saraad* used by Aneurin Owen in his translation. The measure of *sarhaed* has a regular relation to that of *galanas:* see p. 42.

servient slave, Cyfn §47/8. Welsh law recognised two classes of female slave; the servient slave is defined at Bleg 59.27 as a needlewoman (*gwreic wrth y notwyd*), but the corresponding Lat D 340.31-2 has "nec ius eam ad *raw* vel ad molam ire paciatur", which corresponds to the qualifications given in Cyfn. Anglo-Saxon law had a similar gradation of female slaves, but recognised a third grade (presumably working with the spade) as well as the "grinding slave": Abt 10, 11. Frisian law knew a similar distinction, referring to *ancilla quæ nec mulgere nec molere solet:* J. Grimm, *Deutsche Rechtsaltertümer,* fourth edition (Leipzig, 1899; reprinted, Darmstadt, 1974) i.485.

single, Ior §46/2, translating *gweddw,* q.v.

sui juris, p. 125, "of his own right [*or* law], the technical Roman-law term for full legal capacity, when the person had become free of all authority of parent or guardian. The person under such authority was *alieni iuris,* "of another's right"; in Roman law a woman was always *alieni iuris.*

surety, Ior §54/9, translating *mach*, q.v.

swydd, Lat A §53/4, left untranslated in the Latin, where it explains *hereditas*, which normally translates *tref tad* (i.e. *patrimony*, literally "father's holding"). In modern Welsh, and normally in the lawbooks, *swydd* means *office*, and there is no suggestion in the law texts, apart from this passage, that office was hereditary in principle, though the office of *distain* (*steward*, but in effect prime minister) to the prince of Gwynedd became in practice a perquisite of the family of Ednyfed Fychan, and that of *pencerdd* ("chief of song", perhaps also doubling as court judge) a perquisite of the descendants of Meilir. An alternative explanation is that *hereditas* should here be understood as meaning *property,* without any implication of heritability: cf. French *patrimoine,* which can mean *assets,* without any implication that they have been inherited. If so, this is the only hint in the Welsh law material of the concept of office as property which became so important in the later Middle Ages.

swyddogion penadur, Lat A §53/7, *chief officers* (of the court). The combination *swyddogion penadur* does not seem to occur in the thirteenth-century Welsh texts, though WML 24.3-4 requires a larger compensation from the hall doorkeeper if a court officer impeded by him is *penadur*, and MS. *U*, in its version of *Llyfr y Damweiniau* (17 *Y Cymmrodor* 136.22) lists the *pennaduryeit* of the court (whose *ebediw* is £1, whereas that of all the other officers is 120*d.*) as the steward (*distain*), chief groom, chief falconer, chief huntsman, and chamberlain. The same manuscript agrees with other Cyfnerth manuscripts in adding the court justice to the list (in the Laws of Court, WML 8) of the officers whose *ebediw* is £1; that list then agrees with that in Lat A 113.5-6, but in neither list are these officers given a special designation. The more usual designation is *penswyddog*, as in Ior §51/11. For the special position of the court justice, see *ynad*.

taeog, *villein*, cf. *aillt, bilain*. Comparable forms are found in Cornish, where OCorn. *pobel tiogou* glosses *vulgus*, and later Cornish *tyack* means *farmer*; and in Breton, where MBret. *tiec* and Modern Breton *tieg, tieien* mean "head of a family" or *farmer*.

tafodiog, p. 40 n.2. The word is used in the lawbooks in two senses: (*a*) as here, for the man who speaks in court for a person incapacitated by defective speech or legal incapacity, or as the representative appointed by a group of joint owners (DwCol §426); in this sense *tafod* is also used (DwCol §§7, 9); (*b*)for a witness whose unsupported evidence is conclusive: see *Y Naw Tafodiog* at Ior §56/2-9, and cf. MS. *B*'s reading of the end of Ior §47/1, *canys ena e mae nauuet tauodyauc, ac urth henne e mae credadve hy, urth nat oes neythyaurwyr.* A third sense, corresponding to that of *counter* or *narrator* in early English common law practice (see PM i.212-16), seems to be found only at Bleg 45.14-30, = Lat D 354.3-15, which has at lines 3-4 "prelocutorem, id est, *tauodyawc*": see Bleg xvii-xviii.

tâl cynhysgaeth, see *cynhysgaeth.*

tir prid, p. 102: in this context, land acquired by a *prid* transaction, as contrasted especially with *tir priod*, in which the tenant had full proprietary rights created by long-continued inheritance: see *priodor Wallicus.* Originating as the verb-noun of *prynaf* ("I buy") and at one stage apparently used for all modes of acquiring land otherwise than by inheritance (cf. English *purchase*), *prid* came to mean a gage (or pledge) of land, which could be recovered on repayment of the debt which it secured. *Prid* transactions were used to circumvent the rule of Welsh law which prevented an owner from disposing of his land for more than his own lifetime: see the article cited at p. 102 n.26.

tlysau, see *trythgwd.*

toft, privileged, Ior §53/2, Welsh *tyddyn breiniol*, which corresponds to the *eisyddyn arbennig* of Cyfn §73/28, translated *special croft.* Both names clearly refer to a particular part of the patrimony; the word *tyddyn* implies the presence of a house, and a passage in Bleg indicates that the privileged toft is that carrying the house of the man whose patrimony is to be shared. According to Bleg 74.21-22, "Pan ranho brodyr tref eu tat yrydunt, y ieuhaf a geiff tydyn a holl adeil y tat" ("When brothers share their patrimony between them, the youngest is to have the homestead and all the buildings of his father", BBleg 77.21-3); the Latin original of this passage (Lat D 387.1-2), "*tydyn* et edificia patris" could, like the Welsh, be translated "a *tyddyn* and the father's buildings", but the reading of MSS. *L* and *Tr, y tydyn arbenhic* (Bleg p. 148) seems conclusively to identify the privileged toft as that of the father. In Lat A 132.37-8, "iunior debet habere *tygdyn,* id est, edificia, patris sui", "the youngest is entitled to have the *tyddyn*, i.e. the buildings, of his father", the buildings constitute the whole of the *tyddyn*. The various readings of the Iorwerth manuscripts and that of Col §583 (see the note to that passage) suggest that in thirteenth-century Gwynedd there was a tendency to allow the youngest son first choice of toft: if he had stayed at home with his father (as was likely enough) he would probably choose the privileged toft on which he was living. If a daughter living with the father was given in marriage to an alien, it might well happen that he would join her in her father's house, but this would give his sons by her no claim to stay there after their grandfather's death.

traditio, p. 122, "handing-over", see *rhodd ac estyn*.

traean cymell, pp. 55, 97, "enforcing (or compelling) third", claimed by the territorial lord for enforcing payment of composition for homicide; it seems to reflect an early principle found in Welsh law. The Herefordshire Domesday (cited at LTWL 93) records the king's right to a third of the plunder taken by the victim's kin from the offender's kin when one Welshman killed another in Archenfield. In Irish law a third of the *eraic* went to the lord, see CG p. 86.

tremyg, p. 99, *contempt,* one of a series of words incorporating the root -*myg-* (< *mik*), meaning "see, look at", e.g. *edmygaf,* "I admire", cf. Irish *dimicthe*, glossing *despictus*, VKG ii.576. *Tremyg*, with the element *tre-* meaning *through*, is semantically comparable with modern English "she looked through him"; in the lawbooks it occurs regularly for failure to respond to a legal summons, and is represented by *negligencia* in the Latin texts, cf. also *varn tremyc* Bleg 103.19-20 = *iudicium neglectivum* Lat D 352.12.

trithgwd, see *trythgwd*.

trythgwd, Lat A §52/14, Ior §44/11, and *tlysau*, Lat A §52/15, are considered together because they overlap in meaning: whereas in Lat A the *tlysau* are gold and silver, in Lat D 344.31 and Bleg 65.19 "the *tlysau* except for gold and silver" corresponds to "the *trythgwd* except gold and silver" in Lat A. *Tlysau* seem to be essentially "precious things", and the *trythgwd* is similarly "the bag of precious things". The spelling *trithg6t* of Ior (MS. *D*) seems to represent an erroneous modernisation of the archetype's spelling: ct. *pergyng*.

twyll, pp. 31-2, *deception.*

tyddyn, see *croft, toft.*

uchelwr, see *breyr.*

virgin maid, Cyfn §73/13a, translating *morwyn wyry,* see *gwraig.*

wynebwerth, literally *face-value,* is perhaps the oldest word for *honour-price* in Welsh, and is related to several Irish words based on *enech* and connected with honour: see CG pp. 84-6 and cf. WM 459.22, *d6yn dy vyneb di a wnaf,* "I will take away your honour". This notional use of *face* for *honour* seems to be symbolised by the gold plate as broad as his face which forms part of the king's *sarhaed,* cf. the plate named in the Book of Llan Daf as part of the honour-price of a bishop: LL 233. The word *wynebwerth* is also found outside the lawbooks, in the Branwen story for the compensation offered to Matholwch, PKM 33.18. In the law texts it may replace *sarhaed* as the term for compensation for insult in general (see Ior §19/8), but its usual use is for compensation for a sexual offence within marriage. In the triad *Tri anghyfarch gŵr, wynebwerth* is the compensation to a man from his wife for sexual misbehaviour, and as paid to a woman it alternates with *gowyn* as the name for the compensation from her husband for his adultery: see pp. 66-7. For the Breton cognate see p. 49, n.31. The variant form *wynebwarth,* found for instance in MS. *B*'s version of Ior §44/9, seems to be influenced by *gwarth,* "shame".

ynad, p. 104. In modern Welsh *ynadon* are "justices", and a stipendiary magistrate is *ynad cyflog,* whereas a High Court or circuit judge is *barnwr.* In the lawbooks *ynad* and *brawdwr* (corresponding to the later *barnwr*) seem at first sight interchangeable, and the *ynad llys* and *ynad cymwd* (court and commote justices) are surely officials appointed to sit in judgement. The name of the *brawdwr* implies that he gave judgement, and the tendency of southern texts to speak of *brawdwr* rather than *ynad* may reflect the use in Deheubarth of lay judges; like English doomsmen and Continental *scabini,* these judges by status of land (*brawdwyr o fraint tir*) found the judgements but were not trained in the law and were not so sternly dealt with if they gave a wrong decision as were the professionals. The name of the *ynad,* on the other hand, may imply a knowledge of law: earlier spellings, representing *yngnad,* suggest a derivation from the root *gna- (J. Loth, (1930) 47 RC 174-5), so that the *ynad* was he who knew, and he was perhaps in essence a knowledgeable jurist to whom disputes could properly be referred for decision. When the king is said to *estynnu yneidiaeth* to an aspirant attested by the *ynad llys* as competent, he may be "handing-over" (see *rhodd ac estyn*) not office but status. The *ynad llys* himself may have been court jurist rather than court judge, acting as legal advisor on some occasions and judge on others; for the Irish parallel, see D. A. Binchy, "Féchem, Fethem, Aigne", 11 *Celtica* 18-33. The Cyfnerth text shows special respect for the status of the *ynad llys*: he pays no *ebediw*, "for *yneidiaeth* is better than anything temporal", WML 17.12-13; this exemption explains his absence from the list of officers who paid £1 as ebediw, as given in *Llyfr y Damweiniau*: see *swyddogion penadur*.

ysgar, Ior §54/1, translated *parting*; in modern Welsh the normal word for *divorce* in its contemporary technical sense (ct. *divorcium*, q.v.); the sense in the lawbooks is much less precise, and the non-technical *parting* is to be preferred to *separation*, which has a technical meaning in English law.

BIBLIOGRAPHICAL ABBREVIATIONS

AL [Aneurin Owen, ed.], *Ancient Laws and Institutes of Wales*; London, 1841. References of the form AL ii.200 are to pages in the two volumes of the octavo edition.

ALI *Ancient Laws of Ireland*; six volumes, Dublin, 1865-1901.

Arch. Brit. Edward Lhuyd, *Archæologia Britannica*; London, 1707, reprinted, Shannon, 1971.

Abt The Laws of Æthelberht (Liebermann i.3ff).

BBCS *Bulletin of the Board of Celtic Studies.*

BTPTr Thomas Jones (ed. and tr.) *Brut y Tywysogyon, Peniarth MS. 20 version* translated; Cardiff, 1952.

BBleg Melville Richards (ed. and tr.), *The Laws of Hywel Dda (The Book of Blegywryd)*; Liverpool, 1954.

B.Crólige D. A. Binchy (ed.) Bretha Crólige, (1934) 12 Ériu 1-77.

Binchy, *Kingship* D. A. Binchy, *Celtic and Anglo-Saxon Kingship*; Oxford, 1970.

Bleg S. J. Williams and J. E. Powell (ed.), *Cyfreithiau Hywel Dda yn ôl Llyfr Blegywryd*; Cardiff, 1942, second edition, 1961. Page references are the same in both editions, but there are some changes in the notes. See also p. 2 and n.3.

Bowen Ivor Bowen (ed.), *The Statutes of Wales*; London, 1908.

Bracton *Bracton de Legibus et Consuetudinibus Angliæ.* Folio references are to the *editio princeps* of 1569 and are valid for all editions. Woodbine/Thorne references are to the edition by G. E. Woodbine (four volumes, New Haven, 1915-42), re-issued with additional introductions and translation by S. E. Thorne (Cambridge, Mass., 1968, 1977); a fifth volume of commentary is in preparation.

Brissaud   Jean Brissaud, *A History of French Private Law*, translated by Rapelje Howells from *Manuel d'histoire du droit francais* (1898); CLHS iii (192, reprint 1968).

Brunner   H. Brunner, *Deutsche Rechtsgeschichte*, second edition; i, Berlin, 1906; ii (ed. C. von Schwerin), Berlin, 1928.

Bürgschaft   R. Thurneysen, *Die Bürgschaft im irischen Recht; Abhandlungen der preussischen Akademie der Wissenschaften* (1928) nr. 2.

CA   Ifor Williams (ed.), *Canu Aneirin*; Cardiff, 1938.

CG   D. A. Binchy (ed.), *Crith Gablach*; Dublin, 1941. References (unless otherwise indicated) are to lines of the text.

CLHS   The Continental Legal History Series, published under the auspices of the Association of American Law Schools; Boston and London, 1912-28, reprinted, South Hackensack and New York, 1968-9.

CLP   [D. Jenkins (ed.)], Celtic Law Papers, Brussels, 1973.

Calisse   Carlo Calisse, *A History of Italian Law*, translated by Layton B. Register from *Storia del Diritto italiano* (1903); CLHS viii, (1928, reprint 1969).

Chirk Codex   J. Gwenogvryn Evans (ed.), *Facsimile of the Chirk Codex of the Welsh Laws*; Llanbedrog, 1909.

Col   D. Jenkins (ed.), *Llyfr Colan*; Cardiff, 1963. References, unless otherwise indicated, are to numbered sentences.

Contribb.   K. Meyer, *Contributions to Irish Lexicography*; Halle, 1906.

Cyfn   The "Cyfnerth" text: see pp. 2-3. References of the form Cyfn §73/4 are to the numbered sections and sentences of the text in the present volume; for other parts of the Cyfnerth text reference is made to WML.

DC   "Dimetian Code" in AL i.338-617. References (for material not printed in Bleg) are to Book, chapter, and section.

DGG   I. Williams and T. Roberts (ed.), *Dafydd ap Gwilym a'i Gyfoeswyr*, second edition; Cardiff, 1935.

DGVB   L. Fleuriot, *Dictionnaire des gloses en vieux breton*; Paris, 1964.

DwCol   D. Jenkins (ed.), *Damweiniau Colan*; Aberystwyth, 1973. References are to numbered sentences.

EASL   Essays in Anglo-Saxon Law; Boston, 1905; reprinted, South Hackensack, 1972.

GPC   *Geiriadur Prifysgol Cymru, A Dictionary of the Welsh Language*; Cardiff, 1950- .

Geirfa   J. Lloyd-Jones, *Geirfa Barddoniaeth Gynnar Gymraeg*, Cardiff, 1931-63.

Glanvill   *Tractatus de legibus et consuetudinibus regni Anglie qui Glanvilla vocatur*. Reference to book and chapter apply to all editions. Hall: G. D. G. Hall (ed. and tr.), *The Treatise . . . commonly called Glanvill*; London and Edinburgh, 1965: references are to pages.

H   J. Morris-Jones and T. H. Parry-Williams (ed.), *Llawysgrif Hendregadredd*; Cardiff, 1933.

HGK   D. Simon Evans (ed.), *Historia Gruffud vab Kenan*; Cardiff, 1977.

Hn   *Leges Henrici Primi:* ed. L. J. Downer, Oxford, 1972, and in Liebermann, i.547ff.

Hall   see Glanvill.

Hübner   Rudolf Huebner, *A History of Germanic Private Law*, translated by Francis S. Philbrick from *Grundzüge des deutschen Privatrechts* (second edition, 1913); CLHS iv (1918, reprint 1968).

Ior   A. R. Wiliam (ed.), *Llyfr Iorwerth*; Cardiff, 1960. References of the form Ior §52/1 are to the numbered sections and unnumbered sentences of this edition; for the tractate on the Law of Women they refer (unless otherwise stated) to the text printed in the present volume. See also p. 2 and n.3.

Ir. Recht R. Thurneysen (ed.), *Irisches Recht; Abhandlungen der preussischen Akademie der Wissenschaften* (1931) nr. 2.

JD John Davies, *Antiquæ Linguæ Britannicæ . . . Dictionarium Duplex;* London, 1632, reprint, Menston, 1968.

LHEB K. H. Jackson, *Language and History in Early Britain;* Edinburgh, 1953.

LL J. Gwenogvryn Evans (ed.), *The Text of the Book of Llan Dâv;* Oxford, 1893; reprinted, Aberystwyth, 1979.

LTWL H. D. Emanuel, *The Latin Texts of the Welsh Laws;* Cardiff, 1967.

LW W. Wotton and Moses Williams (ed.), *Cyfreithjeu Hywel Dda . . . seu Leges Wallicae;* Lonon, 1730.

Lat A Redaction A in LTWL. For the tractate on the Law of Women, references are to the numbered sections and sentences of the text printed in the present volume.

Lat B Redaction B in LTWL.

Lat D Redaction D in LTWL.

Lat E Redaction E in LTWL.

Lewis I. M. Lewis, *Social Anthropology in Perspective;* Harmondsworth, 1976.

Liad & Cuir K. Meyer, *Liadain and Cuirithir;* London, 1902.

Liebermann F. Liebermann, *Gesetze der Angelsachsen;* three volumes, Halle, 1903-16; reprinted, Aalen, 1960.

LlA   J. Morris-Jones and J. Rhŷs (ed.), *The Elucidarium and Other Tracts from Llyvyr Agkyr Llandewivrevi*; Oxford, 1894.

MWS   T. Jones Pierce, *Medieval Welsh Society* (ed. J. Beverley Smith); Cardiff, 1972.

NLWJ   *National Library of Wales Journal.*

Nicholas   J. K. B. M. Nicholas, *An Introduction to Roman Law*; Oxford, 1962.

PKM   Ifor Williams (ed.), *Pedeir Keinc y Mabinogi*; Cardiff, 1930.

PM   F. Pollock and F. W. Maitland, *The History of English Law before the time of Edward I*; second edition, Cambridge, 1898, re-issued with Introduction by S. F. C. Milsom, 1968.

PRIA   *Proceedings of the Royal Irish Academy.*

Plucknett, *Legislation*   T. F. T. Plucknett, *Legislation of Edward I*; Oxford, 1949.

RBB   J. Rhŷs and J. Gwenogvryn Evans (ed.), *The Text of the Bruts from the Red Book of Hergest*; Oxford, 1890.

RC   *Revue Celtique.*

RLME   P. Vinogradoff, *Roman Law in Medieval Europe*; second edition, ed. F. de Zulueta, Oxford, 1929 and reprints.

Rec. Caern.   [H. Ellis (ed.)], *Registrum vulgariter nuncupatum "the Record of Caernarvon"*; London, 1838.

SC   *Studia Celtica.*

S.Cano   D. A. Binchy (ed.) *Scéla Cano Meic Gartnáin*; Dublin, 1963.

SEIL   M. Dillon and D. A. Binchy (ed.), *Studies in Early Irish Law*; Dublin, 1936.

SOED *The Shorter Oxford English Dictionary.*

SS *Publications of the Selden Society.*

TC *Transactions of the Honourable Society of Cymmrodorion.*

TR Thomas Richards, *Antiquæ Linguæ Britannicæ Thesaurus*; Bristol, 1753.

TRHS/V *Transactions of the Royal Historical Society,* Fifth Series.

VC "Venedotian Code" in AL i.2-335. References (for material not printed in Ior) are to Book, chapter, and section.

VKG H. Pedersen, *Vergleichende Grammatik der keltischen Sprache,* ii; Göttingen, 1913.

WHR Welsh History Review.

WM J. Gwenogvryn Evans (ed.), *The White Book Mabinogion*; Pwllheli, 1907, reprinted with Introduction by R. M. Jones, Cardiff, 1973.

WML A. W. Wade-Evans (ed.), *Welsh Medieval Law*; Oxford, 1909.

WTL or *Welsh Tribal Law* T. P. Ellis, *Welsh Tribal Law and Custom in the Middle Ages*; Oxford, 1926.

Wer The tractate *Wergeldzahlung*, Liebermann i.

X Book X in AL ii.306-95. References are to the numbered chapters and sections of the Book.

XII Book XII in AL ii.450-75. References are to the numbered plaints in the Book.

XIV Book XIV in AL ii.568-743. References are to the numbered chapters and sections of the Book.

ZCP *Zeitschrift für celtische Philologie.*

ZRG *Zeitschrift der Savigny-Stiftung für Rechtsgeschichte (Germanistische Abeilung).*

INDEX TO
PASSAGES CITED

References to *words* are to the articles in the Glossary under the respective keywords.

75.19-22:	82 n.63
75.24-5:	19 n.38, 75 n.26, 101 n.22
79.5:	*llys*
79.11:	28 n.11
81.8:	*croft*
81.22:	*gwartheg dyfach*
82.4:	64 n.97
84.25:	*dial*
92.5:	*llys*
94.3:	*llys*
110.1-5:	64 n.98
111.20:	116 n.8
111.21-2:	37
111.24-8:	33, 52 n.49
112.3-8:	32
112.3-16:	69 n.2
112.26-32:	*gwaed cyn delwawd*
114.28-9:	118 n.15
116.1-2:	64 n.98
116.3:	116 n.8
116.24:	67 n.115
116.27-9:	21 n.43, 37, *cywyres*
116.29-117.6:	34, 48 n.30
119.8:	116 n.8
119.8-18:	10 n.10
119.11-14:	116
119.14:	18 n.32
119.15:	81 n.61
119.15-16:	76 n.29
122.20-25:	34
128.25:	62 n.87
128.28:	62 n.86

Chirk Codex (J. G. Evans, *Facsimile of the Chirk Codex*, 1909)

34.7-9:	67 n.108

Col (D. Jenkins, *Llyfr Colan*, 1963): references, unless otherwise noted, are to the numbered sentences of the text.

p.45:	82 n.63
1 and n.:	18 n.32, 51 n.38
7,8:	73 n.15
14n:	*aillt*
23:	77 n.34, 78 n.39, 118 n.15

26, 27:	89 n.96
29	52 n.49
34n:	28 nn.12,13
42:	49 n.31
42-45:	116 and n.8
48:	28, 88 n.93
49:	82 n.64, 100 n.16
50:	82 n.66, 100 n.16
54:	48 n.27, 71 n.7
55, 56:	72 n.13
58:	55 n.59
63:	72 n.9
64:	105 n.39
65:	90 n.98
66:	48 n.29, 67 n.112, 116 n.8
67:	78 n.44
113n:	*lady*
133-5n:	*amod*
140:	77 n.34, 118 n.15
249:	63 n.94
264, 265:	56 n.67
278:	63 n.93
283-7:	63 n.96
305:	44 n.16
332:	*gwaed cyn delwawd*
393:	*daered*
529:	77 n.37
531:	62 n.87
578:	55 n.62
580:	*cynnwys*
583:	*toft*
600:	75 n.27
601, 602:	55 n.63
606:	*alltud, bonheddig canhwynol*
607:	*bonheddig canhwynol*
649n:	*gafael*
654:	*casual acquisitions*
658:	*pencenedl*

Cyfn (the parts of the Cyfnerth text published here: for other "Cyfnerth" material, see WML)

33/2:	75 n.24
73/2:	76 n.33
73/2a:	79 n.48

GENERAL INDEX

Key words are in the order of the English alphabet, and references to *Cyfn* in the order of the text here printed, where that differs from numerical order. References to the glossary are not included in the index.

yoke, Cyfn §73a/7, Lat A §52/9, Ior
  §44/6
    of God, 7
ysgar, 28, 124